THE IRISH MARTYRS

IRISH THEOLOGICAL QUARTERLY MONOGRAPH SERIES

General Editor: D. Vincent Twomey, SVD

1 P.J. Corish & B. Millett, *The Irish Martyrs*
2 Denis the Carthusian, *Spiritual writings*, translated by I. Ní Riain

The Irish Martyrs

EDITED BY

Patrick J. Corish
Benignus Millett OFM

Prepared for publication by Mark Bennett

FOUR COURTS PRESS

Set in 11 on 14 Bembo for
FOUR COURTS PRESS LTD
7 Malpas Street, Dublin 8, Ireland
e-mail: info@four-courts-press.ie
http://www.four-courts-press.ie
and in North America
FOUR COURTS PRESS
c/o ISBS, 920 N.E. 58th Avenue, Suite 300, Portland, OR 97213

ISBN 1–85182–858–3

Printed in Great Britain
by MPG Books Ltd, Bodmin, Cornwall.

Contents

Foreword by Cardinal Desmond Connell   7

List of abbreviations   11

1 Historical background   19

2 Patrick O'Healy and Conn O'Rourke   32

3 Matthew Lambert, Robert Meyler, Edward Cheevers,
  Patrick Cavanagh and companions   57

4 Dermot O'Hurley   66

5 Margaret Ball (née Bermingham)   81

6 Maurice MacKenraghty   86

7 Dominic Collins   95

8 Conor O'Devany and Patrick O'Loughran   107

9 Francis Taylor   138

10 Peter Higgins   148

11 Terence Albert O'Brien   157

12 John Kearney   165

13 William Tirry   176

Appendix: The historiography of the martyrs   184

List of contributors   203

Foreword

The beatification of seventeen Irish martyrs in 1992 was an event of great spiritual significance in the history of the Church in Ireland. It represented the first fruits of the work of Cardinal Moran, and later Archbishop Walsh, who, a century ago, led the movement to promote the process of beatification and canonization of our martyrs. A special tribute is due to Archbishop Ryan who sought and obtained the willing and generous cooperation of the most distinguished scholars who are expert in the history of the Church in Ireland: Monsignor Patrick J. Corish, Father Benignus Millett, OFM, Father Proinsias Ó Fionnagáin, SJ, Father Hugh Fenning, OP, Father Francis X. Martin, OSA, Dr Ciarán Brady, Dr Colm Lennon, and Father Kevin Kennedy. Thanks to their work, which was approved and much admired by the Roman authorities, the beatification of Blessed Dermot O'Hurley and sixteen companions was celebrated by His Holiness Pope John Paul II.

To me was given the unforgettable privilege of presenting to the Pope a request for the beatification at a solemn celebration of Mass in St Peter's Square. It was a Eucharistic moment of special communion with the Pope in commemoration of those who had given their lives as witnesses to Catholic faith in the Eucharist and in the apostolic mission of Peter's successors.

In writing this preface I am thinking of the heroic archbishop of Cashel, Blessed Dermot O'Hurley, raised up on the scaffold on a mid-summer morning in what is now the centre of Dublin. I see the sudden red burst of the winter sun lighting up the last moments of Conor O'Devaney, bishop of Down and Connor, and of his priest companion Patrick O'Loughran. I remember those other bishops and priests, religious and lay people, who bore witness to their faith through torture and death. Were they tempted to despair of the cause for which they were ready to die? Was not the future in the hands of a government that must always feel threatened for as long as the people remained true to their Catholic faith? And how could all this be happening in Ireland, the land which had received the faith from St Patrick without shedding the blood of a single martyr, the land which had lived the faith for a thousand years without the taint of religious persecution? Yes, strange things have happened in the course of our history.

Not far down the road from the scene of Blessed Dermot's execution, Blessed Margaret Ball may still have been alive. Did she feel that the faith for which she was suffering could hardly survive long after her death? What could one elderly woman like Margaret do, cut off from the world in a prison cell and powerless to influence the course of events?

The martyrs could not foresee the constancy of Irish Catholics in the following centuries of trial, a constancy that owed so much of its strength to the heroic stand they had taken. And may we not feel helpless, caught up in the swirl of a tide flowing strongly against us? The example of the martyrs is there to help us to find our feet and their prayers are strong to assist us. Remember what Jesus told the apostles just before he went to his agony: 'In the world you will have trouble, but have courage: I have overcome the world' (Jn 16:33). These are the words I myself found inscribed on a stone by the wayside near Rome one day as I was making my retreat in preparation for my consecration.

A share in the courage shown by the martyrs – the courage to which the Holy Father exhorted us in the words of Christ on the occasion of his inauguration in the Petrine ministry: 'Do not be afraid' (Lk 5:10) – is a gift of the Holy Spirit. It is he who brings strength to our hope in God, in whose hands we leave the future. I am speaking of hope, which is not the same thing as optimism. Optimism takes the view that all will be right whatever the appearances may be. And so it rests content to await the outcome with undisturbed complacency. But hope lives in the real world. It knows that for which it longs and the distance that has to be crossed before it can be attained. It knows the obstacles that render the outcome uncertain. It turns to God in prayer and it gets down to the task that must be accomplished, not refusing the labour, the trials, the suffering inseparable from the following of Christ. Our hope is in the Lord who made heaven and earth and who is preparing the new world through the work to which he has called us; we live that hope in fidelity to the task that is ours.

The bishops stand prominently before the people and find themselves exposed today to forms of publicity that create new demands on their ministry. Failures, whether real or alleged, are used to embarrass the Church. It is difficult to convince a world, so driven by the imagery of media rhetoric, that prominence is not the same thing as importance. Who would have thought the Wexford sailors important? We know nothing about them except that they lived with the kind of love of the Church that proved itself throught the mouth of their spokesman, Blessed Matthew Lambert. At his trial he said: 'I believe in the faith of my mother, the holy Catholic Church.' Our lay martyrs are calling us to afford our lay people the opportunity to grow in the service of the Church. This must be the response to the new summons to the laity to play that active part to which the Holy Father has called them. Each member of the Church is important, in each is reflected the entire spiritual glory of the Church as the Mystical Body of Christ.

The witness of the martyrs requires us especially to value and to foster our communion with our Holy Father the Pope. For them the issue that cost them the ultimate sacrifice is succintly expressed by Monsignor Corish in the question: 'Pope or Queen?' Inspired by the example of John Paul II, and faithful to his teaching, we remain in the communion that unites us under the leadership of Peter's successor.

The witness of the martyrs likewise proclaims the centrality of the holy Eucharist as the source and the summit of Christian life (*Lumen gentium*, 11). The martyred priests offer a special inspiration to all engaged in the service of the ministerial priesthood. As the Second Vatican Council reminds us, their entire ministry is directed to the central act of the Eucharistic sacrifice and therein it finds its completion. Their ministry, which begins with the preaching of the Gospel, 'draws its force and power from the sacrifice of Christ and tends to this, that "the whole redeemed city, that is the whole assembly and community of the saints, should be offered as a universal sacrifice to God through the Hight Priest who offered himself in his passion for us that we might be the body of so great a Head"' (*Presbyterorum ordinis*, 2). May the witness of the priest-martyrs encourage our priests, renew the conviction of their faith in their sacramental identity with Christ, and inspire them to promote vocations above all by the example of their lives.

The readiness of the martyrs to forgive and to defend the rights of those who accused them, so wonderfully shown by the Dominican priest, Blessed Peter Higgins, summons us to work in sincerity for reconciliation and peace with those with whom we differ. In a land that now by its pluralism professes to value difference, it should not be taken amiss that we should value our own identity when fidelity to our faith and convictions poses no threat to the rights of fellow citizens. May this record of heroic apostolic faith and communion be for us a source of encouragement and joy.

On Pentecost Day, the apostles went into the streets and onlookers were taken aback when they saw them; some even thought they had been drinking too much (Acts 2:13). They were intoxicated for sure, but under the influence of the Spirit of joy. We share their joy and we cannot keep that joy to ourselves. That is the meaning of evangelization. A joyful people spreads a contagion of joy: and in that joy it gives itself generously to the tasks of evangelization. We are not like those men on the road to Emmaus, our faces downcast. We have met the Lord in the breaking of bread and in our hearts is a joy that no man can take from us (Jn 16:22). May the Church in Ireland be renewed by that joy and in it may we find the key to a new proclamation of the Gospel.

Cardinal Desmond Connell

Abbreviations

AAS	*Acta Apostolicae Sedis* (Rome, 1909–)
A.C. Cause	Archivio della Sacra Congregazione per le Cause dei Santi
A.C. Cause, Pos. Decr. et Resc.	—, Positiones Decretorum et Rescriptorum
A.C. Cause, Reg. Decr.	—, Registra Decretorum in Causis Servorum Dei
A.C.H.	Archivum Collegii Hibernorum de Urbe, i.e. archives of the Irish College, Rome
AFM	*Annála Ríoghachta Éireann: Annals of the kingdom of Ireland by the Four Masters from the earliest period to the Year 1616*, ed. and trans. John O'Donovan (7 vols., Dublin, 1851; reprint, New York, 1966)
AGA	Archivum Generale Augustinianorum, Rome
AGOFM	Archivum Generale Ordinis Fratrum Minorum, Rome
AGOP	Archivum Generale Ordinis Praedicatorum, Rome
A.G. Sim.	Archivo General de Simancas
ALC	*The Annals of Loch Cé: a chronicle of Irish affairs, 1014–1590*, ed. W.M. Hennessy (2 vols., London, 1871; facsimile reprint, Dublin, 1939)
APF	Archivo Storico della Sacra Congregazione per l'Evangelizzazione dei Popoli o *de Propaganda Fide*
APF, Atti	—, Atti, or Acta, i.e. the minutes of the General Meetings
APF, SOCG	—, Scritture Originali Riferite nelle Congregazioni Generali
ARSI	Archivum Romanum Societatis Iesu
ARSI, MSS Castell.	—, MSS provinciae Castellanae
ARSI, MSS Hist. Soc.	—, MSS Historiae Societatis
ASI	Archives of St. Isidore's College, Rome
AU	*Annála Uladh, Annals of Ulster; otherwise Annála Senait, Annals of Senat: a chronicle of Irish affairs, 431–1131, 1155–1541*, ed. W.M. Hennessy and B. MacCarthy (4 vols., Dublin, 1887–1901)
AV	Archivio Segreto Vaticano
Acta Nunt. Gall.	*Acta Nunciaturae Gallicae* (Rome/Paris, 1961–)
Acts and Ordinances Interregnum	*Acts and ordinances of the Interregnum, 1642–1660*, ed. C.H. Firth and R.S. Rait (3 vols., London, 1911)
Acts Privy Council, 1542–7 [etc.]	*Acts of the privy council of England, 1542–7* [etc.] (London, 1890–)
Acts Privy Council, Ire., 1556–71	'Acts of the privy council in Ireland, 1556–1571', ed. J.T. Gilbert, in *H.M.C. rep. 15*, app. iii (London, 1897)
Alegambe, *Mortes Illustres*	Philippe Alegambe, *Mortes Illustres et Gesta eorum de Societate Iesu qui in odium fidei, pietatis, aut cuiuscunque, virtutis ab ethnicis, haereticis, vel aliis, morte confecti sunt* (Rome, 1657)
Anal. Boll.	*Analecta Bollandiana* (Brussels/Paris, 1882–)

Anal. Hib.	*Analecta Hibernica, including the reports of the Irish Manuscripts Commission* (Dublin, 1930–)
Anc. Rec. Dublin	*Calendar of Ancient Records of Dublin, in the possession of the municipal corporation*, ed. Sir J.T. Gilbert and Lady Gilbert (19 vols., Dublin, 1889–1944)
Ann. Min.	Luke Wadding, *Annales Minorum seu Trium Ordinum a S. Francisco Institutorum* (8 vols., Lyons/Rome, 1625–54; 3rd ed. (with continuations), Quaracchi [etc.] 1931–)
Annates, Ulster	*De Annatis Hiberniae: a calendar of the first fruits' fees levied on papal appointments to benefices in Ireland, A.D. 1400–1535, extracted from the Vatican and other Roman archives*, vol. i: *Ulster*, ed. M.A. Costello and Ambrose Coleman (Dundalk, 1909; reprint Maynooth, 1912)
Archiv. Fr. Praed.	*Archivum Fratrum Praedicatorum* (Rome, 1930–)
Archiv. Hib.	*Archivum Hibernicum: or Irish Historical Records* (Maynooth, 1912–)
BL	British Library (formerly called British Museum), London
BL, Add. MSS	—, Additional MSS
BR	Bibliothèque Royale Albert 1er, Brussels
BV	Biblioteca Apostolica Vaticana
BV, MSS Barb. Lat.	—, MSS Barberini Latini
BV, MSS Urb. Lat.	—, MSS Urbinati Latini
Bagwell, *Stuarts*	Richard Bagwell, *Ireland under the Stuarts* (3 vols., London, 1909–16; reprint, 3 vols., London, 1963)
Bagwell, *Tudors*	Richard Bagwell, *Ireland under the Tudors with a succinct account of the earlier history* (3 vols., London, 1885–90; reprint, 3 vols., London, 1963)
Ball, *Judges*	F.E. Ball, *The judges in Ireland, 1221–1921* (2 vols., London, 1926)
Bellesheim, *Gesch. Der Kirche*	A. Bellesheim, *Geschichte der katholischen Kirche in Irland von in Irland der Einführung des Christenthums bis auf die Gegenwart* (3 vols., Mainz, 1890–91)
Bibl. Mazar.	Bibliothèque Mazarine, Paris
Bodl.	Bodleian Library, Oxford
Bourchier, *Historia*	Thomas Bourchier, *Historia Ecclesiastica de Martyrio Fratrum Ordinis divi Francisci* (Paris, 1582; 2nd ed., Ingolstadt, 1583)
Bradshaw, *Dissolution*	Brendan Bradshaw, *The dissolution of the religious orders in Ireland under Henry VIII* (Cambridge, 1974)
Bradshaw, *Ir. Const. Rev.*	Brendan Bradshaw, *The Irish constitutional revolution of the sixteenth century* (Cambridge, 1979)
Brady, *Ep. Succ.*	W. M. Brady (ed.), *The episcopal succession in England, Scotland, Ireland, A.D. 1400 to 1875* (3 vols., Rome, 1876–7)
Brady, *Ir. Ch. Eliz.*	W. M. Brady (ed.), *State papers concerning the Irish Church in the time of Queen Elizabeth* (London, 1868)
Burke, *Hib. Dom.*	Thomas Burke (de Burgo), *Hibernia Dominicana* (Cologne, 1762)
Cal. Carew MSS, 1515–74 [etc.]	*Calendar of the Carew manuscripts preserved in the archiepiscopal Library at Lambeth, 1515–74* [etc.], ed. J.S. Brewer and William Bullen (6 vols., London, 1867–73)
Cal. Papal Letters, 1198–1304	*Calendar of entries in the papal registers relating to Great Britain [etc.] and Ireland: Papal Letters, 1198–1304* [etc.] (London, 1893–)
Cal. Pat. Rolls Ire., Hen. VIII-Eliz.	*Calendar of patent and close rolls of chancery in Ireland, Henry VIII to 18th Elizabeth*, ed. James Morrin (Dublin, 1861)

Cal. Pat. Rolls Ire., Eliz.	*Calendar of patent and close rolls of chancery in Ireland, Elizabeth, 19th year to end of reign*, ed. James Morrin (Dublin, 1862)
Cal. Pat. Rolls Ire., Jas I	*Irish patent rolls of James I: facsimile of the Irish record commissioners' calendar prepared prior to 1830*, with foreword by M.C. Griffith (Dublin, 1966)
Cal. Pat. Rolls Ire., Chas I	*Calendar of patent and close rolls of chancery in Ireland, Charles I, years 1 to 8*, ed. James Morrin (Dublin, 1864)
Cal. S.P. Ire., 1509–73 [etc.]	*Calendar of state papers relating to Ireland, 1509–73* [etc.] (24 vols., London, 1860–1912)
Cal. S.P. Rome, 1558–71 [etc.]	*Calendar of state papers relating to English affairs, preserved principally at Rome, in the Vatican Archives and Library, 1558–71* [etc.], ed. J.M. Rigg (2 vols., London, 1916–26)
Cal. S.P. Spain, 1485–1509 [etc.]	*Calendar of letters, despatches, and state papers relating to the negotiations between England and Spain, preserved in the archives at Simancas and elsewhere, 1485–1509* [etc.] (London, 1862–)
Cath. Bull.	*Catholic Bulletin* (29 vols., Dublin, 1911–39)
Cath. Encycl.	*The Catholic Encyclopedia* (17 vols., New York, 1913–22)
Cath. Rec. Soc. Publ.	*Catholic Record Society Publications*, Record series (London, 1905–)
Census Ire., 1659	*A census of Ireland circa 1659, with supplementary material from the poll money ordinances (1660–1661)*, ed. Séamus Pender (Dublin, 1939)
Civil Survey	*The Civil Survey, A.D. 1654–56*, ed. R.C. Simington (10 vols., Dublin, 1931–61)
Clogher Rec.	*Clogher Record* ([Monaghan], 1953–)
Cloulas, *Correspondance*	Ivan Cloulas (ed.), *Correspondance du nonce en France Anselmo Dandino (1578–1581)* (Rome/Paris, 1970) [i.e. *Acta Nunt. Gall.*, viii]
Collect. Hib.	*Collectanea Hibernica: sources for Irish history* (Dublin, 1958–)
Comment. Rinucc.	Richard O'Ferrall and Robert O'Connell, *Commentarius Rinuccinianus, de Sedis Apostolicae Legatione ad Foederatos Hiberniae Catholicos per annos 1645–9*, ed. Stanislaus Kavanagh (6 vols., Dublin, 1932–49)
Commons' Jn. Ire.	*Journals of the House of Commons of the Kingdom of Ireland* ... (1613–1791, 28 vols., Dublin, 1753–91; reprinted and continued, 1613–1800, 19 vols., Dublin, 1796–1800)
Conry, *Threnodia*	[Maurice Conry], *Threnodia Hiberno-Catholica, sive planctus universalis totius cleri et populi regni Hiberniae* (Innsbruck, 1659)
Coppinger, *Theatre*	[John Coppinger], *The Theatre of Catholique and Protestant Religion* ([Saint-Omer], 1620)
Corish, *Ir. Catholicism*	P.J. Corish (ed.), *A history of Irish Catholicism* (Dublin/Melbourne, 1967–) [A co-operative work, in separate fascicules, beginning with vol. i, I]
DDA	Dublin Diocesan Archives
DHGE	*Dictionnaire d'Histoire et de Géographie Ecclésiastiques* (Paris, 1912–)
DNB	*Dictionary of National Biography*, ed. Sir Leslie Stephen and Sir Sidney Lee (66 vols., London, 1885–1901; reprinted with corrections, 22 vols., London, 1908–9)
DTC	*Dictionnaire de Théologie Catholique* (15 vols., Paris, 1903–50; tables générales, 1951–72)

Dunlop, *Commonwealth*   *Ireland under the Commonwealth: being a selection of documents
                                 relating to the government of Ireland from 1651 to 1659*, ed.
                                 Robert Dunlop (2 vols., Manchester, 1913)

Edwards, *Church and State*   R. Dudley Edwards, *Church and State in Tudor Ireland*
                                 (Dublin, 1935)

Éigse   *Éigse: a Journal of Irish Studies* (Dublin, 1939–)

FLK   Franciscan Library, Killiney, County Dublin

Father Luke Wadding   *Father Luke Wadding commemorative volume*, ed. Franciscan
                                 Fathers, Killiney (Dublin, 1957)

Fiants Ire., Hen. VIII [etc.] 'Calendar to fiants of the reign of Henry VIII ...' [etc.], in
                                 P.R.I. Rep. D.K. 7–22 (Dublin, 1875–90)

Fitzsimon, *Brittannomachia*   Henry Fitzsimon, *Brittannomachia Ministrorum in plerisque et
                                 fidei fundamentis et fidei articulis dissidentium* (Douai, 1614)

Fitzsimon, *Catalogus*   Henry Fitzsimon, *Catalogus Praecipuorum Sanctorum
                                 Hiberniae* (Liège, 1619)

Gilbert, *Contemp. Hist., 1641–52* Sir J.T. Gilbert (ed.), *A contemporary history of affairs in
                                 Ireland, from A.D. 1641 to 1652...* (3 vols., Dublin, 1879)

Gilbert, *Ir. Confed.*   Sir J.T. Gilbert (ed.), *History of the Irish Confederation and
                                 the war in Ireland, 1641–9...* (7 vols., Dublin, 1882–91)

Gonzaga, *De Origine*   Franciscus Gonzaga, *De Origine Seraphicae Religionis
                                 Franciscanae* (Rome, 1587)

HBC   *Handbook of British Chronology*, ed. Sir F. Maurice Powicke
                                 and E.B. Fryde (2nd ed., London, 1961)

HMC   Historical Manuscripts Commission

HMC Rep. 1 [etc.]   —, *First* [etc.] *Report* (London, 1870–)

HMC Rep. Egmont MSS   —, *Egmont Manuscripts* (2 vols., London, 1905)

Hier. Cath.   *Hierarchia Catholica Medii et Recentioris Aevi*, ed. C. Eubel, P.
                                 Gauchat, R. Ritzler, P. Sefrin (Münster [then Padua],
                                 1898–)

Hist. Jn.   *The Historical Journal* (Cambridge, 1958–)

Hist. Studies   *Historical Studies: papers read before the Irish Conference of
                                 Historians* (vols. i–viii, London/Dublin, 1958–71; in
                                 progress)

Hogan, *Distinguished Irishmen* Edmund Hogan, *Distinguished Irishmen of the sixteenth
                                 century* (London, 1894)

Howlin, *Perbreve Compend.*   John Howlin, *Perbreve Compendium in quo continentur
                                 nonnullorum nomina, qui in Hybernia regnante impia Regina
                                 Elisabetha, vincula, martirium et exilium perpessi sunt*, MS in
                                 Maynooth, Salamanca MSS, legajo xi, no. 4

Hughes, *Patentee officers*   *Patentee officers in Ireland, 1173–1876, including high sheriffs,
                                 1661–1684 and 1761–1816*, ed. James L.J. Hughes (Dublin,
                                 1960)

Hughes, *Ref. Eng.*   Philip Hughes, *The Reformation in England* (3 vols.,
                                 London, 1950–54; 5th ed., London, 1963)

IER   *Irish Ecclesiastical Record* (5 series in 172 vols., Dublin,
                                 1864–1968)

IHS   *Irish Historical Studies: the Joint Journal of the Irish Historical
                                 Society and the Ulster Society for Irish Historical Studies*
                                 (Dublin, 1938–)

Inq. Cancell. Hib. Repert.   *Inquisitionum in Officio Rotulorum Cancellariae Hiberniae ...
                                 Repertorium* (2 vols., Dublin, 1826–9)

Ir. Cath. Hist. Comm. Proc.   *Proceedings of the Irish Catholic Historical Committee* (Dublin,
                                 1955–)

Ir. Geneal.   *The Irish Genealogist: Official Organ of the Irish Genealogical
                                 Research Society* (London, 1937–)

Ir. Jurist	*The Irish Jurist*, new series (Dublin, 1966–)
Ir. Sword	*Irish Sword: the Journal of the Military History Society of Ireland* (Dublin, [1949]–)
Ir. Theol. Quart.	*Irish Theological Quarterly* (17 vols., Dublin, 1906–22; Maynooth, 1965–)
JEH	*Journal of Ecclesiastical History* (London/Cambridge, 1950–)
Jones, *Counter-Reformation*	F.M. Jones, 'The Counter-Reformation', in Corish, *Ir. Catholicism*, iii, III
Liber Lovan.	*Liber Lovaniensis*, ed. Cathaldus Giblin (Dublin, 1956)
Liber Mun. Pub. Hib.	*Liber Munerum Publicorum Hiberniae*, ed. Rowley Lascelles (2 vols., London, 1852)
Lodge, *Desiderata*	John Lodge, *Desiderata Curiosa Hibernica* (2 vols., Dublin, 1772)
Lodge, *Peerage Ire.*	John Lodge, *The peerage of Ireland*, revised by Mervyn Archdall (7 vols., Dublin, 1789)
Louvain Papers	*Louvain papers, 1606–1827*, ed. Brendan Jennings; prepared for publication by Cathaldus Giblin (Dublin, 1968)
Lynch, *De Praesulibus Hib.*	John Lynch, *De Praesulibus Hiberniae potissimis Catholicae Religionis in Hibernia, serendae, propagandae, et conservandae authoribus*, ed. J.F. O'Doherty (2 vols., Dublin, 1944)
MacCarthy, *Florence MacCarthy Reagh*	Daniel MacCarthy, *The life and letters of Florence MacCarthy Reagh, tanist of Carbery, MacCarthy Mór* (London, 1867)
Measgra Ui Chléirigh	*Measgra i gCuimhne Mhicil Ui Chléirigh*, ed. Sylvester O'Brien (Dublin, 1944)
Millett, *Ir. Franciscans*	Benignus Millett, *The Irish Franciscans, 1651–1665* (Rome, 1964)
Moran, *Analecta*	*The analecta of David Rothe, bishop of Ossory*, ed. P.F. Moran (Dublin, 1884). Reprint of David Rothe, *De processu martyriali quorundum fidei pugilum in Hibernia, pro complemento Sacrorum Analectorum* (Cologne, 1619)
Moran, *Hist. Cath. Abps*, i	P.F. Moran, *History of the Catholic Archbishops of Dublin since the Reformation*, i (Dublin, 1864)
Moran, *Spicil. Ossor.*	P.F. Moran (ed.), *Spicilegium Ossoriense: being a collection of original letters and papers illustrative of the history of the Irish Church from the Reformation to the year 1800* (3 vols., Dublin, 1874–84)
Mullan, *Idea Tog.*	John Mullan (Molanus), *Idea Togatae Constantiae, sive Francisci Tailleri Dubliniensis praetoris in persecutione congressus et religionis Catholicae defensione interitus* (Paris, 1629)
Mullan, *Epitome Tripartita*	*Epitome Tripartita Martyrum fere omnium qui in Britanicis Insulis nostra patrumque memoria de haeresi gloriose triumpharunt (Paris, 1629)*. This work, with separate title-page, is printed at the end of his *Idea Togatae Constantiae*.
NCE	*New Catholic Encyclopedia* (15 vols., New York, 1967; supplementary vols., 1974–)
NHI	*A new history of Ireland*, ed. T.W. Moody, F.X. Martin, F.J. Byrne and others (Oxford, 1976–)
N.L.I.	National Library of Ireland
Nieremberg, *Ideas*	J.E. Nieremberg, *Ideas de virtud en algunos claros varones de la Compañia de Iesus* (Madrid, 1643)
O'Laverty, *Dioc. Down and Connor*	James O'Laverty, *An historical account of the diocese of Down and Connor, ancient and modern* (5 vols., Dublin, 1878–95)

O'Mahony, *Brevis Synopsis*	Francis O'Mahony, *Brevis Synopsis Provinciae Hyberniae Fratrum Minorum*, in A.S.I., MS W 28. 2; printed in *Anal. Hib.* 6 (1934), 174.
Ormonde MSS	*Calendar of the manuscripts of the marquess of Ormonde, preserved at Kilkenny Castle* (11 vols., London, 1895–1920)
O'Sullivan Beare, *Hist. Cath. Ibern.*	Philip O'Sullivan Beare, *Historiae Catholicae Iberniae Compendium* (Lisbon, 1621)
PRO	Public Record Office of England
PROI	Public Record Office of Ireland
P.R.I. Rep. D.K. 1 [etc.]	*First* [etc.] *report of the Deputy Keeper of the Public Records in Ireland* (Dublin, 1869–)
Pacata Hibernia	[Thomas Stafford], *Pacata Hibernia: Ireland appeased and reduced, or An historie of the late warres in Ireland, especially within the province of Mounster under the government of Sir George Carew* (London, 1633)
Past	*The Past: the Organ of the Uí Ceinnsealaigh Historical Society* (Wexford, 1920–)
Perrott, *Chron. Ire., 1584–1608*	Sir James Perrott, *The chronicle of Ireland, 1584–1608*, ed. Herbert Wood (Dublin, 1933)
Phillips, *Ch. of Ire.*	W. A. Phillips (ed.), *History of the Church of Ireland* (3 vols., Oxford, 1933–4)
R. Hist. Soc. Trans.	*Transactions of the Royal Historical Society* (London, 1872–)
RIA	Royal Irish Academy
RIA Proc.	*Proceedings of the Royal Irish Academy* (Dublin, 1836–)
RSAI Jn.	*Journal of the Royal Society of Antiquaries of Ireland* (Dublin, 1892–)
Rec. Comm. Ire. Rep. 1811–15 [etc.]	*Reports of the commissioners appointed by his majesty to execute the measures recommended in an address of the House of Commons respecting the public records of Ireland; with supplement and appendices* (3 vols., London, 1815–25: i, rep. 1–5, 1811–15; ii, rep. 6–10, 1816–20; iii, rep. 11–15, 1821–5)
Renehan, *Collections*	*Collections on Irish church history, from the MSS of … Laurence F. Renehan*, ed. Daniel McCarthy (2 vols., Dublin, 1861–73)
Reportorium Novum	*Reportorium Novum: Dublin Diocesan Historical Record* (Dublin, 1955–)
Ronan, *Ref. Ire. Eliz.*	M.V. Ronan, *The Reformation in Ireland under Elizabeth, 1558–1580* (London, 1930)
Rothe, *Analecta*	[David Rothe], *Analecta Sacra Nova et Mira, de rebus Catholicorum in Hibernia pro fide et religione gestis, divisa in tres partes* (2 vols., Cologne, 1617–19)
Rothe, *De Processu Martyriali*	[David Rothe], *De processu martyriali quorundum fidei pugilum in Hibernia, pro complemento Sacrorum Analectorum* (Cologne, 1619)
SPO	State Paper Office of Ireland, Dublin Castle
Salamanca MSS	MSS from the Archives of the former Irish College, Salamanca, now preserved in the Library of St Patrick's College, Maynooth
Seanchas Ardmhacha	*Seanchas Ardmhacha: Journal of the Armagh Diocesan Historical Society* ([Armagh], 1954–)
Silke, 'Hugh O'Neill'	J.J. Silke, 'Hugh O'Neill , the Catholic Question and the Papacy', in *I.E.R.*, 5th series, civ (1965), 66–79
Silke, *Kinsale*	J.J. Silke, *Kinsale: the Spanish Intervention in Ireland at the End of the Elizabethan wars* (Liverpool, 1970)

Stat. Ire.	*The statutes at large passed in the Parliaments held in Ireland...* (2 vols., Dublin, 1786–1801)
Stat. of Realm	*The statutes of the realm ...* [of England and Great Britain, to 1713] (9 vols. in 10 and 2 index vols., London, 1810–28)
Steele, *Proclamations*	Robert Steele (ed.), *A bibliography of Royal proclamations of the Tudor and Stuart sovereigns* (2 vols., Oxford, 1910)
TCD	Trinity College, Dublin
Tanner, *Societas Iesu*	Mathias Tanner, *Societas Iesu usque ad Sanguinis et Vitae Profusionem Militans* (Prague, 1675)
Theiner, *Vetera Mon.*	Augustine Theiner, *Vetera Monumenta Hibernorum et Scotorum* (Rome, 1864)
Verstegan, *Theatrum*	Richard Verstegan, *Theatrum Crudelitatum Haereticorum nostri temporis* (Antwerp, 1587)
Wadding Papers	*Wadding papers, 1614–38*, ed. Brendan Jennings (Dublin, 1953)
Wadding, *Scriptores*	Luke Wadding, *Scriptores Ordinis Minorum* (Rome, 1650)
Walsingham Letter-Bk	*The Walsingham letter-book, or Register of Ireland*, ed. James Hogan and N. McNeill O'Farrell (Dublin, 1959)

CHAPTER I

Historical background

Patrick J. Corish

In the century between the accession of Elizabeth I in 1558 and the restoration of Charles II in 1660, two things happened in Ireland that were unique in the history of western Europe. Though a State Church rejecting Roman authority had been established, Roman nominations to the historic episcopal sees were continued, and the great majority of the people opted for a religion which was not that of their civil ruler. These developments took place against a background of legal proscription of Catholicism, frequently escalating into active persecution, civic pressure on Catholics, and wars of conquest that in the end left Catholics largely despoiled of their property and without a political voice.

CATHOLIC CHURCH GOVERNMENT

The consolidation of the formal Reformation establishment in the last decade of the reign of Henry VIII (1537–47) was followed in swift succession first by the introduction of Protestantism in the reign of Edward VI (1547–53) and then by the restoration of Catholicism under Mary (1553–8). In this rapidly changing religious situation the final outcome was quite uncertain, and it is frequently difficult to define the relationships between individual bishops and the Holy See. It may, however, be said with certainty that only a small number actively supported the Reformation, and the pressure the government could put on the bishops as a body to conform was exceedingly limited.[1]

Between 1558 and 1570, the Holy See retained some hope that Elizabeth might not have taken a final decision in religious affairs. Rome continued to make episcopal nominations, especially to sees more remote from the central authority, while carefully avoiding any political confrontation with

[1] As is only to be expected, it is sometimes hard to be certain of the situation in any given diocese in the sixteenth century. Detailed information will be found in the two basic works of reference: *Hier. Cath.*, iii–iv, and *NHI*, ix (Oxford, 1984), 332–438.

the government. This had been the policy recommended by David Wolfe, SJ, who had been named papal nuncio to Ireland in 1560.

Political confrontation came with the papal excommunication of Elizabeth in 1570. As the power of her government in Ireland was gradually extended, Roman episcopal nominations became more intermittent, with the exception of the years 1580–82, when Pope Gregory XIII named twelve bishops in the context of a papally backed but hopeless war against the queen.[2]

The grip of her government in Ireland tightened after the failure of the Spanish Armada in 1588. In addition, Pope Clement VIII (1592–1605) abandoned the policy of confrontation pursued by his predecessors. There was now better material from which to choose pastors for the Catholic Church in Ireland. For some years young Irishmen had been going abroad to study for the priesthood in seminaries in Catholic Europe. Because of the political fragmentation of the country, it had been difficult to establish an Irish seminary in Europe, but the first was opened at Salamanca in 1592, and within a few years there were a number of small Irish seminaries, principally in Spain and the Spanish Netherlands.

The policy inaugurated by Clement VIII was to put these seminary-trained priests in charge of Irish dioceses, not as bishops, but as vicars apostolic without episcopal orders. Bishops were appointed only in exceptional circumstances. This policy was continued after the death of Elizabeth in 1603. By this date armed resistance to the crown had come to an end, but the great bulk of the population had opted for the Catholic Church. As it became clear that the Church might be able to maintain its organization in these highly exceptional circumstances, the Holy See moved cautiously towards the appointment of diocesan bishops. This development was speeded up after the foundation of the Congregation *de Propaganda Fide* in 1622.

During the 1640s, a Catholic civil administration controlled much of Ireland. In these years, every Irish see was filled, with the exception of Derry. All these bishops were swept aside by the Cromwellian conquest (1649–53), but already in 1657 the Holy See nominated two bishops and thirteen vicars apostolic. No further episcopal nominations were made until 1669, but within less than three years after this date bishops had again been

---

2 Research in Irish Tudor history over the past decade has left the older work dated. However, works like R. Dudley Edwards, *Church and state in Tudor Ireland: a history of penal laws against Irish Catholics, 1534–1903* (1972) and G.A. Hayes McCoy in *NHI*, iii, 39–141, may still be consulted for an understanding of the general framework.

nominated in considerable numbers and the pattern of a diocesan episcopate restored.[3]

CIVIL AUTHORITY, CATHOLICISM, AND MARTYRDOM

Elizabeth I (1558–1603)

The task of enforcing the Reformation in their Irish kingdom was far more
demanding than the one which the Tudors successfully completed in
England. Unlike its larger neighbour, sixteenth-century Ireland was a
deeply divided and seriously undergoverned country. Riven by divisions of
an ethnic and factional character, the Anglo-Irish and Gaelic communities
of the island waged constant, if limited, feudal warfare against one another
and among themselves. Though many native leaders paid a formal allegiance to the crown, they tended to heed the authority of their English
sovereigns in practice only when compelled to do so by force.[4] For the
Tudors, then, the objective of enforcing a new religious settlement upon the
whole country had necessarily to wait upon the primary task of the establishment of their rule in matters secular.

The instruments available to the Tudors to impose such government were,
however, quite inadequate to the task. In theory the constitutional and insti-
tutional structure of the Irish polity was a close copy of that of the kingdom
of England, but in actual fact it was something very different. There was an
Irish parliament with a House of Lords and a House of Commons, and it was
hoped that in time the entire political nation of Gaelic and Anglo-Irish
Ireland would be represented in it. It was summoned only six times in the
period 1536–1603, however, and it remained throughout this time a small,
narrow and grossly unrepresentative institution. Thus parliament, the crucial
instrument for the endorsement and enforcement of the Reformation in
England, was incapable of serving such a function for the Tudors in Ireland.
The other instruments of Tudor rule were almost equally unsatisfactory. The
royal courts of law in Ireland were closely modelled upon those in England,
but they remained severely restricted in range and influence in the country.
Where they existed, local courts were the preserve of local elites.[5]

---

3 P.J. Corish, *The Catholic community in the seventeenth and eighteenth centuries* (Dublin, 1981),
18–72. 4 For a comprehensive survey of Ireland in the early Tudor period, see D.B. Quinn
and K.W. Nicholls in *NHI*, iii, 1–38; more detailed accounts of Gaelic and Anglo-Irish
society will be found in K.W. Nicholls, *Gaelic and Gaelicised Ireland in the Middle Ages* (Dublin,
1972), and James Lydon, *Ireland in the later Middle Ages* (Dublin, 1973). 5 The best modern

Because these formal means of government lacked any real strength, the Tudors were forced to rely, when occasion demanded, upon a set of extraordinary or informal methods, which were only rarely employed in England. The crown's will was frequently asserted in Ireland simply through royal proclamation without any pretence at securing parliamentary consent.[6] Presidential courts, which dispensed law by virtue of the royal prerogative, were established in the provinces of Munster and Connacht. They were given an authority and breadth of jurisdiction far in excess of those in operation in Wales and the north of England. But more commonly, in order to impose their authority, officers of the crown, acting at national, regional or local level, had recourse to martial law and frequently sheer force of arms. Most important of all, the Tudors were forced to maintain an increasingly large standing army in the country in order to defend their Irish charge. At bottom such peace and order as existed in Ireland in the sixteenth century were sustained by military might.[7]

The heavy cost of such dependence on military force tended, however, to counsel the parsimonious Tudors towards caution in their proceedings in Ireland. They preferred where possible to avoid the expense of outright confrontation and to secure compliance by persuasion, by intrigue, and by the sheer passage of time; they faced up to conflict only where no other options seemed available. Tudor policy towards Ireland thus tended to oscillate between long periods of neglect or cautious toleration and sudden crises of frenetic, forceful action. This was to be particularly true of their enforcement of religious change.[8]

The progress of the Reformation in Ireland followed closely the pattern established in England. Thus the statutes passed in England between 1529 and 1536 were largely repeated in the parliament held in Ireland in the years

---

account of English administrative structures is Penry Williams, *The Tudor regime* (Oxford, 1979). Nothing comparable is as yet available for Ireland. But on parliament, see T.W. Moody, 'The Irish Parliament under Elizabeth and James I', in *RIA Proc.*, sect. C, xlv (1939), 41–81; V.W. Treadwell, 'The Irish Parliament of 1569–71', in *RIA Proc.*, sect. C, lxv (1966–7), 55–89; Brendan Bradshaw, 'The beginnings of Modern Ireland', in Brian Farrell (ed.), *The Irish parliamentary tradition* (Dublin, 1974), 68–87. On local government see D.B. Quinn, 'Anglo-Irish Local Government, 1485–1534', in *IHS* i (1939), 354–81. For the full treatment of the central courts, see S.G. Ellis, *Reform and renewal* (Woodbridge, 1986), 106–64.   **6** See *Tudor royal proclamations*, ed. P.L. Myles and J. Larkin (3 vols, New Haven, 1964–9), passim. **7** Presidents and other provincial military governors are discussed in N.P. Canny, *The Elizabethan conquest of Ireland: a pattern established, 1565–1576* (Hassocks, 1976), and Penry Williams, 'The Munster Presidency in the Later Sixteenth Century', in *Irish Committee of Historical Sciences Bulletin*, new series, viii, no. 94 (1961), 20–3.   **8** The most recent narratives of the political polity of sixteenth-century Ireland are R.D. Edwards, *Ireland in the age of the Tudors* (London, 1978), and G.A. Hayes-McCoy in *NHI*, iii, 39–141.

1536–7. Similarly, an attempt was made to enforce in Ireland the radical doctrinal changes, which were enacted in England during the reign of Edward VI. Queen Mary's re-establishment of Catholicism was formally given effect in Ireland by the parliament held there in 1556–7, and the Irish parliament of 1560 re-established Protestantism as the official religion of Ireland under the terms of the Elizabethan settlement of 1559.[9]

The Irish experience of that settlement tended if anything towards greater flexibility than was the case in England. The Act of Uniformity passed in Ireland in 1560, for example, allowed for greater latitude in the use of the Book of Common Prayer than was granted in England.[10] The moderate character of the religious settlement in Ireland became more pronounced in later decades as repeatedly the government failed to enforce the coercive legislation passed against recusants in England. Attempts by the executive to do so were repeatedly forestalled by firm opposition in the Irish parliaments of 1569–71 and 1585.[11]

The difficulty encountered by the Dublin administration in following the pattern set by the English parliament is a reflection of its general problems in enforcing the Reformation. In the first decade of Elizabeth's reign, little was done to give practical effect to the Anglican settlement either by the reform and improvement of the Established Church or by the enforcement of the penal clauses in the legislation because of the governors' predominant concern with political and financial matters. Even for some years after the publication of the papal bull *Regnans in excelsis*, the Irish government, despite the occasional admonitions of the crown and the periodic recognition on the part of the administration of the need for greater effort, remained remarkably lax. It was only in the latter half of the 1570s, when a series of internal crises in Ireland coincided with a larger international threat to the Elizabethan regime, that a policy of strict conformity and the severe oppression of dissent was embarked upon.[12]

The failure of the Irish administration in the critical years before 1575 to

9 The standard account of State religious policy remains Edwards, *Church and State*. Edwards's work has been significantly revised in Brendan Bradshaw, 'The opposition to the ecclesiastical legislation in the Irish Reformation parliament of 1536–7', in *IHS* 16 (1969), 285–303, and 'The Edwardian Reformation in Ireland', in *Archiv. Hib.* 34 (1975–6), 83–99. 10 2 Eliz., c. 2 (*Stat. Ire.*, i, 284–9). 11 See articles by Treadwell and Bradshaw cited in note 5 above. 12 The most detailed accounts of government policy in the 1560s and 1570s remain G.V. Jourdan, 'The transitional stage of reform', in Phillips, *Ch. of Ire.*, ii, 292–375, and Ronan, *Ref. Ire. Eliz.* For a recent debate on the character and progress of the Reformation in this period, see Brendan Bradshaw, 'Sword, word and strategy in the Reformation in Ireland', in *Hist. Jn.* 21 (1978), 475–502, and N.P. Canny, 'Why the Reformation failed in Ireland: *une question mal posée*', in *JEH* 30 (1979), 423–50.

enforce the Reformation statutes was to be decisive in two ways. In the first place it was to leave sections of the population unaware of and indifferent to the established religion. But more importantly, the government's inaction provided an opportunity for a revitalized and dynamic Catholicism to gain ground among a small but influential section of the clergy and laity.[13] Clerics like Dermot O'Hurley and Patrick O'Healy, who had been educated abroad at the universities of Douai, Louvain, and Salamanca for the Counter-Reformation mission, returned to Ireland imbued with Counter-Reformationary zeal to propagate the faith.[14] Lay people like Margaret Bermingham and the Wexford townsmen who were becoming more confident in their commitment to Catholicism received the words of the missioners with enthusiasm.

The administrative neglect and uncertainty, which was creating such a serious threat to the government's religious policy, had already produced an equally grave and much more immediate challenge to the Tudor attempt to enforce law and order in secular terms. Between 1579 and 1603, the government of Ireland was engulfed by a series of crises which threatened to overthrow the entire structure of Tudor rule there and galvanized it into immediate action. In 1579, rebellion, which had been simmering for some time in Desmond, erupted into full-scale revolt that lasted until 1583. Simultaneously, a widespread conspiracy, which was uncovered in the heart of the Pale itself, produced a rebellion in which were implicated such leading Anglo-Irish families as the Nugents of Delvin in County Westmeath and the Eustaces of Kilcullen in County Kildare. Increasing troubles in Gaelic Ulster in the later 1580s resulted in the rebellion of the great northern chieftains, O'Neill and O'Donnell, which lasted from 1594 to the end of the reign and involved the entire island.[15]

13 On the general context of the early Counter-Reformation in Ireland, see Colm Lennon, 'Recusancy and the Dublin Stanyhursts', in *Archiv. Hib.* 33 (1975), 101–10, and 'Richard Stanihurst (1547–1618) and Old English Identity', in *IHS* 31 (1978), 121–43. 14 On the continental seminaries, see John Brady, 'The Irish Colleges in Europe and the Counter-Reformation', in *Ir. Cath. Hist. Comm. Proc.* (1957), 1–8, and 'Father Christopher Cusack and the Irish College at Douai', in *Measgra Uí Chléirigh*, 98–117; Helga Hammerstein, 'Aspects of the Continental education of Irish students in the reign of Elizabeth I', in *Hist. Studies* 8 (1971), 137–54; T. J. Walsh *The Irish Continental College movement* (Dublin, 1973); John Brady (ed.), 'The Irish Colleges in the Low Countries', in *Archiv. Hib.* 14 (1949), 66–91; D.J. O'Doherty (ed.), 'Students of the Irish College, Salamanca', in *Archiv. Hib.* 2 (1913), 1–36, 3 (1914), 87–112; Brendan Jennings, 'Irish students in the University of Louvain', in *Measgra Uí Chléirigh*, 74–97; Canice Mooney, 'The Golden Age of the Irish Franciscans', ibid., 21–33; Edmund Hogan, *Ibernia Ignatiana*, i (Dublin, 1880), and Hogan, *Distinguished Irishmen*. 15 On the closing stages of Tudor rule in Ireland see Hayes-McCoy in *NHI*, iii, 94–141; a specific study of the Baltinglass rebellion and the Nugent conspiracy is to be found in David

Although the causes of these upheavals were fundamentally political, the rebel leaders often justified their defiance of the crown in religious terms.[16] By declaring their causes to be spiritually inspired, they hoped to attract aid from Catholic powers, particularly Spain, and also to strengthen unity and loyalty among their followers. The government's response in the face of these manifestations of dissent was based on an undiscriminating perception of the issues. The same forceful measures which were applied to rebels in the field were used to prosecute Catholic dissidents, including martial law and the presidency courts. It was in these circumstances that many Catholic clerics such as Dermot O'Hurley and others, whose involvement was non-political, were put to death.

James I (1603–25)

When the threat to the State was lifted with the ending of the Nine Years War in 1603, the government determined to avail itself of the peaceful conditions obtaining throughout the country and of the opportunity provided by conquest to enforce the State religion in a more systematic way.[17] The growing influence of the Catholic clergy was attested to by the issuing of a proclamation in 1605 ordering priests to quit the realm. Also in that year, the laity were instructed to attend Divine Service in accordance with the law, and 'mandates' were issued to several aldermen and prominent citizens of Dublin, requiring them to accompany the Governor to church.[18] For the first time since the Elizabethan settlement was enacted in 1560, recusants were penalized systematically and on a geographically widespread basis. Repressive measures were suspended only when civil unrest threatened to coincide with military rebellion, as in the case of the O'Doherty revolt of 1608, or when the foreign policies of the Jacobean government dictated that a conciliatory approach be adopted towards Irish Catholics. Government attempts in the parliament of 1613–15 to pass into law some of the measures introduced by proclamation failed because of the virulence of the Catholic opposition in the House of Commons.[19]

That the measures which actually were enforced proved ineffective is evidenced by the fact, for example, that the proclamation against priests was reissued in 1611 and 1624.[20] Large sums were gathered by the State by way of recusancy fines. By the end of the reign, a new resident Catholic

---

Mathew, *The Celtic peoples and Renaissance Europe* (London, 1933), ch. x. **16** See J.J. Silke, *Ireland and Europe, 1559–1607* (Dundalk, 1966), and 'The Irish Appeal of 1593 to Spain', in *IER*, 5th series, 92 (1959) 270–90, 362–71. **17** See Aidan Clarke in *NHI*, iii, 187–232. **18** Steele, *Proclamations*, ii, 17 (no. 184). **19** Moody, loc. cit. **20** Steele, *Proclamations*, ii, 20, 26 (nos. 203, 247) (13 July 1611, 21 Jan. 1624).

episcopate was competing successfully with the Established Church structure.[21] In its efforts to enforce conformity the government used a mixture of established legal forms and extraordinary or prerogative instruments. The difficulty experienced in securing convictions for recusancy before the jury courts forced the government to make use of the prerogative court of Castle Chamber. Before this court were brought those who had failed to obey the 'mandates' of 1605, those who refused to take the Oath of Supremacy on being elected to public office, and empanelled jurors who failed to find a verdict for the crown in recusancy cases. The court was not bound by the scale of penalties imposed by statute law: the normal sentence was a heavy fine and, frequently, imprisonment during pleasure.[22]

Charles I (1625–49)

In Ireland as in England, conditions improved for Catholics with the accession of Charles I in 1625. The social and political situation in Ireland was complex. The adherents of the Established Church were known as the 'New English'. The title was reasonably descriptive, for most of them had arrived from England since the Reformation. They had amassed considerable wealth in the confiscations, and they sought the monopoly of political power, which was theirs by the letter of the law. The 'Old English' were the descendants of settlers who had come from England before the Reformation.[23] As a body, they were now firmly committed to the Catholic Church. They had lost little in the confiscations and were still a wealthy group. They sought to retain the political power which was generally accepted to be the natural concomitant of property. The Old Irish, descendants of the original Gaelic stock, had been largely despoiled of property. They were coming to place most of their hopes in an insurrection with Spanish support.[24]

The Catholic Church had the allegiance of the great bulk of the population. The precarious toleration it had enjoyed was sufficient to allow the establishment of a diocesan jurisdiction and even the beginnings of a parish

---

21 On the recovery of the Catholic clergy and laity under James see P.J. Corish, 'The Reorganisation of the Irish Church, 1603–1641', in *Ir. Cath. Hist. Comm. Proc.* (1957), 9–14, and *The Catholic community in the seventeenth and eighteenth centuries* (Dublin, 1981), ch. ii; see also John Meagher (ed.), 'Presentments of Recusants in Dublin, 1617–18', in *Reportorium Novum* 2 (1957–60), 269–73. 22 See Herbert Wood, 'The Court of Castle Chamber', in *RIA Proc.*, sect. C, xxxii (1913–16), 152–70; the records of the court *c.* 1573–1620 are printed in *HMC Rep. Egmont MSS*, i, 1–16. 23 For an account of how this title had come to be adopted by this social group by the early years of the seventeenth century, see N.P. Canny, *The formation of the Old English elite in Ireland* (Dublin, 1975). 24 See especially Aidan Clarke, *The Old English in Ireland, 1625–42* (London, 1966), and in *NHI*, iii, 187–288.

system. Religious Orders could begin to live in community.[25] The early years of the reign of Charles I were particularly favourable because England was engaged in foreign wars, and the strain this placed on the government enabled the Catholics to strike a bargain. In return for a sum of money, they received the 'Graces', a royal assurance in the areas of religion, property and political office. However, the government did not have the strength to implement its promises, even had it had the will. When the wars came to an end, Lord Deputy Falkland (1622–9) issued a proclamation dated 1 April 1629 forbidding the exercise of ecclesiastical jurisdiction derived from Rome and ordering all houses of Catholic religious to be closed or in default confiscated. Catholics suffered considerable harassment for some time after this proclamation, but the resources of the State were insufficient to maintain it, and, when it died down early in 1631, it had proved to have been an inconvenience rather than a disaster.

A new lord deputy was appointed in 1633, Thomas Wentworth (created earl of Strafford in 1640). He was to remain in office until 1641.[26] His policy was to restore the authority of the crown against all groups that threatened it. These included the New English Protestants. As for the practice of the Catholic religion, he proposed to eradicate that in time, but he judged that, for the moment, repressive measures were provocative and ineffective, and in consequence not to be pushed. However, in matters of property and political office, he gave every indication that he would not honour the 'Graces'. When parliament met in March 1640, Strafford faced a combined opposition of New English Protestants and Old English Catholics. He was recalled to England.

Parliament was still in session when the Old Irish of Ulster rose in arms on 23 October 1641.[27] The Old English Catholics offered their services to the government to help in suppressing them. When these offers were rejected by a government now dominated by the New English Protestants, they reluctantly joined the Old Irish in a 'confederacy' to protect their common interests. Similar groups were taking shape at this time in both England and Scotland, and the situation was to lead to a decade of civil war.

By the spring of 1642, the Confederate Catholics held most of Ireland, though the Protestants in Ulster were able to defend most of their possessions, and the government held sizeable areas around Dublin and Cork. Then in June 1642, the Irish Catholics met at Kilkenny to organize their

25 Corish, *The Catholic community*, op. cit. 18–42. **26** See especially H.F. Kearney, *Strafford in Ireland, 1633–41* (Manchester, 1959). **27** P.J. Corish, 'The origins of Catholic Nationalism', in Corish, *Ir. Catholicism*, iii, VIII, and in *NHI*, iii, 289–335.

confederacy. They emphasized their loyalty to the king, but demanded 'free exercise of the Roman Catholic faith and religion'. Long-drawn-out negotiations with the king began in September 1643. The different interests proved irreconcilable. The most the king could envisage was 'prerogative' toleration, that is, toleration by royal clemency without formal repeal of the penal laws. The Old English would have liked more, but they were prepared to accept this, provided their civic and social status was assured. It was totally unacceptable to the papal nuncio, Archbishop Rinuccini, who arrived in October 1645. He won the support of the Old Irish. These dissensions tore the Confederation of Kilkenny apart. Rinuccini left Ireland in February 1649, after the Old English, in the name of the Confederate Catholics, had reached an agreement with the lord lieutenant, the marquis of Ormond.

The Commonwealth (1649–60)

By the time the Irish Catholics had signed their agreement with Ormond, the Civil War had ended in England. The king was executed at the end of January 1649. On 15 August, Oliver Cromwell arrived in Ireland to begin a ruthless war of conquest against divided opposition, that ended with piecemeal surrenders in the first half of 1653.[28] Civil government had been restored with the arrival from England of Charles Fleetwood in September 1652. He came with instructions to put the laws of England into operation in Ireland 'as far as present affairs will permit'. On 6 January 1653, the civil authorities in Ireland issued an order that all priests should leave the country within twenty days under penalty of an English statute of 1585 (27 Eliz., c. 2). This statute had made all priests who failed to leave automatically guilty of treason, and those who abetted them guilty of felony. A similar proposal had failed to pass an Irish parliament, also in 1585, but it was now deemed to be law in Ireland.

From 2 March 1653 there was a de facto union of England and Ireland. Irish members sat in the Westminster parliaments of 1653, 1654–5, 1656–8 and 1659. However, no legislation was passed formally uniting the two kingdoms.[29]

In a reform of the treason laws, dated 19 January 1654, it was explicitly declared that the laws passed against Catholics in England under Elizabeth I and James I still held good.[30] These laws decreed among other things that

---

28 For a general survey of the events of the Commonwealth period, see P.J. Corish in *NHI*, iii, 336–86, and T.C. Barnard, *Cromwellian Ireland* (Oxford, 1975).   **29** T. C. Barnard, 'Planters and policies in Cromwellian Ireland', in *Past and Present* 61 (Nov. 1973), 60–5, and *Cromwellian Ireland*, 28–49.   **30** *Acts and Ordinances, Interregnum*, ii, 834–5.

priests ordained by authority of the see of Rome were guilty of high treason by the very fact of their presence in the country.

THE MEMORY OF THE MARTYRS

It is clear from the accounts of individual martyrs that they were remembered in Ireland. There are references to pilgrimages to their graves and to veneration of their relics. However, this had to be done very discreetly as Catholicism became more and more effectively a legally proscribed religion. The memory faded almost to extinction during the long trial of the eighteenth century. As in so many other things, the most permanent legacy derived from Irish exiles in Catholic Europe. It was here for the most part that the lives of the martyrs were committed to writing, and more often than not printed. An account of these 'martyrologies' is given in the Appendix.

By the end of the Penal Code, at the beginning of the nineteenth century, the Irish Catholic memory was not far from being a *tabula rasa*, and its recovery was inevitably slow. In the early stages a crucial role was played by Maynooth College, founded in 1795 to train Catholic priests, in place of the many centres in Catholic Europe that had been confiscated during the French Revolution. By its second generation, say about 1830, it was beginning to take a leading part in the intellectual recovery of the Irish Catholic heritage, though inevitably hampered by the fact that there was little immediately to hand by way of source material. Two names in particular stand out. One was Matthew Kelly, who died in 1858 at the age of forty-four. He concentrated on the preparation of new critical editions of the seventeenth-century exile publications. The second was Lawrence Renehan, who died in 1857, aged fifty-nine. He had a longer life, but it was filled with other duties. To begin with, he had been appointed to teach Scripture, and he was the kind of person towards whom administrative tasks gravitated (he became president of the College in 1845). Nevertheless, he found time to collect sources for Irish Catholic history, still existing in many manuscript volumes in the College Library, and he planned – and in great part achieved – a survey of the Irish Catholic archbishops and bishops from the Reformation onwards.

Meanwhile, archival sources for Irish history were being opened up, in London and Dublin and, though a bit more tardily, in Rome. The pioneer explorer of the Irish heritage in the papal archives was, beyond all question,

Patrick Francis Moran. He was also the first to focus specifically on the Irish martyrs. He developed his interest when he was vice-rector of the Irish College, Rome, between 1855 and 1866, with the active encouragement of his uncle, Archbishop Paul Cullen of Dublin. Moran came back to Dublin in 1866, as secretary to Cullen, now a cardinal. Their active interest in the martyrs continued, even after Moran had left Dublin to become in turn bishop of Ossory and cardinal archbishop of Sydney. He had fitted the collection and publication of a great corpus of historical material into a very busy life.

The canonical presentation of this material was organized under Archbishop William Walsh (1885–1921). By 1917, the relevant Roman Congregation had approved the introduction of the causes of 260 Irish martyrs. Progress now depended on historical expertise. What was required was to show from credible testimony that any given person died in defence of his or her Catholic faith. An extensive documentation was assembled and forwarded to Rome in 1930. There was in fact a steady growth in historical understanding of the complexities of Irish history in the sixteenth and seventeenth centuries – here the establishment of the National University of Ireland in 1908 was a key factor – but resources were still unequal to the great number of causes proposed. In 1936, the Roman Congregation sensibly demanded that a selection be made, but also kept insisting that the full documentation be completed to its satisfaction, and this long process was finished only in 1978.

In 1975, Archbishop Dermot Ryan set up a Diocesan Commission for Causes, composed of professional historians. The members of the Commission were (from 1981): Patrick J. Corish (chairman), Benignus Millett, OFM (secretary), Kevin Kennedy, PP, Francis Finegan, SJ, F.X. Martin, OSA, Drs Ciaran Brady and Colm Lennon. The following auxiliary members were co-opted: John J. Meagher, PP, James Coombes, PP, Kieran Devlin, PP, and Augustine Valkenburg, OP.

Their remit was to determine with all possible accuracy the facts of the life and death of each martyr proposed. It would appear that quite simply the time was ripe, and only now ripe, in that the historical background was sufficiently well understood and a competent team could be assembled. Experience had also shown the need to be selective. Twelve causes were chosen, comprising seventeen individuals. This short list aimed to be as representative as possible, of bishops, diocesan clergy, religious orders, laymen and laywomen. For each cause, all the documentation had to be presented, in a new critical edition, and on the basis of this a 'biographical conspectus' drawn up. It is these lives of the martyrs that are presented here. The person named in connection with each study had the primary responsibility for drawing it up. The texts, with annotation, are as submitted in 1988. (They were individually reprinted in the *Irish Theological Quarterly* over the years 1999, 2000 and 2001.)

The work of the Commission was transmitted to the Roman Congregation for the Causes of Saints in 1988. After due consideration the Congregation issued its Decree of Approval on 6 July 1991. The seventeen martyrs were beatified by Pope John Paul II in St Peter's Square on 27 September 1992. They were:

h = hanged; h.d.q. = hanged, drawn and quartered

I.	PATRICK O'HEALY, OFM			
	Bishop of Mayo	h.	Kilmallock	*c.* 13 August 1579
	CONN O'ROURKE, OFM			
	Priest	h.	Kilmallock	*c.* 13 August 1579
II.	MATTHEW LAMBERT			
	Layman	h.d.q.	Wexford	July 1581
	ROBERT MEYLER			
	Layman	h.d.q.	Wexford	July 1581
	EDWARD CHEEVERS			
	Layman	h.d.q.	Wexford	July 1581
	PATRICK CAVANAGH			
	Layman	h.d.q.	Wexford	July 1581
III.	DERMOT O'HURLEY			
	Archbishop of Cashel	h.	Dublin	20 June 1584
IV	MARGARET BALL			
	(née BERMINGHAM)			
	Laywoman	died in prison	Dublin	*c.* 1584
V.	MAURICE MacKENRAGHTY			
	Secular priest	h.	Clonmel	20 April 1585
VI.	DOMINIC COLLINS, SJ			
	Lay Brother	h.	Youghal	31 October 1602
VII.	CONOR O'DEVANY, OFM			
	Bishop of Down and Connor	h.d.q.	Dublin	1 February 1612
	PATRICK O'LOUGHRAN			
	Secular priest	h.d.q.	Dublin	1 February 1612
VIII.	FRANCIS TAYLOR			
	Layman	died in prison	Dublin	30 January 1621
IX.	PETER HIGGINS, OP			
	Priest	h.	Dublin	23 March 1642
X.	TERENCE ALBERT O'BRIEN, OP			
	Bishop of Emly	h.	Limerick	30 October 1651
XI.	JOHN KEARNEY, OFM			
	Priest	h.	Clonmel	11 March 1653
XII.	WILLIAM TIRRY, OSA			
	Priest	h.	Clonmel	2 May 1654

In 1998, a further list of eighteen causes, comprising forty-two individuals, was submitted to the Congregation for the Causes of Saints.

CHAPTER 2

Patrick O'Healy, OFM, and Conn O'Rourke, OFM

Benignus Millett

EARLY LIFE: PATRICK O'HEALY

Nothing is known for certain of the early life of Bishop Patrick O'Healy. There is no definite evidence about when or where he was born. In a letter dated 24 June 1575, which is preserved in the Archivo General de Simancas in Spain, he is called 'fray Patricio Oheli de Petra'.[1] This geographical description could stand for *Petra Patricii*, a Latinization of *Carraig Phádraig*, the old Gaelic name for the hill on which the friary of Dromahaire, in County Leitrim, was built. If so, it could be taken that O'Healy was a native of Dromahaire or, alternatively, was an alumnus of the friary at that place. *Petra* alone, standing for *Carraig* or *Carrick*, is too vague to be identified with any degree of probability.

Thomas Bourchier, an English Franciscan who lived with O'Healy in Paris in 1578–9 and knew him reasonably well, records that this Irish friar had a good education in his youth, that he was intellectually brilliant, and that he went to Spain to study at the University of Alcalá, where he outstripped all his contemporaries.[2] The information is given in the chapter which he devoted to the two Irish martyrs in his book on the martyrs of the Franciscan Order. This work was read with avid interest by Father Juan Campoy, who translated it from Latin into Spanish and inserted details of the courses of studies pursued in Spain by Patrick O'Healy, with whom he had been acquainted. From the information given in his manuscript (now lost) by Campoy and transmitted by José Corbalán in his *Hierarchia Tripartita*[3]

1 'Haura ocho dias que llego aqui fray Patricio Oheli de Petra y me dio la carta de V Md de los xxi de Março.' Juan de Cuniga, ambassador, to Philip II, Rome, 24 June 1575; deciphered copy in Archivo General de Simancas, Secretaria de Estado: Negociaciones de Roma, leg. 925 (only partly foliated); the letter is to be found *c.* ff. 81–4. This and other relevant letters dealing with this petition to the pope and the king of Spain have been briefly described by Canice Mooney in *Breifne* 1 (1961), 338. 2 Bourchier, *Historia*, 234–62. 3 José Corbalán, *Hierarchia tripartita venerabilium servorum ac famularum Dei provinciae seraphicae*

a general outline of O'Healy's activities between 1562 and 1574 emerges. In 1562 the young Patrick O'Healy arrived in Rome from Ireland and sought out Francisco Zamora, the minister general of the Observant Franciscans. It seems that he had already made his novitiate and taken his vows, and that his religious superiors in Ireland had sent him to the minister general to arrange further religious formation and ecclesiastical studies; there is no mention by the Spanish historians of a canonical novitiate in Spain.

Zamora, who was a native of Cuenca, was deeply impressed by the zealous young man, showed him many kindnesses, and sent him to his own Franciscan province of Cartagena to be trained and educated. O'Healy, after studying grammar for two years in the friary of St Francis in Molina de Aragón, was transferred to the friary in San Clemente, where he was taught philosophy for four years. While there he was incorporated into the province of Cartagena.[4] He then went to the friary in Cuenca to study theology. The record of his ordination to the priesthood has not been found.[5] His superiors next sent him to Alcalá de Henares where, as a boarder at the university, he completed his theological training. He was a fluent speaker of Catalan and a very effective preacher. O'Healy was a very young man when he met Zamora in Rome in 1562. If he were then between sixteen and nineteen years of age, he would have been born between 1543 and 1546.

Having completed his studies, he was anxious to return to Ireland and labour as a priest among his afflicted fellow-countrymen. In 1574–5 there were in Spain a number of prominent Irish clerics who were endeavouring to persuade Philip II to give assistance to the Catholics of Ireland. They would have been pleased to avail themselves of the services of this young Franciscan priest because of his competence and the respect in which he was held. Most active among those agents was Maurice MacGibbon, OCist,

Carthaginensis, 1688, AGOFM, MS T/16, 19–24 [hereafter Corbalán, *Hierarchia tripartita*]; printed in José Corbalán, *Hierarchia tripartita venerabilium servorum ac famularum Dei provinciae seraphicae Carthaginensis*, ed. Antonio Martín (Vich, 1925), 17–19.1. 'Haura ocho dias que llego aqui fray Patricio Oheli de Petra y me dio la carta de V Md de los xxi de Março.' Juan de Cuniga, ambassador, to Philip II, Rome, 24 June 1575; deciphered copy in Archivo General de Simancas, Secretaria de Estado: Negociaciones de Roma, leg. 925 (only partly foliated); the letter is to be found *c*. ff. 81–4. This and other relevant letters dealing with this petition to the pope and the king of Spain have been briefly described by Canice Mooney in *Breifne* 1 (1961), 338. **4** Melchor de Huélamo, *Hystoria de las personas illustres y notables en santidad, de la santa provincia de Carthagena, de la orden de nuestro seraphico padre San Francisco* (Cuenca, 1617), f. 73r. **5** In the diocesan archives of Cuenca the earliest register of ordination records covers the years 1566–71. It does not contain any reference to Patrick O'Healy. The next register preserved there begins in 1602. Moreover, there is no mention of O'Healy in the bundle of documents relating to ordinations which is also in the archives.

the papal archbishop of Cashel.[6] Clearly O'Healy was approached by MacGibbon or someone close to him with a definite proposal to place before the king and the pope. It was not a new plan but one which some of the Irish Catholic leaders had been urging for about five years.[7]

The earliest reference to Patrick O'Healy in extant contemporary documentation occurs in the letter of 24 June 1575 already mentioned. This letter was written by Don Juan de Cuniga, the Spanish ambassador at the papal court, to Philip II. The ambassador states that O'Healy arrived in Rome eight days earlier (i.e. 16 June), presented to him a paper from the king, presumably a letter of recommendation, dated 21 March, and explained that the purpose of his visit was to request the pope to grant letters patent and supplies to a leading Irish Catholic nobleman (i.e. James Fitzmaurice, who is not named) who was prepared to lead Irish Catholics in a rebellion against the heretical queen of England and acknowledge Don Juan of Austria as king of Ireland. The ambassador asked for more detailed information. O'Healy remained in Rome, urging his case through Cardinal Alciati, protector of Ireland, and the cardinal bishop of Como, Tolomeo Galli. He made a favourable impression on the ambassador, and Cuniga commended him to the king in another of his letters.[8]

Bourchier relates that the young friar discussed the plight of the Irish Catholics with his minister general, Christopher Cheffontaine, and Gregory XIII. On 4 July 1576, Pope Gregory provided Patrick O'Healy to the diocese of Mayo, at the instance of Cardinal Alciati.[9] The relevant minute of this meeting of the consistory shows that he was an Observant Franciscan and implies that he was in Rome at the time of his appointment. Between this date and the autumn of 1578 there is frequent reference to him in the correspondence of various papal representatives, and four letters written by him and four addressed to him have survived. From this documentation he emerges as a clear historical figure.

About 10 November 1576, the papal secretary of state, Tolomeo Cardinal Galli, wrote to the king of Spain and to Don Juan of Austria, then governor of Flanders, and informed them that the pope was sending each of them a brief.[10] Galli told them that certain Irishmen, and especially the Observant

---

6 Moran, *Spicil. Ossor.*, i, 59–71.   7 See, e.g., *Cal. S.P. Rome 1558–71*, 379–85; *Cal. S.P. Spain 1568–79*, 159, 210, 147, 193, 308, 309, 315.   8 'Fray Patricio o helio de petra ha andado aqui solicitando su pretension por medio del Cardl Alciato que es protector de Irlanda y el Card de Como ... fray Patricio queda aqui, esperando esta respuesta. Ha tratado este negocio con menos reydo y con mejor termino que otros que han venido por aca con semejantes demandas.' A.G. Sim., Secretaria de Estado: Negociaciones de Roma, leg. 925, f. 201. 9 *Archiv. Hib.* 5 (1916), 173.   10 'Venendo a questa Corte il Padre Frate Patrizio creato da

Franciscan Patrick, whom the pope had appointed bishop of Mayo, intimated on several occasions to His Holiness the willingness of the Irish to surrender Ireland to His Catholic Majesty or to whomsoever he should approve. Because of the distance involved, wrote Galli, the pope was unable to lend such aid as he would wish, but both he and Galli were entirely in favour of the plan because it was a question of restoring the Catholic faith. Accordingly, the bishop of Mayo was to put the plan before the king.

At this point the sources make no mention of James Fitzmaurice at the papal court. Towards the end of February 1577, he was in Rome and intended going to Ireland via Portugal, where he wished to visit his young son who was at school in Lisbon.[11] On 2 April, Galli informed Don Juan of Austria that the pope had sent Fitzmaurice to Portugal with substantial financial aid, there to embark for Ireland to assist his friends-in-arms against the heretical queen.[12] By 31 May 1577, Fitzmaurice was in Madrid with Bishop O'Healy and Father David Wolfe, the former Jesuit.[13] On 29 June, Antonio Clementini, secretary to the nuncio, reported to Galli from Spain that the king, to avoid arousing suspicions, had decided that Fitzmaurice should not go to the royal court, but that O'Healy and Nicholas Sanders were there.[14] The sources next show Bishop O'Healy in Portugal. On 14 November 1577, he wrote from Lisbon to Canobio, the papal collector, thanking him for using his influence with the Spanish king's ambassador in

Nostro Signore vescovo Maionense per supplicare Sua Maestà Catholica a non perdere l'occasione che si presenta di restituire nel la patria sua d'Hibernia la fede Catholica con l'acquisto del domino di quel regno che puo servire anche ad altre cose maggiori, Sua Santità non potendo, come sarebbe suo desiderio, per la lontananza de' paesi, giovare a questa impresa con altro, ha scritto sopra di cio a la Maestà sua, et a Vostra Altezza come vedrà nel suo breve, ed ha voluto che io ancora con questa mia le raccomandi di questa negotiatione, la quale con il servizio di Dio, e di Sua Maestà Catholica è anco indirizzata a l'honore e grandezza di Vostra Altezza, come meglio intenderà da detto Padre.' Cardinal Galli to Don Juan of Austria, Rome, 10 November 1576 (copy), in AV, Fondo Borghese, series IV, 214, f. 94; printed in *Archiv. Hib.* 4 (1915), 219. See also two papal briefs in AV, Arm. LII, 31; English summary of same in *Cal. S.P. Rome, 1572–8*, 286–7. **11** *Archiv. Hib.* 7 (1918–21), 85–6; *Cal. S.P. Rome, 1572–8*, 293. On 15 March Fitzmaurice was in Genoa (ibid., 295). O'Healy, in his letter of 31 March 1578 to Galli (Patrick O'Healy to Tolomeo Cardinal Galli, Paris, 31 March 1578: AV, Segretario di Stato, Francia, 12, ff. 78r–79v.), says that he acted on behalf of Fitzmaurice during his first visit to Rome (i.e. in 1575), but not during his second visit. This, of course, does not take into account his arrival in Rome as a young friar in 1562, when he had no contact with Galli. This statement of 1578 seems to imply that his second visit to Rome may have coincided, for a brief period, with that of Fitzmaurice, for whom others were then acting as agents. Accordingly, O'Healy may have gone back to Rome during the summer of 1576 and remained there until the opening days of 1577. **12** *Cal. S.P. Rome, 1572–8*, 298. **13** Ibid., 311; *Archiv. Hib.* 7 (1918–21), 86: '... ho ancora parlato de la impresa Anglicana ... et insieme de le cose Irlandesi, et di Jacopo Mauriti capitato qui col Vescovo Franciscano Maionen. et col padre David.' **14** *Cal. S.P. Rome, 1572–8*, 317.

Portugal to procure a ship to carry O'Healy and his associates to Ireland and expressing unbounded confidence that God would grant them victory over their enemies.[15]

Bishop O'Healy accompanied Fitzmaurice when he set sail from Lisbon on 18 November 1577. A severe storm forced them to hug the coast of Spain for more than a month. In the harbour of Bayona they repaired the damage to the ship and set out again, only to be compelled to seek shelter in the harbour of Monuiero, near Corunna in Galicia, where they spent twenty days. The Breton captain with his crew was committed to prison when he refused to carry out his contract and proceed with the voyage. On the night of 5 January 1578 they broke out of jail. They took over their ship and sailed out of the harbour early the next morning, while Fitzmaurice was attending Mass for the Feast of the Epiphany. He then returned to find his ship gone, with all its war material and also his personal baggage as well as that of the bishop. He rightly suspected that the captain had sailed for Brittany. To recover their property, Fitzmaurice and O'Healy followed them to France, Fitzmaurice going on to Saint-Malo and the bishop proceeding to Paris to procure a royal warrant for restitution of the stolen goods. The details of what happened on that ill-fated voyage are given by Patrick O'Healy in a long letter which he wrote to Cardinal Galli from Paris on 31 March 1578.[16]

The bishop ended his narrative with a strong plea for practical papal aid for Fitzmaurice, and then came these strangely prophetic words:

> but please also remember that with the help of God's grace I shall be much more free and ready to give up life and blood and all I have, should need there be, for the safety and exaltation of the Apostolic See, for the propagation of the Catholic faith, and the spread of the Christian religion, and that I have every confidence in the bountiful liberality of His Holiness, which in my experience I have found to be great and prompt.

He said that he was writing in a similar strain to Francesco Cardinal Alciati. He added a postscript informing Galli that he had lost the bulls of

15 Patrick O'Healy to Giovanni Francesco Mazza di Canobio, Papal Collector, Lisbon, 14 November 1577: AV, Secretaria di Stato, Spagna, 11, f. 81r (copy); English summary in *Cal. S.P. Rome, 1572–8*, 350. **16** Patrick O'Healy to Tolomeo Cardinal Galli, Paris, 31 March 1578: AV, Segretaria di Stato, Francia, 12, ff. 78r–79v; English translation in Ronan, *Ref. Ire. Eliz., 1558–1580* (London, 1930), 568–71, and in *Catholic Bulletin* 19 (1929), 49–52; English summary in *Cal. S.P. Rome, 1572–8*, 395–6.

appointment to Mayo when his personal effects were stolen, and that he was anxious that they be reissued to him. On 7 April, while at Paris, he obtained a royal mandate addressed to the seneschal of Nantes, who was instructed to compel Thomas Strubec of Le Croisic, the ship's master, to restore their stolen property to Fitzmaurice and O'Healy.[17]

The difficulties, unpleasantness and prolonged negotiations which this venture engendered appear to have made O'Healy think seriously about revising his personal plans. Fitzmaurice remained in Brittany for many months, during which he made at least one visit to Paris. After his property had been seen to and a grant of 1,000 gold crowns had been received from the pope, he set out for Spain to finalize his arrangements for the expedition or crusade to Ireland. But the bishop did not accompany him; instead he chose to remain in France, in or near Paris, until he set out privately for Brittany, whence he hoped to sail to Ireland. He is mentioned in correspondence between Anselmo Dandino, nuncio in France, and the papal secretary of state.[18] Some letters exchanged between the bishop and Cardinals Galli and Alciati are also extant.[19]

O'Healy undoubtedly retained his interest in a Fitzmaurice expedition or crusade to Ireland. But at some stage he changed his mind about taking part in it. Perhaps, as he had written to Galli, he wished to feel 'much more free'. It was some unnamed person, not O'Healy, who was Fitzmaurice's agent in Paris in mid-July 1578, although the bishop accompanied the agent on a visit to Archbishop Frangipani, the papal legate.[20]

In the summer of 1578, O'Healy was reported on and betrayed to the English ambassador in Paris by an Irish Franciscan named Denis Molan. The bishop discovered this and denounced the friar, whom he regarded as an

---

17 *Cath. Bull.* 19 (1929), 52–3. **18** *Archiv. Hib.* 7 (1918–21), 126, 138, 144; *Cal. S.P. Rome, 1572–8*, 425, 449; Cloulas, *Correspondance*, 149, 159, 162, 169, 172, 207. **19** [a] Francesco Cardinal Alciati to Patrick O'Healy, Rome 5 May 1578: London, Public Record Office of England, S.P., 63/60/59; brief English summary in *Cal. S.P. Ire., 1574–85*, 133. [b] Tolomeo Cardinal Galli to Patrick O'Healy, Rome, 2 June 1578: AV, Segretaria di Stato, Francia, 11, f. 289rv (draft); printed in Bellesheim, *Gesch. der Kirche in Irland*, ii, 699–700, and with some slight alterations in *Archiv. Hib.* 7 (1918–21), 139; English summary in *Cal. S.P. Rome, 1572–8*, 449. [c] Patrick O'Healy to Tolomeo Cardinal Galli, Paris, 5 June 1578: AV, Segretaria di Stato, Francia, 14, f. 189r. [d] Tolomeo Cardinal Galli to Patrick O'Healy, Rome, 14 June 1578: AV, Arm. XLIV, 28, ff. 109v–110r (copy); English translation in *Cal. S.P. Rome, 1572–8*, 452–3. [e] Patrick O'Healy to Tolomeo Cardinal Galli, Paris, 22 June 1578: AV, Segretaria di Stato, Francia, 12, f. 166rv; printed in Bellesheim, *Gesch. der kirche in Irland*, ii, 700–1, and in *Archiv. Hib.* 7 (1918–21), 143–4; English summary in *Cal. S.P. Rome, 1572–8*, 456–7. [f] Tolomeo Cardinal Galli to Patrick O'Healy, Rome, 11 August 1578: AV, Arm. XLIV, 28, f. 110rv (draft); printed in Bellesheim, *Gesch. der Kirche in Irland*, ii, 701; English translation in *Cal. S.P. Rome 1572–8*, 485–6. **20** *Archiv. Hib.* 7 (1918–21), 148; *Cal. S.P. Rome, 1572–8*, 469–72.

apostate and heretic, to the nuncio, with a request that Rome be warned against Molan.[21] Perhaps it was this unpleasant affair which finally convinced Bishop O'Healy that it would not be wise or safe for him to take part in the Fitzmaurice crusade.

The bishop's first biographer, Thomas Bourchier, who in 1581 wrote a detailed account of the capture, imprisonment, and execution of O'Healy and his companion, and published it in 1582,[22] lived with the bishop of Mayo in the same Religious community in Paris. O'Healy, according to Bourchier, stayed in Paris for seven or eight months, residing in the Franciscan friary (perhaps the *grand couvent*) or elsewhere in the city. If this period is to be reckoned from midsummer 1578, when Bourchier himself took up residence in Paris, then the bishop of Mayo would have been there up to January or February 1579. His holy life, especially his humility and charity, made a deep impression on many, and in particular on his own brethren, including the young friars whom he helped to train. The bishop participated in academic exercises, and his outstanding intellectual gifts were noted. In due course, after he had received news from Ireland that the religious situation there had deteriorated, he set out for Brittany accompanied 'by a certain student of noble birth', i.e. Conn O'Rourke, OFM, and his plan was to await there a friendly ship's captain and favourable weather to take them home to Ireland. The bishop's anxiety to keep the English spies from learning of his proposed journey explains why nothing is known of his movements in Brittany.

EARLY LIFE: CONN O'ROURKE

Conn O'Rourke was still pursuing his studies, presumably in Paris, when he was appointed by his superiors, or he willingly opted, to become the *socius* of the bishop of Mayo for his journey back to Ireland. Seven sources – the Annals of Loch Cé,[23] Bourchier,[24] Verstegan,[25] Gonzaga,[26] Mooney,[27] Coppinger[28] and O'Mahony[29] – state that he was a Friar Minor. Two tell us that he was a priest – Bourchier, in reference to the imparting of absolution, and Gonzaga.

21 Cloulas, *Correspondance*, 209, 223; *Archiv. Hib.* 7 (1918–21), 165; *Cal. S.P. Rome, 1572–8*, 488; see also Ronan, *Ref. Ire. Eliz.*, 571–3. 22 Bourchier, *Historia*, 234–62. 23 Ad an. 1579, *A.L.C.*, ii, 426, 428; English translation, ibid., 427, 429. 24 Bourchier, *Historia*. 25 Verstegan, *Theatrum*, 80. 26 Gonzaga, *De Origine*, 846–7. 27 Donagh Mooney, *De Provincia Hiberniae S. Francisci*: BR, MS 3195, 9, 54, 89; printed in *Anal. Hib.* 6 (1934), 25, 75, 112. 28 Coppinger, *Theatre*. 29 O'Mahony, *Brevis Synopsis*.

Very little is known for certain about Conn O'Rourke before his capture. However, two important pieces of information are available. The first, which relates to his origins, is given in the Annals of Loch Cé in the entry for 1579, which records the capture and death of the two Franciscans.[30] It describes him as 'the son of Ó Ruairc, i.e. Connbráthair, the son of Brian, son of Eoghan Ó Ruairc'. This identifies him with precision. It gives the familiar diminutive of his Christian name, Conn.[31] It states that he was Connbráthair, i.e. 'Conn the friar', who was the son of Brian and grandson of Eoghan O'Rourke. He was, therefore, from Breifne in the heart of Gaelic Connacht, which had not yet been subjugated by the English, and he was the son of the Gaelic chieftain of the area, Brian Ballach O'Rourke of Breifne O'Rourke. He was of noble birth and in fact could point to a family tree more noble and more ancient than that of many contemporary royal and noble families in Europe. With the aid of extant genealogies,[32] a modern historian has traced his ancestry back in direct line through twenty-one generations to that first Ruarc in the latter half of the ninth century who gave his name to the *clann*, the eponymous ancestor of the O'Rourkes of Breifne.[33] The annalist deliberately styled him 'Conn the friar' to distinguish him from two other sons of Brian Ballach who were also named Conn.[34]

The second piece of information is contained in an intelligence report from France,[35] which was sent without date but was endorsed at Cork on 19 February 1577. Written probably towards the end of 1576 or early in 1577, this spy's report stated that the two friars who had arrived in France from Sligo, one of whom was the illegitimate son of O'Rourke, were living in Paris, where their board and lodging were being paid for by James Fitzmaurice. This claim that Friar Conn was a 'bastarde son' may have been

---

30 *A.L.C.*, ad an. 1579. **31** The Gaelic name *Conn* was frequently Latinized as *Cornelius*. Bourchier (*Historia*) calls him *Connacius*, which may have been the version O'Rourke himself used in France. Howlin uses *Conaldus* as the Latin equivalent (Howlin, *Perbreve Compend.*). **32** See M.V. Duignan (ed.), 'The Uí Briúin Breifne genealogies', in *RSAI Jn* 64 (1934), 90–137, 213–56; Séamus Pender (ed.), 'The O Clery Book of Genealogies', in *Anal. Hib.* 18 (1951), 103–5. **33** 'Conn the friar' was the son of Brian Ballach (d. 1562), son of Eoghan (d. 1528), son of Tighernán (d. 1468), son of Tadhg (d. 1434), son of Tighernán Mór (d. 1418), son of Ualgarg (d. 1346), son of Domhnall, son of Amhlaidh (d. *c*. 1258), son of Art (d. 1210), son of Domhnall, son of Fearghal, son of Domhnall (king of Connacht), son of Tighernán, son of Ualgarg (d. 1085), son of Niall (d. 1047), son of Art Oirdnidhe (king of Connacht), son of Aodh (d. *c*.1015), son of Sean-Fheargal (d. *c*.966), son of Art, son of Ruarc (d. 898). Canice Mooney, 'Some Leitrim Franciscans of the past', in *Breifne* 1 (1961), 342. **34** The first Conn rebelled against his father and was slain in 1540. The second Conn died in 1577. **35** Intelligence Report from France, endorsed Cork, 19 February 1576 [1577 N.S.]: London, PRO, S.P., 63/58/2 i.

accurate because in Ireland the canon law of marriage was still to a great extent ignored in the Gaelic and Gaelicized districts.[36] The obvious place of residence at Paris for the two Religious, who apparently had gone abroad to complete their studies, was the Franciscan friary known as the *grand couvent*.

James Archer, SJ, who saw Conn O'Rourke the night before his execution in August 1579, told Malachy Hartry, who has recorded the information,[37] that O'Rourke was then scarcely thirty years of age. If that statement was reasonably accurate, then Conn O'Rourke must have been born *c.*1549. It is safe to assume that he entered religious life at Dromahaire Friary, which had been founded for Observant Franciscans in 1508 by his grandfather Eoghan and his wife Margaret O'Brien.[38] Eoghan died in 1528 in the habit of St Francis and was buried in the friary.[39] Despite the military and diplomatic pressures on the O'Rourkes from the Crown representatives, the Franciscans remained in undisturbed possession of their friary at Dromahaire. A report of 1574 shows them still in possession.[40] No records of Friar Conn's religious profession and priestly ordination have been found.

ARREST AND IMPRISONMENT

The arrival in Ireland of O'Healy and O'Rourke, and their capture, imprisonment and subsequent execution, are mentioned in a letter written from Askeaton on 10 October 1579.[41] The writer was Gerald Fitzjames Fitzgerald, fifteenth earl of Desmond, a first cousin of James Fitzmaurice

---

36 The twelfth-century reformers had failed in their efforts to Christianize the ancient Irish laws on marriage, which permitted easy divorce. It was not uncommon in late medieval Ireland for men and women of the higher social strata to have a succession of spouses. Moreover, the Irish in practice usually married their kinsfolk. As a result, in sixteenth-century Ireland a large number of clerics in the Gaelic districts were the children of parents related within the forbidden degrees, or of parents remarried in violation of canon law. See Kenneth Nicholls, *Gaelic and Gaelicised Ireland in the Middle Ages* (Dublin, 1972), 73–7; Canice Mooney, 'The Irish Church in the Sixteenth Century', in *IER* 99 (1963), 106–7. **37** Malachy Hartry, *Synopsis nonnullorum illustrium Cisterciensium Hibernorum*, 1649. Thurles, Cashel and Emly Diocesan Archives, MS 25, 1, f. 44r; printed in Malachy Hartry, *Triumphalia Chronologica Monasterii Sanctae Crucis; de Cisterciensium Hibernorum viris illustribus*, ed. Denis Murphy (Dublin, 1891), 258. **38** *Anal. Hib.* 6 (1934), 161, 200; *AFM*, ad an. 1508. **39** See *ALC*, ad an. 1528; *AU*, ad an. 1528; *AFM*, ad an. 1528. **40** For report, see *Cal. Carew MSS, 1601–3*, 471–6. **41** Gerald Fitzjames Fitzgerald, fifteenth earl of Desmond, to Thomas Butler, tenth earl of Ormond, Askeaton, 10 October 1579: London, PRO, S.P., 63/69/51 (contemporary copy) [hereafter Letter of Desmond].

Fitzgerald, who had led the Spanish expeditionary force to Ireland in the summer of that same year.[42] Because of the involvement of his family in the Munster revolt, and because he was aware that his own temporising had aroused the suspicions of Lord Justice Sir William Drury and others,[43] the earl wrote this letter to prove his loyalty. It was addressed to his arch-rival, Thomas Butler, tenth earl of Ormond, who had become general of the crown's forces in Munster after Drury's death. He mentioned a series of events to demonstrate to Ormond his firmness in dealing with opponents of the crown and began with his treatment of the bishop and his companion:

> First, before the Traitour [i.e. James Fitzmaurice] arrived, there landed at Smerwicke Haven three Irish scholars in mariners attire, which [i.e. whom] upon suspicion I caused to be examined and sent to the Gaol at Limerick, who in fyne were known to be gentlemen, and one of them a Bishop, who was sent by the Traitoure to practise with the North to join with him, for which they were by my Lord Justice executed.

The earl of Desmond clearly states that they landed before Fitzmaurice arrived, that they came ashore at Smerwick, and that he arranged for them to be interrogated and taken to Limerick city to be imprisoned there. This passage must refer to Bishop O'Healy and Conn O'Rourke. The identification of the bishop does not create a problem because O'Healy was the first Catholic bishop put to death in Ireland by the English since Henry VIII broke with the papacy. The third man, also a scholar or a student, is not known. He is not mentioned in any other source.

The Fitzmaurice expedition sailed from Ferrol in Galicia on 20 June 1579. Among the clergy on board were two Spanish Franciscans (one of them being Mateo de Oviedo, who later became archbishop of Dublin), a Franciscan bishop (Donnchadh Óg O'Gallagher of Killala) and two Irish Franciscan priests (Shane O'Farrell of Askeaton and James O'Hea of Youghal).[44] O'Healy and O'Rourke were not among them and had no

---

42 See Lodge, *Peerage Ire.*, i, 73–7; see relevant entries in the *DNB*. **43** After James Fitzmaurice was killed on 18 August, the earl's brother John assumed leadership in Fitzmaurice's place (see reference in letter of Lord Justice Drury to the Queen, Cork, 24 Aug. 1579, printed in *Walsingham Letter-Bk*, 139). Writing to the lord chancellor and the archbishop of Dublin on 1 Sept. 1579, Drury and four other crown officials stated: 'The earl of Desmond is a rebell' (ibid., 148). **44** See J. B. Wainewright (ed.), 'Some letters and papers of Nicolas Sander, 1562–1580', in *Cath. Rec. Soc. Publ.* 26 (1926), 19. There were also two

contact with them. After a brief stop at Dingle, the Fitzmaurice expedition then put in at Smerwick harbour on 18 July. It was there, according to the earl of Desmond, that O'Healy and his companions had landed. This has led one modern scholar to the false conclusion that the Franciscan bishop who accompanied the crusading force was Patrick O'Healy.[45] Neither James Fitzmaurice nor any of those who came with him had had any contact with O'Healy for a long time, perhaps for more than a year, and they were quite unaware that he had arrived in Ireland before them. There is not even one mention of the bishop of Mayo in the letters and reports which were sent abroad within two months or so of the arrival of the expeditionary force in mid-July. In August they heard nothing of his capture, imprisonment and death. Accordingly, Mateo de Oviedo had nothing to report on Bishop O'Healy to the papal officials when he reached Madrid on 23 August.

The relevant entry for 1579 in the Annals of Loch Cé notes that the bishop and the friar 'came from the east' (i.e. from Brittany) to Smerwick, not from the south (Spain). This agrees with the account given by Bourchier, who says that after waiting for some time in Brittany they left by ship in favourable weather and landed at a remote corner of the Irish coast. Gonzaga gives the same information, seemingly taken from Bourchier. John Coppinger is the only martyrologist who says that they came from Spain.

According to Bourchier's account, they both went almost immediately to visit the earl of Desmond – presumably at Askeaton, though this is not stated. In the absence of the earl, his wife Eleanor received them hospitably. After three days the two Franciscans set out for Limerick, intending to journey on from there and make contact with those who supported the Catholics. In other words, they intended to cross the river Shannon into Connacht, there to engage in pastoral work. What the bishop had in mind was to get away from the districts controlled by the forces of the crown and go to the relative safety of his diocese or his native area. But, unsuspected by them, the countess had betrayed the two Franciscans by sending word secretly to the crown authorities at Limerick about the two arrivals. Accordingly the mayor, James Goold, was expecting them and captured them on the way. He had them transferred to Kilmallock, where they were imprisoned. John Howlin, however, says, as does the earl of Desmond,[46] that they were first jailed in Limerick city and after they were court-martialed and condemned to death they were removed to Kilmallock.

English secular priests, Dr (Roger?) Allen and Dr Nicholas Sanders, and Fitzmaurice's chaplain, Laurence Moore. **45** John Hagan, writing in *Cath. Bull.* 19 (1929), 1122. **46** Letter of Desmond.

Coppinger has a slightly different sequence. He says that the bishop and O'Rourke were arrested by the sheriff and officers of Dingle, the nearest town to Smerwick, and sent by them to the countess of Desmond, who, for her own reasons, handed them over to James Goold. He gives the reasons: the countess, who was seriously worried – and with good cause – because Drury and other crown officials suspected that her husband the earl was not loyal, endeavoured to convince them of the loyalty of the earl and his immediate family by handing over her eldest son as a hostage and also by giving them the bishop and young Religious as prisoners.

TRIAL

There was no formal trial. What was allowed to substitute for it was an interrogation, or several interrogations, and then a condemnation to death on a charge of treason by a court-martial administering martial law. Therefore there are no judicial records.

In his letter of 10 October 1579, the earl of Desmond says in reference to O'Healy and O'Rourke: 'which [i.e. whom] upon suspicion I caused to be examined and sent to the Gaol at Limerick'. He claimed that the prisoners were interrogated on his orders and imprisoned in Limerick.

John Howlin says of the bishop that he, together with O'Rourke, was captured by the heretics, locked up in prison and detained for a long time, and he adds that O'Healy endured patiently considerable hardship and suffering in prison. The sources agree that it was Lord Justice Sir William Drury, lord president of Munster, who condemned them; and it can be established when he was in Limerick and, approximately, when he was in Kilmallock. O'Healy and O'Rourke arrived in Ireland before Fitzmaurice landed on 18 July, although how long before can only be guessed at. They spent three days with the wife of the earl after their journey from the end of the Dingle peninsula to County Limerick. And their execution took place in mid-August. It is clear from the State Papers that Drury was at Limerick on 2 August 1579 and was still there on 10 August.[47] But he was in Cork on 22 August.[48] His journey there would have taken him through Kilmallock.

According to Thomas Bourchier, the two captives were thrown into prison in Limerick, and from there the bishop, as one guilty of *lèse-majesté*,

---

47 *Cal. S.P. Ire. 1574–85*, 178, 180; *Walsingham Letter-Bk*, 112–14, 126. **48** *Cal. S.P. Ire., 1574–85*, 182; *Walsingham Letter-Bk*, 135–7.

and his companion were sent to Kilmallock, where Drury was then residing. Bourchier implies that the interrogation was held in Kilmallock. Howlin, however, clearly states that it took place before the prisoners were transferred from Limerick to Kilmallock and that sentence was passed on them in Limerick. So does Coppinger.

The prisoners – especially Bishop O'Healy – were interrogated by the lord justice. The 'forum Iudiciale' mentioned by Howlin was not a court of common law. It is quite clear that Drury tried the bishop and his companion by martial law; both Bourchier and Coppinger expressly say so. The interrogation, or part of it, was carried out before the trial. The practice of resorting to martial law was devised in the sixteenth century to deal with certain alleged criminals (e.g. rebels, traitors) who could not be easily or speedily convicted in a court of common law. It meant that the prisoner would not be tried in public; that, after the charges were read out, he would be given no opportunity to reply or defend himself; that there would be no jury, thus eliminating the danger of his being acquitted; that the judge or presiding official, without having to wait for a defence, proceeded to pronounce judgement as he thought fit.

The right to try prisoners by martial law was considered to belong to the royal prerogative. In Ireland during the reign of Elizabeth, it was customary to issue martial law commissions to certain crown officials. A royal commission was issued on 26 June 1576 to Sir William Drury, as lord president of Munster, to execute martial law in the counties of Waterford, Tipperary, Limerick, Cork and Kerry, and in all cities and corporate towns, and to punish by death or otherwise any persons found to be felons, rebels, enemies or notorious evil-doers; but the powers did not extend against anyone having a £5 freehold or against £40 chattel holders.[49] In 1577, Drury, the queen's archbishop of Cashel, and other officials, ecclesiastical and lay (including the mayor of Limerick), were appointed by the crown to be commissioners of ecclesiastical causes in the province of Munster and were empowered to inquire *by all means* into offences against the Acts of Supremacy and Uniformity, and to administer the Oath of Supremacy to all ecclesiastical persons.[50] Therefore Drury, according to a law devised by the crown for its own ends, did not act illegally, though it could be questioned whether he was legally correct in proceeding to sentence O'Healy and O'Rourke as men of little or no property.

Both Bourchier and Howlin state that O'Healy was asked by Drury to

---

49 *Fiants Ire., Eliz.,* no. 2868; see also no. 218.   **50** Ibid., no. 3156; see also no. 3047.

acknowledge the queen as the supreme head of the Church. When he adamantly refused to admit the royal supremacy and insisted that the pope was the supreme head of the Church, he was declared a traitor and guilty of *lèse-majesté*, and for that he and his companion were condemned to death. Howlin also states that O'Healy was falsely accused of many other crimes besides that of being a papal bishop and that he was able to show that such charges were groundless. According to Bourchier, O'Healy told Drury that he had come to Ireland as a bishop in order to promote the cause of religion and work for the salvation of souls. When the lord justice pressed him to tell them what plans the pope and the king of Spain had made for the invasion of Ireland, the bishop remained silent, even under torture, when they drove sharp spikes through his fingers, some of which were severed from his hands. Then Drury condemned the two prisoners to death.

It is clear that at some stage during the interrogation O'Healy was tortured. This is mentioned by Bourchier and Howlin, who do not, however, say that O'Rourke was subjected to the same treatment. It was not common practice to torture prisoners during interrogation. But occasionally, from the late 1570s until the end of the reign, prisoners suspected of political or religious offences were questioned under torture, especially in the hope of extracting from them some useful information of a political nature. Drury, as a dedicated official of the crown, acted in defence of what he saw as the national interest, and, seemingly, within the terms of his commissions. But with Bishop O'Healy torture failed to produce the desired results. The lord justice then resorted to bribery.

Bourchier says that Drury offered the bishop full title to and possession of his benefice (the diocese of Mayo) and other emoluments on condition that he would deny the faith and reveal his entire business. O'Healy replied that he would not exchange the faith for any earthly possessions or honours, that the purpose of his coming to Ireland was episcopal and pastoral, and that he would accept death rather than the alternative offered him. Government officials, when faced with a recalcitrant Catholic priest, had begun to try every means to get him to admit the royal supremacy and to act against his conscience. Elizabethan society was a hierarchical one, in which great store was put on social roots, social status and economic position. But in those parts of Ireland where the crown had authority, the external signs of status, the social supports, were to a great extent denied to the recusant priest or bishop. He had no part in the ecclesiastical structure, with its hierarchy, benefices and recognized status, which had passed to the post-Reformation cleric of the Established Church. Moreover, his priest-hood could not be professed openly.[51] Drury held out a strong economic and social enticement to the Franciscan bishop to return to the normal web of relationships which defined and gave meaning to people's lives. This offer was made after the torture, and perhaps also after sentence of death had been pronounced, as a kind of final plea 'ad terrorem'. It was rejected.

MARTYRDOM

Sir William Drury sentenced the two prisoners to die by hanging. All the sources agree on this. The sentence was carried out at Kilmallock, a small town about twenty miles from Limerick city. They were taken there under military escort, with their hands tied behind their backs and their feet fastened with ropes, 'upon garrans', i.e. small Irish horses.[52] During the journey the bishop, according to Howlin, spoke with the bystanders, among whom were some Catholics in disguise; he gave salutary advice to all, confirmed the Catholics in the faith, and urged the schismatics to repent.

Before the execution took place, O'Healy, according to Thomas Bourchier, first asked permission for the prisoners to recite the litanies and impart absolution to each other, and this was granted. When they reached the place selected for the hanging, the bishop encouraged the young Conn O'Rourke to face death intrepidly. O'Healy then addressed the bystanders, speaking at some length about the need for faith and about his Franciscan and episcopal vocation. He told them that he and his companion joyfully faced death for the name of Christ. Howlin too records the bishop's final address. He says that it was a sermon on faith and on the authority of the Roman Church and the supreme pontiff, and that the bishop asked those Catholics who were present to pray for him and his companion. The two prisoners were then hanged by the neck until dead.

From the dates given above for Drury's presence in Limerick (2 and 10 August 1579) and in Cork (22 August) it is clear that the hanging of O'Healy and O'Rourke at Kilmallock must have taken place c.13 August. Filippo Sega, the nuncio in Spain, later wrote an account of his nunciature in which he said that the bishop of Mayo and another were martyred by the English shortly before the death of Fitzmaurice (18 August).[53]

51 See Arnold Pritchard, *Catholic Loyalism in Elizabethan England* (London, 1979), 187–8.
52 Howlin, *Perbreve Compend.*; Coppinger, *Theatre*. 53 Report of Filippo Sega, former

The two corpses were left hanging on the gibbets for quite some time. During that time they were mocked and ill-treated by the soldiers, but were not savaged in any way by wolves, which were then in great numbers in that area, or by birds. After a week or so John Fitzgerald of Desmond buried them.

The severe illness and then the death of Sir William Drury, which occurred shortly afterwards, are noted in the sources[54] and seen as a just punishment by God. Two of the martyrologists report that the bishop foretold this.[55]

MOTIVE FOR MARTYRDOM

Why were these two clerics executed? Their death was ordered because they refused to renounce their allegiance to the pope and acknowledge, in accordance with the Act of Supremacy, that the English queen was the head of the Church in her realms. That was the real reason.

It was referred to briefly by the official who sentenced them to death, Sir William Drury, in a letter[56] which he wrote from Cork to Queen Elizabeth on 24 August 1579. Most of that letter deals with military matters – the killing of Fitzmaurice and the campaign to defeat his expeditionary force. But towards the end of the letter Drury changes topics. He suggests to the queen that she should summon to her presence the earl of Kildare to explain

> what unstedfastness the forraine practises and promise of alteration of relligion hathe bread in your people and what execution hathe been don uppon some of the Popes prelates and Agentes that have been the instrumentes to seduce your subjectes from their dueties and loyalties.

This must refer to O'Healy and O'Rourke (and perhaps other unknown clerics) who were put to death about two weeks earlier on his orders. Bishop O'Healy was the first Catholic prelate put to death in Ireland since Henry VIII rejected the papacy. Drury calls their death an 'execution' and

nuncio in Spain, to Tolomeo Cardinal Galli, *c.* 1584. AV, Fondo Borghese, series III, 129D, f. 437r. See *Cath. Bull.* 19 (1929), 1124. From internal evidence it appears that Sega's report was not written before 1584. **54** *ALC*, ad an. 1579; Bourchier, *Historia*; Howlin, *Perbreve Compend.*; Coppinger, *Theatre.* **55** Howlin, *Perbreve Compend.*; Coppinger, *Theatre.* **56** Sir William Drury, Lord Justice, to Queen Elizabeth I, Cork, 24 August 1579. PRO, MS 30/5/4; *Walsingham Letter-Bk.*, 140.

says that it was ordered because they were papal agents sent to confirm her Irish subjects in their opposition to the queen's religious policy. He implies that this new breed of clergy, trained abroad and backed by the papacy, had persuaded many of the laity to reject the Church by law established. The lord justice gave no details about the martyrdom, perhaps because he was not sure how the queen would react to the news that he had had a bishop executed. Clearly he believed that this new and much tougher policy against Catholic bishops and priests was necessary in the disturbed Ireland of 1579, with what he calls at the beginning of his letter 'the troubles stirred in this your state by forraine practise'.

Drury does not associate these clerics whom he executed with James Fitzmaurice and his invading force. He does not mention them when treating of the military campaign, led by himself, to suppress the rebels in Munster. He refers to their execution when he begins to discuss matters of religion. They were disloyal clergy who rejected the queen's ecclesiastical supremacy and attempted to make her Irish subjects do likewise. In punishing them with death did he have other motives and evidence which he suppressed in his letter?

There is no clear evidence to support the statement of the earl of Desmond in his letter of 10 October[57] that Bishop O'Healy returned to Ireland as an active agent of James Fitzmaurice for the express purpose of persuading the chieftains of the north to support the revolt. This statement must be seen as part of Desmond's plan to keep his real intentions and loyalties hidden and play both sides. For James Fitzmaurice's success, it was essential for him to win the support of his cousin the earl, and he communicated with him immediately on his arrival; he also sought help from other Munster Lords and from the northern chiefs. Lord Justice Drury mustered an army against Fitzmaurice and sent Henry Davells to confirm the earl of Desmond in his allegiance. Davells was murdered by the earl's brother, Sir John, who assumed leadership when Fitzmaurice was killed on 18 August in a chance encounter with the Limerick Burkes. It was a matter of critical importance for the queen's representatives in Ireland, including the earl of Ormond, who succeeded Malby as general in Munster after Drury died, whether the earl of Desmond would back the queen or the pope. Desmond was not a man of pronounced religious convictions, unlike James Fitzmaurice. He would have preferred to remain neutral, for he did not trust the government. Indeed, during the period from July to September

57 Letter of Desmond.

1579, he had given Drury only half-hearted co-operation. In October, after Drury's death (on 3 October), he knew he had relentless men to deal with in Ormond and the new lord justice, Sir William Pelham; indeed, Pelham was to proclaim him a traitor on 2 November.[58] So he wasted no time but penned this letter to Ormond, despite the jealousy which had existed between them, as he admitted in the opening sentence. This letter of 10 October was a deliberate attempt by Desmond to exaggerate his own part in the arrest of O'Healy and O'Rourke, and in the obstruction of the Fitzmaurice revolt, in order to demonstrate to the crown officials his loyalty.

Desmond knew that O'Healy and O'Rourke had not come with James Fitzmaurice. He says so. He must also have been aware that the bishop had not come as an agent of Fitzmaurice. The earl made it his business to know what was going on on both sides. From contacts made with Fitzmaurice he would have learned that Fitzmaurice had sent his emissary to contact the northern chieftains, and that the Franciscan bishop of Killala had landed with Fitzmaurice and then been taken off by boat to Connacht. So his statement to Ormond about Bishop O'Healy was a bluff. But did Drury execute O'Healy in the mistaken belief that he was a political agent? This cannot have been the case. Bourchier, Gonzaga[59] and Campoy as recorded by Corbalán[60] have noted that Patrick O'Healy made a deep and favourable impression on his contemporaries in Spain, at Rome and at Paris. He impressed them as a man of remarkable integrity, of exceptional charity and humility, and as a man who was both scholarly and intellectually brilliant. The chronicler who made the entry in the Annals of Loch Cé[61] noted his exceptional holiness. The shrewd, experienced Drury, after interrogating the bishop, must have quickly realized that he was telling the truth. Moreover, immediately after the execution there was a strong *fama martyrii* among the Catholic Irish — both the Old Irish and the Anglo-Irish — who had a firm conviction that these two men had been killed for religious, and not for political, reasons. They considered that these two were not like the hundreds of others whom Drury had executed in the two years immediately before this. The stories about their cruel death, and about what happened to their bodies afterwards, spread abroad quickly.

What was Drury's real intention? Apart from Desmond's statement in his letter to Ormond, is there any evidence to show that the Lord Justice

---

58 The most recent study of this politico-military situation is by G.A. Hayes-McCoy in *NHI*, iii, 94–141; see especially 105–7. **59** Gonzaga, *De Origine.* **60** Corbalán, *Hierarchia Tripartita.* **61** *ALC*, ad an. 1579.

sentenced the two prisoners on a purely political charge? Drury's action must be seen in its contemporary setting. In England and Ireland official attitudes to priests and religious had changed from 1577 onwards. For almost the first twenty years of her reign the ultimate penalties of the anti-papal legislation had not been used by Elizabeth against priests and religious. In England this legislation was contained principally in the acts of 1559 (1 Eliz., c. 1) and 1563 (5 Eliz., c. 1) and the acts of 1571 (13 Eliz., cc. 1 and 2) prescribing certain actions as treason and forbidding the introduction of papal bulls into the realm; in Ireland there was only the equivalent of the 1559 act, i.e. the Ecclesiastical Acts passed by the Irish parliament of 1560. Towards the end of the 1570s the queen and her officials had become alarmed. By about 1577 or 1578 the crown officials were convinced that they were dealing with less pliant, more hardened Catholics than those confronting them at the beginning of Elizabeth's reign. They were aware that some priests, Jesuits and friars, with the new seminary formation and theological training envisaged by the Council of Trent, had entered England and Ireland to re-evangelize and toughen the laity. Among the Tudor statesmen there was emerging a determination to destroy Catholicism, a Catholicism which at last had manifestly begun to make a stand.[62]

Stricter measures would have to be taken against papally sponsored campaigns and the activities of seminary-trained priests, Jesuits and friars, and, in the case of Ireland, bishops sent from Rome. The pope was seen as the great enemy, sending these men to encourage the Catholics of the queen's realm to disobey the queen's laws about religion. Sir William Drury and Sir Nicholas Malby in Ireland were as conversant with official thinking and policy as men like Sir Walter Mildmay and Sir William Cecil (Lord Burghley) at Westminster. Elizabeth's leading councillors were constantly anxious that she should not tolerate Catholicism, and they sponsored anti-Catholic propaganda based on the assumption that Catholic meant traitor. They spoke openly and forcefully about Dr Sanders and others. And the papally financed expedition from Spain to Ireland provided welcome evidence of Catholic disobedience and ill will. Their reiterated theme was that Catholics were a danger to the realm. Accordingly, in their view, the execution of priests, Jesuits, friars and bishops at this time would reinforce this propaganda and strengthen the position of these councillors by fixing the fear as a reality in the public mind.[63]

62 It was about this time that the first killing of priests and religious in Ireland occurred.
63 For the change in attitude and policy, see Hughes, *Ref. Eng.*, iii, 292–316, 335–44, 353–9; Edwards, *Church and State*, 249–73. The hanging of Friar Tadhg Ó Dálaigh at Limerick in

It is against this background and this policy of the top-ranking crown officials that the sentencing and execution of Patrick O'Healy and Conn O'Rourke in mid-August 1579 must be viewed. They were arraigned as traitors, but their treason was the rejection of the crown's religious policy by their refusal to acknowledge the queen as supreme governor in all things spiritual and ecclesiastical in the realm. They were staunch adherents of the pope, the arch-enemy, and therefore in the eyes of Elizabeth's Irish officials a menace to the crown. To Drury, Malby and their group, this bishop and this friar constituted a real danger – and especially at this time of panic – for they would strengthen the resistance of the laity. In this sense, then, it could be said that they were tried on a political charge, that of opposition to Tudor policy, but primarily to the religious policy. Religion and politics had become intertwined.

Moreover, to crown officials in Ireland and England it was known that O'Healy had been closely associated with James Fitzmaurice overseas in 1576–8. But there is no evidence that he had any link with the expedition in its final stage. Not that this would have mattered to Drury, who had boasted in 1578 that about four hundred had been executed 'by justice and martial law' in Munster.[64] By the late summer of 1579 the Spanish expeditionary force had landed in south-west Munster and something akin to panic had set in among the crown officials.[65] Drury was not going to display much mercy in his campaign throughout the province. To have captured a papal bishop at this time was a piece of good fortune, for an example could be made of him. Probably any Catholic bishop would have suited his purpose, especially one just arrived from abroad. But the fact that it was the bishop of Mayo, who was known to have had dealings with James Fitzmaurice in the past, would help to bolster the crown's propaganda. The questioning of O'Healy by Drury and the tactics he employed, as reported by Bourchier and Howlin, resemble closely those which were used a few years later by Loftus and Wallop, the lords justices, when dealing with Archbishop Dermot O'Hurley of Cashel.

The legislation enshrined in the anti-papal act of 1563 (5 Eliz., c. 1) passed by the parliament of Westminster was not passed by the Irish parlia-

---

1578 by Drury was made legal only by invoking martial law; see Brady, *Ir. Ch. Eliz.*, 24. **64** Sir William Drury to the Privy Council at Dublin, Waterford, 24 March 1578. See Brady, *Ir. Ch. Eliz.*, 24. **65** Indicative of the panic are the words written by Sir Humphrey Gilbert to Drury early in August 1579: '... the loss of Ireland wilbe the loosinge of England, and of your life and honnour, for assure your selfe that this sparke of rebellion is attended with bellowes, both Frenche, Spanishe, Portingals, Italians, and of all sortes of papistes thoroweout Christendome ... I thinke this an universall conspiracie' (*Walsingham Letter-Bk*, 121).

ment of 1569–70. But the 1560 acts were on the Irish statute book.[66] The ultimate penalty for a third offence of usurping and maintaining papal authority in the realm of Ireland was death. But there had to be two previous convictions, and the offender charged for the third time had to be tried in a court of law and convicted. Drury, listening to the bishop's answers under interrogation, was convinced that he could not get any Irish jury to convict O'Healy. No papal bishop had been executed in Ireland up to this date. So in the case of O'Healy – as Elizabeth was to advise in 1584 regarding Archbishop Dermot O'Hurley – it would be better 'to take a shorter way with him by martial law'.[67] However, if there was a question of charging O'Healy with treason committed in foreign parts through plotting with the pope and others against the queen, it would also have been necessary to have him executed under martial law, because the relevant English statute was not law in Ireland.[68] Drury was a ruthless man who would not hesitate at dispatching opponents of the crown when the circumstances so demanded. But, being also a typical Tudor official, he would wish to give the appearance of legality to his acts.

He resorted to martial law to give his acts legal standing. But Drury, as well as being ruthless, was also shrewd. Why, then, did he take the risk of putting a bishop to death, when such had never been done before? For him it was a calculated risk. Among the senior officials of the crown in Ireland and England there was panic, or something very like it, when the news was received that the Spanish expeditionary force had landed in Ireland. The officials were desperately worried about the ultimate dimensions of this invading force and the support it might receive in Ireland. In Drury's view radical decisions were called for. Accordingly, he would put to death this captured papal bishop and his companion, and this could serve as an example to frighten and subdue the Irish, and thus lessen the danger of major support for the revolt.

The lord justice could not have charged O'Rourke with being a papal bishop. And O'Rourke could not have been justly accused of plotting abroad to overthrow the queen's authority. No evidence could be produced to support such a charge, if it were made. O'Rourke had gone overseas to study. Desmond in his letter described him, like his companions, as a scholar who was dressed as a sailor. The legal title for sentencing him was his refusal to accept the royal supremacy. For the death sentence to be legal there

---

66 *Stat. Ire.*, i, 101–29. **67** Brady, *Ir. Ch. Eliz.*, 79. **68** 13 Eliz., c. 1. See G.W. Prothero (ed.), *Select statutes and other constitutional documents illustrative of the reigns of Elizabeth and James I* (2nd ed., Oxford, 1898), 57–60.

would have to be two previous convictions and now a full trial and conviction. So it was again necessary to resort to martial law. Almost certainly,
Drury knew that this prisoner was a priest and a Religious but did not
know his real identity. Very few, if any besides Bishop O'Healy, knew that
he was the son of Brian Ballach O'Rourke, and it seems that very few knew
that he was a Friar Minor. The Annals of Loch Cé imply, but do not state
openly, that O'Healy and O'Rourke were killed because they were priests.

FAMA MARTYRII

Patrick O'Healy and Conn O'Rourke acquired an instant reputation of
martyrdom among the Catholics of Ireland, for the execution of a bishop
shocked many and ensured that his killing would be remembered. News of
the two deaths was carried northwards to O'Rourke's family. In due course,
perhaps even that same year, the martyrdom was recorded in the Annals of
Loch Cé.[69] This was the only martyrdom in the sixteenth century which
was noted in a native Irish source.

The written word played a major part in spreading and perpetuating this
fama martyrii. News of the sufferings and death of the two friars reached
Paris quickly, and the English Franciscan Thomas Bourchier[70] wrote an
account of their martyrdom, which was completed in 1581 and published
at Paris in 1582 as part of his history of Franciscan martyrs. A second edition
appeared at Ingolstadt in 1583. In Spain, Juan Campoy translated his work
into Spanish and added new material on Patrick O'Healy, whom he knew
well.

Five years after the first appearance of Bourchier's work, the English
recusant Richard Verstegan printed an account of this martyrdom in his
book dealing with the cruelties inflicted on Catholics by contemporary
heretics.[71] In this work he inserted an engraving which was a composite
iconographic representation of the two martyrs and Archbishop Dermot
O'Hurley. At least eight editions of Verstegan's work appeared within twenty
years (1587–1607). This publication and that by Bourchier enhanced considerably the *fama martyrii*. When the English priest John Bridgewater brought
out at Trier in 1588 an enlarged edition of the English martyrology
Concertatio Ecclesiae Catholicae in Anglia, he published in it an account of the
death of O'Healy and O'Rourke taken word for word from Verstegan.

---

69 *ALC*, ad an. 1579.   **70** Bourchier, *Historia*.   **71** Verstegan, *Theatrum*.

In 1591 an Oratorian named Tommaso Bozio included the names of O'Healy and O'Rourke in a list of Franciscan martyrs.[72] This was published at Rome, where already it was accepted that O'Healy had died a martyr's death. When a successor was being provided to the diocese of Mayo on 29 July 1585, it was recorded in the official acts of this meeting of the Secret Consistory that the Church of Mayo was 'vacant by the death of Patrick Oheli of holy memory, killed for the Catholic faith by English heretics'.[73] Bozio took the names of these two Irish Franciscan martyrs from a work which appeared at Rome in 1587. This was a bulky history of the Franciscan Order by Francesco Gonzaga of Mantua, minister general 1579–87, who printed a lengthy account of the martyrdom of the two Irish friars[74] which was based to no small extent on Bourchier's.

The first contemporary Irish martyrology, compiled by the Jesuit, John Howlin, was completed *c.*1590, probably at Lisbon, and it too contained an account of the martyrdom.[75] To a large extent this is a testimony to the reputation of martyrdom from sources independent of Bourchier and Verstegan. This martyrology remained unpublished for almost three centuries, until Patrick F. Moran edited it.[76] But the manuscript was consulted by scholars such as David Rothe and Luke Wadding.

The memory of the sufferings and death of O'Healy and O'Rourke was kept fresh by the writings of their Franciscan confrères, both Irish and non-Irish. In 1617–18 the Irish minister provincial, Donagh Mooney, wrote his history of the Franciscan province of Ireland, in which he made three references to these two martyrs.[77] Francis O'Mahony, who was minister provincial 1626–9, also wrote a history of the Irish Franciscans which he finished in 1629, and in its martyrological section he included Patrick O'Healy and Conn O'Rourke.[78] Apart from the living oral tradition in Ireland and among the Irish in exile, between 1582 and 1630 the works of Bourchier, Gonzaga, Verstegan, and their derivatives were especially responsible for the spread and growth of the *fama martyrii*. Then another and more influential pen took over, when Luke Wadding, the official historian of the Franciscan Order, received copies of histories written by Mooney and O'Mahony[79] and made good use of them. In his *Annales Minorum* he

72 Thomas Bozius, *De Signis Ecclesiae Dei* (2 vols, Rome, 1591–2), i, 554.   **73** Minutes of the Secret Consistory held on 29 July 1585. AV, Acta Camerarii, 12, f. 27v; BV MSS Barb. Lat., 2871, f. 200v (copy); printed in *Archiv. Hib.* 5 (1916), 176–7, and in Brady, *Ep. Succ.*, ii, 156.   **74** Gonzaga, *De Origine*.   **75** Howlin, *Perbreve Compend.*   **76** Moran, *Spicil. Ossor.*, i, 82–109.   **77** Mooney, *De Provincia.*   **78** O'Mahony, *Brevis Synopsis.*   **79** See Wadding, *Scriptores*, 104, 123, where he mentions that he has copies of the two manuscript histories.

referred twice to the martyrdom of O'Healy and O'Rourke.[80] Other authors, particularly Franciscans, quoted Wadding. One such was the Franciscan martyrologist Arthur Monstier, who printed an entry on O'Healy and O'Rourke, and listed fourteen sources, which are an impressive testimony to the *fama martyrii*.[81] Wadding, who obtained considerable information from the publications of David Rothe, the greatest of the Irish martyrologists, got very little on O'Healy and O'Rourke from Rothe's *De Processu Martyriali*, which has but a brief entry on their death.[82] In 1650, when he published at Rome his Franciscan bibliography or *Scriptores*, Luke Wadding printed at the end of it, as an appendix, a Franciscan martyrology which contains twenty Irish Franciscan martyrs, including Patrick O'Healy and Conn O'Rourke.

John Coppinger's *Theatre of Catholique and Protestant Religion*[83] appeared in 1620, too early to be influenced by Wadding. While he may have read the relevant works of Bourchier, Verstegan, Howlin and Rothe, his account of the martyrdom of O'Healy and O'Rourke would appear to have relied to no small extent on a living oral tradition. Philip O'Sullivan Beare also printed an account of the martyrdom,[84] without citing any source, as did John Mullan,[85] who depended on Rothe. These writers, as well as Henry Fitzsimon, SJ, who included Bishop O'Healy among the Irish saints in his *Catalogus Praecipuorum Sanctorum Hiberniae* (Liège, 1619), helped to keep the *fama martyrii* alive. Anthony Broudin's account of the two martyrs in his *Propugnaculum Catholicae Veritatis* (Prague, 1669), 433–7, depends on Gonzaga, and also to some degree on Monstier, and on Wadding's list of martyrs at the end of the *Scriptores*.

During the eighteenth century the memory of martyrdom of very many Irish martyrs weakened but, because of the enduring value of Luke Wadding's annals and his Franciscan bibliography, the reputation of martyrdom of O'Healy and O'Rourke was sustained. Moreover, a second edition of the *Annales Minorum* appeared in 1731–6. Several historians and chroniclers of the Franciscan Order, especially in Spain, used Wadding's annals and mentioned these martyrs, thus contributing to the *fama martyrii*. In the nineteenth century, and indeed up to recent years, Monstier's *Martyrology* was read publicly each day in the refectory of every Franciscan friary, thus helping to keep fresh the memory of O'Healy and O'Rourke

80 *Ann. Min.*, ad an. 1291, no. LI; ad an. 1302, no. XII. **81** Arthur Monstier, *Martyrologium Franciscanum* (2nd ed., Paris, 1653), 448–9. **82** Rothe, *De Processu Martyriali*, unpaginated section following the preface. Reprinted in Moran, *Analecta*, 382. **83** Coppinger, *Theatre*. **84** Philip O'Sullivan Beare, *Hist. Cath. Ibern.*, ff. 90r-91v. **85** Mullan, *Epitome Tripartita*.

among their religious brethren. The reprinting of O'Sullivan Beare's history in 1850 and of Rothe's martyrology in 1884, and the publication in 1868 and 1896 of comprehensive works on the Irish martyrs by Myles O'Reilly and Denis Murphy, reawakened the memory of the martyrdom among many non-Franciscans.

The reputation of martyrdom of Bishop Patrick O'Healy and Friar Conn O'Rourke was examined, together with the evidence for their martyrdom, during the Ordinary Process held at Dublin in 1904 and was presented to the Holy See. The General Promoter of the Faith, after reviewing the evidence in his *Disquisitio*, 51–4, concluded with this favourable verdict:

> *Quam ob rem horum Servorum Dei causam ad sacram Congregationem censeo posse deferri.*

Accordingly, the cause of Patrick O'Healy and Conn O'Rourke was among those approved by Benedict XV for examination during the Apostolic Process, which was conducted at Dublin in the years 1917–30. The findings were then presented to the Holy See.

Matthew Lambert, Robert Meyler, Edward Cheevers, Patrick Cavanagh and companions

Patrick J. Corish

EARLY LIFE

The early lives of these men, a baker and five sailors from the town of Wexford, are known to us only from incidental references in the accounts of their deaths. These references may be convincingly set against a background of what is known of the political and religious history of the town in the first twenty years of the reign of Queen Elizabeth I.

All of them were poor men. While Matthew Lambert is stated to have owned a bakery, the same source[1] stresses that he was 'a simple and completely unlettered' man (*simplex et literarum omnium ignarus*). To this might be added the fact that his name does not occur in any of the surviving records of the town (people listed in these sources would be the people of substance). While Matthew Lambert owned his own business, it is clear that this business was a modest one.[2]

Howlin states that five sailors in all suffered martyrdom, and there is no reason to doubt the accuracy of his statement. One is unnamed. Another appears as 'John O'Lahy' in the less reliable Catholic sources.[3] The name is not local to Wexford, and in view of the other errors of detail in these sources, the identity of this man must remain uncertain. Of the three whose names have been preserved with certainty, Meyler and Cheevers, like Lambert, are of Norman origin, while Cavanagh is the patronymic of the principal Gaelic sept in County Wexford.

The southern part of this county, and more particularly the town of Wexford and the area surrounding it, had been settled by the Normans immediately on their arrival in the twelfth century. It had remained consciously English and English-speaking, all the more so because in a Gaelic revival in the fourteenth and fifteenth centuries the great Irish sept of the Cavanaghs had reasserted their authority over much of County

---

1 Howlin, *Perbreve Compend.*; printed, with some inaccuracies, in Moran, *Spicil. Ossor.*, i, 59–71. **2** Ibid. **3** Coppinger, *Theatre*, 584–5; Anthony Bruodin, *Propugnaculum Catholicae Veritatis* (Prague, 1669), 442–3.

Wexford and regularly posed a threat to the 'English' lands to the south. By the reign of Elizabeth I, the English monarchy, here as elsewhere, had begun the task of subjugating the independent Irish lordships to the authority of the crown. As the Gaelic system came under pressure, individuals from time to time sought a livelihood outside it. One of these was Patrick Cavanagh, who became a sailor in the port of Wexford.

As in the larger and wealthier 'English Pale' surrounding Dublin and Drogheda, all the traditions of 'English Wexford' disposed it to be loyal to the crown. As one of the new English adventurers, Sir Henry Wallop, wrote from Wexford on 8 June 1581 to Sir Francis Walsingham:

> This countye of Wexford was the first place our nation landyd and inhabityd in, to this day they generally speke owle Inglische and are best affected to owre nation and easyest to be governed had they dyscrete offycers.[4]

The people of 'English Wexford' were disposed to welcome the increased presence of the English administration in that it promised to control the neighbouring Cavanaghs who had threatened them for centuries. By this time also the 'English of Ireland', under humanist influence, had come to see themselves as the natural civilising force as far as their Gaelic neighbours were concerned.

However, latent tensions began to surface in the reign of Elizabeth. The subjugation of the native Irish was expensive, and the government demanded taxation to pay for it.[5] This was much resented in a society which for centuries had had to rely on self-defence but was now expected to pay tax to support the queen's administration and the queen's army. In County Wexford, as elsewhere, most of the profits from the subjugation of the Gaelic lordships went to newly arrived and more thrusting Englishmen. The poor people seem to have found these even more oppressive than their native gentry had been.[6]

---

4 PRO, S.P., 63/83/41, *Cal. S.P. Ire.*, *1574–85*, 306. 5 Sir Henry Sidney, Lord Deputy of Ireland, to the English Privy Council, Kilmainham, 15 May 1577. London, PRO, S.P., 63/58/25; briefly calendared in *Cal. S.P. Ire.*, *1574–85*, 115; printed in P.H. Hore, *A history of the town and county of Wexford* (6 vols, London, 1900–11), v, 178–9. 6 'A Breviate of the Proceedings of the Right Honourable Sir William Pelham, Knight, lord justice of her majesty's realm of Ireland, during the time of his government there, which began the 11th of October 1579 and ended the 7th September 1580'. London, Lambeth Palace Library, Lambeth MS 597, ff 39–40; briefly calendared in *Cal. Carew MSS. 1575–88*, 312–314; printed, with some omissions and inaccuracies, in Hore, op. cit., v, 184 [hereafter: *Breviate*].

By this time the religious issue was also emerging as a source of tension. By and large, 'English Ireland' seems to have had few hesitations in accepting Henry VIII (1509–47) as in some sense 'head of the Church', if only because this had little or no impact on daily life. Religious changes did begin to impinge, however, when the Book of Common Prayer was introduced in the reign of Edward VI (1547–53). This change in the Sunday religious service was widely and positively resented.

By the 1570s 'recusancy', or an unwillingness to follow the government religion, was being strengthened by the influence of the Catholic Counter-Reformation, as may be seen in the case of the priest Richard French[7] and even more strikingly with the merchants and shipowners like Jasper Codd, Richard Sinnott and Patrick Hay.[8] These had clearly taken what must have been a very difficult decision, namely, to commit themselves to political and even military action against Queen Elizabeth in the light of the papal excommunication of 1570.[9]

Matthew Lambert and the sailors were arrested because they had helped Viscount Baltinglass, and his Jesuit chaplain, Robert Rochford, in what proved to be an unsuccessful attempt to flee the country through the port of Wexford at a time when Baltinglass had decided that he had no further hope of maintaining his revolt against the queen.[10] On 18 July 1579 James Fitzmaurice had landed at Smerwick in County Kerry, proclaiming, with papal authority, a war for the defence of the Catholic religion against the deposed and heretical queen. What hopes there may have been of initiating such a war became much slimmer when he was killed a month later. His own family, the powerful Fitzgeralds of Desmond, rose in revolt, and there were outbreaks in Connacht and among the Gaelic septs of Leinster. However, the struggle in Munster developed into what was primarily an old-fashioned dynastic conflict, between the Desmond Fitzgeralds and their long-standing rivals, the Butlers of Ormond, who took the side of the crown.

The government was even more alarmed when in July 1580 James

---

7 Howlin, *Perbreve Compend.*   **8** Sir William Drury, lord president of Munster, to Sir Francis Walsingham, chief secretary, Dungarvan, 14 April 1577. London, PRO, S.P., 63/58/2 I; briefly calendared in *Cal. S.P. Ire., 1574–85*, 112; printed in Hore, op. cit., v, 178. Howlin, *Perbreve Compend.* Rothe, *De Processu Martyriali*, unpaginated section following the preface; reprinted in Moran, *Analecta*, 391. Coppinger, *Theatre*. Mullan, *Epitome Tripartita*, 86–7.   **9** See in particular Brendan Bradshaw, 'Sword, word and strategy in the Reformation in Ireland', in *Hist. Jn.* 21 (1978), 475–502; N.P. Canny, 'Why the Reformation failed in Ireland: *une question mal posée*', in *JEH* 30 (1979), 423–50; Colm Lennon, *Richard Stanihurst the Dubliner, 1547–1618* (Dublin, 1981).   **10** The Catholic sources are in error in stating that Baltinglass and Father Rochford did in fact escape through Wexford.

Eustace, Viscount Baltinglass, took up arms and proclaimed his cause to be support for the pope and refusal to accept the queen's Church. There is no satisfactory study of Baltinglass, but the sincerity of his religious motivation is beyond question.[11] He came from near Dublin, and from a social group regarded as essentially loyal. Though many of the gentry of the Pale came under suspicion, the greater magnates did not give him active support, and he had to rely on some of the lesser gentry and Gaelic septs of Leinster. These included the O'Byrnes of Wicklow, hereditary foes of his own family, and the Cavanaghs, hereditary foes of the people of 'English Wexford'.

Despite a heavy defeat of the government forces at Glenmalure in the Wicklow mountains on 25 August 1580, when the new lord deputy, Lord Grey de Wilton, rashly tried to penetrate the stronghold of the O'Byrnes, Baltinglass was unable to extend his control beyond the mountains. Inevitably his war linked up with the fighting in Munster. In the middle of September, Spanish forces landed at Smerwick, and Baltinglass moved into Munster,[12] but on 9 November Smerwick surrendered to the English and the garrison was massacred. Baltinglass returned to Leinster with only a small following.[13] He made confused and uncertain attempts to surrender, but they came to nothing and he decided to flee the country. This was early in February 1581.[14]

It was natural that he should think of the port of Wexford.[15] He had no hopes in Dublin, to the north of the mountains. The way south to Wexford lay through Cavanagh lands, and Father Rochford was a native of 'English Wexford'[16] and might reasonably expect some help there.

As already indicated, the magnates of the Dublin Pale had refused help

11 See in particular his letters to the earl of Ormond (undated, but before 27 July 1580) and to an unnamed merchant of Waterford (18 July 1580) in *Cal. Carew MSS, 1575–88*, 289–90. The account of Baltinglass in David Mathew, *The Celtic peoples and Renaissance Europe* (London, 1933), 183–270, is still worth reading.   **12** Wallop to Walsingham, Dublin, 9 Oct. 1580, in PRO, S.P., 63/77/22 (*Cal. S.P. Ire., 1574–85*, 259); Sir Richard Bingham to Walsingham, Smerwick, 23 Oct. 1580, in PRO, S.P., 63/77/51 (*Cal. S.P. Ire., 1574–85*, 262). **13** Thomas Wadding, Ormond's chief justice in Tipperary, to James Sherlock, mayor of Waterford, Clonmel, 15 Nov. 1580, in PRO, S.P., 63/78/45 iii (*Cal. S.P. Ire., 1574–85*, 269). **14** Robert Pypho to Walsingham, Dublin, 11 Dec. 1580, in PRO, S.P., 63/79/11 (*Cal. S.P. Ire., 1574–85*, 274); Grey to Walsingham, Dublin, 22 Dec. 1580, in PRO, S.P., 63/79/24 (*Cal. S.P. Ire., 1574–85*, 275); Sir William Gerrard to Walsingham, Dublin, 5 Feb. 1581, in PRO, S.P., 63/80/52 (*Cal. S.P. Ire., 1574–85*, 285); Grey to Sir William Morgan, Mullingar, 14 Feb. 1581, in PRO, S.P., 63/80/76 i (*Cal. S.P. Ire., 1574–85*, 288).   **15** What may be taken as confirming the fact that they moved south to Wexford is to be found in Wallop to Walsingham, Dublin, 28 Jan. 1582, in PRO, S.P., 63/88/46 (*Cal. S.P. Ire., 1574–85*, 346). Listing the arrests and executions after the flight of Baltinglass, he notes: 'the messenger from Viscount Baltinglass to the County of Wexford apprehended'.   **16** For a notice of Rochford's life, see Hogan, *Distinguished Irishmen*, 17–20.

to Baltinglass, though there can be little doubt that at least some of them were sympathetic to his cause. Numbers of the gentry of 'English Wexford' seem to have committed themselves more openly,[17] though the motives of some of them, such as Nicholas Devereux of Ballymagir,[18] must have been mixed. This wealthy landed family was the most prominent in 'English Wexford'. Nicholas's brother Alexander had been abbot of the Cistercian abbey of Dunbrody at the time of its dissolution in the 1530s. He had become Henry VIII's bishop of Ferns in 1539, and held his see, alternating between Catholicism and Protestantism from one reign to another, until his death in 1566. He was succeeded by his nephew, John Devereux (1566–78).[19] It is unlikely that the family were crusaders for Catholicism in 1580.

In any case, when Baltinglass reached Wexford his cause was clearly lost, and it would appear that he found no person of wealth or standing to help him, not even in the town, where several merchants had in previous years committed themselves deeply to the Catholic cause. It was only a handful of obscure men who gave succour to Baltinglass and Father Rochford – Matthew Lambert the baker who gave them lodging, and a group of sailors who tried to arrange a passage for them, though without success.[20]

ARREST AND IMPRISONMENT

In the early summer of 1581, the crown was reasserting its authority in County Wexford, both in 'English Wexford' and in the Cavanagh territories.[21] It is fairly clear that the executions carried out among the Cavanaghs were under martial law.[22] In 'English Wexford', however, the assizes of

---

17 Lord Deputy Grey to the English privy council, Wexford, 10 June 1581. London, PRO, S.P., 63/88/45; briefly calendared in *Cal. S.P. Ire., 1574–85*, 307. *A nineteenth-century calendar of the Journal of the Irish privy council*, Dublin, National Archive; printed in *Anal. Hib.* 24 (1967), 119 – the original was lost in 1922 [hereafter: *Journal of the Irish privy council*]. Lord Deputy Grey to the English privy council, Dublin, 10 July 1581. London, PRO, S.P., 63/84/12; briefly calendared in *Cal. S.P. Ire., 1574–85*, 310. **18** *Journal of the Irish privy council*; Lord Deputy Grey to the English privy council, Dublin, 10 July 1581 (note 17). **19** *HBC*, 371. **20** Baltinglass and Rochford finally escaped 'in a Scottish ship' at the beginning of November 1581 (see Geoffrey Fenton to Burghley, Dublin, 12 Nov. 1581, in PRO, S.P., 63/86/65 (*Cal. S.P. Ire., 1574–85*, 329); John Daniel to Walsingham, Dublin, 23 Nov. 1581, in PRO, S.P., 63/86/77 (*Cal. S.P. Ire., 1574–85*, 330)). **21** Lord Deputy Grey to the English privy council, Wexford, 10 June; Dublin, 10 July 1581 (note 17). See also Wallop to Walsingham, Wexford, 8 June 1581, in PRO, S.P., 63/83/41 (*Cal. S.P. Ire., 1574–85*, 311); Grey to the queen, Dublin, 10 Aug. 1581, in PRO, S.P., 63/84/24 (*Cal. S.P. Ire., 1574–85*, 314). **22** Lord Deputy Grey to the English privy council, Wexford, 10 June 1581 (note 17).

queen's bench had been regularly held every year,[23] and those accused of favouring Baltinglass were in prison awaiting trial. They included many men of standing and substance, and also Matthew Lambert and the group of sailors. There is no record of the date of imprisonment, but their stay in prison may be assumed to have been a short one. It may also be assumed that they were imprisoned in the royal castle in Wexford town.

TRIAL

The records of the court of queen's bench for the reign of Elizabeth were lost in 1922. In consequence, information has to be gleaned from two letters of Lord Deputy Grey,[24] an entry in a nineteenth-century calendar of the minute book of the privy council,[25] and the accounts given by the Catholic writers, more particularly John Howlin.[26] From Grey's letters the date of the trial can be fixed with reasonable accuracy. The sessions had not begun by 10 June.[27] At least one trial – a politically important one and probably taken early – had been concluded before 18 June.[28] The whole series of trials in Wexford was over before 10 July, and clearly some time before this date, for in his letter[29] the lord deputy refers to further trials in New Ross, and these must have taken place some time before he wrote this letter on 10 July after his return to Dublin.

There must have been quite a number on trial. Many had been arraigned, including 'the best of the whole shire, Nicholas Devereux'. What

---

23 Sir Henry Sidney, lord deputy of Ireland, to the English privy council, Kilmainham, 15 May 1577. London, PRO, S.P., 63/58/25. (See note 5). *Breviate* (note 6). Lord Deputy Grey to the English privy council, Wexford, 10 June; Dublin, 10 July 1581 (note 17). The plea rolls, the official records of these court proceedings, were destroyed in the fire at the Dublin Public Record Office in 1922. The Wexford historian Philip H. Hore (1841–1923) had a transcript of the Wexford material made. The rolls were in poor condition and the transcriber reported that much was illegible. Even more unfortunately, at the time the transcript was made material had been located only down to 1578 (see *Rec. Comm. Ire. Rec., 1810–15,* 14, 413; *1816–20,* 42, 47, 79–125, 842; *1821–5,* 3, 7, 11, 19, 23). Later the Wexford material for the remainder of the reign of Elizabeth came to light, including the records for the sessions of 1581 (see *P.R.I. Rep. D.K. 28* [1896], 48–9), but this had not been transcribed before everything was lost in 1922. Hore's transcript is now in his MS collection in St. Peter's College, Wexford (unbound MS no. 4). He printed what could be deciphered in his *History of the town and county of Wexford,* v, 169–70, and in 'The barony of Forth', in *Past* 1 (1920), 83–5. 24 Lord Deputy Grey to the English privy council, Wexford, 10 June; Dublin, 10 July 1581 (note 17). 25 *Journal of the Irish privy council* (note 17). 26 Howlin, *Perbreve Compend.* 27 Lord Deputy Grey to the English privy council, Wexford, 10 June 1581 (note 17). 28 *Journal of the Irish privy council* (note 17). 29 Lord Deputy Grey to the English privy council, Dublin, 10 July 1581 (note 17).

happened in his case illustrates the difficulty in securing the conviction of a great landed magnate in the courts of common law. According to the lord deputy, he had publicly confessed 'matter worthy death', but the local jury simply refused to convict him.[30] He and four other gentlemen then had to bind themselves personal security for the then very considerable sum of £300 each that he would personally appear before the lord deputy and council in Dublin on the first day of the next Michaelmas law term.[31] The lord deputy and council exercised judicial functions as the prerogative court of castle chamber, and as a prerogative court were not bound by the procedures of the courts of common law. There is, however, no record of the fate of Nicholas Devereux in the surviving records of this court.

The lord deputy was naturally anxious that exemplary and public punishment should be meted out in Wexford. The poor men, Matthew Lambert and the sailors, were the obvious victims. Details of their trials have been preserved by John Howlin, who was quite possibly an eye-witness of the events he so graphically describes. At his preliminary hearing Matthew Lambert was at least threatened with torture, and quite probably was tortured. He was questioned on his loyalty to the pope and to the queen. To this he replied simply that he was a Catholic, that he believed what the Catholic Church believed, and that he did not understand these controversies. It would appear that he repeated these statements when he came before the court. But, since the papal deposition of Elizabeth in 1570, a profession of loyalty to the pope was necessarily a profession of disloyalty to the queen. In consequence, he was condemned to be hanged, drawn and quartered as a traitor.[32]

Howlin states explicitly that the sailors were tortured. Despite this and despite the entreaties of their families, they persisted in professing the Catholic faith, and continued to do so in open court (*publice*). In consequence, they too were condemned to die as traitors.

MARTYRDOM

All were hanged, drawn, and quartered at Wexford. There are conflicting testimonies as to the exact date of martyrdom, but it may be assumed that death followed quickly on sentence. It has already been argued that the assizes had finished in Wexford by the end of June, or at the very latest in

---

30 Ibid.   **31** *Journal of the Irish privy council* (note 17).   **32** Howlin, *Perbreve Compend.*

the first days of July. It is quite possible that Rothe has preserved the correct date of the martyrdom of the sailors, 5 July.[33] Howlin's date of 25 July seems much too late. Matthew Lambert would have suffered at the same time, quite probably on the same day.

MOTIVE FOR MARTYRDOM

While the legal charge was treason, there is no reason to believe that these simple and unlettered men were conscious traitors to the queen. The political leaders, James Fitzmaurice and Viscount Baltinglass, had consciously concluded that after 1570 their loyalty to the pope implied that they must be disloyal to the queen, but Matthew Lambert is to be believed when he said that he did not understand these things: he acted as he did simply because he was a Catholic. The sailors were concerned to make the same point.[34]

FAMA MARTYRII

John Howlin is the primary witness to the fact that these men suffered as martyrs for the Catholic faith. David Rothe had had some access to Howlin's manuscript and so may not be an altogether independent witness. However, he was a native of neighbouring Kilkenny and may well have had access to other information circulating in south-eastern Ireland at the time he wrote (it has been noted that he may have silently corrected Howlin's date for the executions). Mullan[35] is only Rothe dressed out in rhetoric. Coppinger, however, does seem to represent an independent tradition: he could scarcely have described Matthew Lambert as a priest had he seen Rothe's text. Bruodin[36] appears to derive from Coppinger: with him Matthew Lambert is a parish priest from near Dublin. This line of tradition has also preserved, though probably in garbled form, the name of another sailor – 'John O'Lahy'. In the case of Patrick Cavanagh, a misreading by Rothe ('Canavasius') and by Moran ('Canavan') is hard to explain. Howlin's clear italic script obviously reads 'Cavanagh', a local name much more plausible than 'Canavan', with its Galway associations. Robert Meyler appears

---

33 Rothe, *De Processu Martyriali*. **34** Howlin, *Perbreve Compend.* **35** Mullan, *Epitome Tripartita*. **36** Anthony Bruodin, *Propugnaculum Catholicae Veritatis* (Prague, 1669), 442–3.

correctly ('Meiler', 'Meilerus') in Howlin and Rothe, but has become 'Miller' in Coppinger and Bruodin.

Some such indecisiveness in detail might perhaps be expected, given their social position, but these working men from Wexford became firmly established in the canon of the Irish martyrs. They are listed by the nineteenth-century hagiographers O'Reilly and Murphy (with both Matthew Lambert retains his role as parish priest).[37] When the Ordinary Process *de fama martyrii* was held in Dublin in 1904 for the Irish martyrs of the sixteenth and seventeenth centuries the evidence for their reputation of martyrdom was examined and approved. It was then forwarded, with the other findings of the tribunal, to the Holy See. In due course, the General Promoter of the Faith gave his verdict on their case. Having reviewed the evidence concerning Matthew Lambert, he stated in his Disquisitio, 69–70:

> *Igitur videtur fidei Catholicae odio occisus eiusque martyrii posse causa institui.*

Concerning the sailors, Robert Meyler, Edward Cheevers, 'John O'Lahy' and Patrick 'Canavan', having likewise reviewed the evidence, he stated (ibid., 70–1):

> *Quare horum quatuor causam ad sacram Congregationem deferri posse existimo.*

In February 1915, the five were included in the 257 named martyrs for the introduction of whose cause authorization was granted. Accordingly, their case was examined at the Apostolic Process held in Dublin 1917–30. The findings were then presented to the Holy See.

In the light of the closest scrutiny of the historical evidence, it was judged appropriate in 1988 to present their cause under the title 'Matthew Lambert, Robert Meyler, Edward Cheevers, Patrick Cavanagh and companions, laymen', and they were beatified by Pope John Paul II on 27 September 1992 as 'Matthew Lambert, baker, and Robert Meyler, Edward Cheevers and Patrick Cavanagh, sailors'.

---

37 Myles O'Reilly, *Memorials of those who suffered for the Catholic faith in Ireland* (London, 1868), 47–8; Denis Murphy, *Our martyrs* (Dublin, 1896), 119–20.

CHAPTER 4

Dermot O'Hurley

J.J. Meagher

EARLY LIFE

Dermot O'Hurley was born *c.*1530 at, or near, Emly,[1] County Tipperary. He was the son of William O'Hurley, an agent of the earl of Desmond, and Honora O'Brien.[2] He had one sister, Honora, who towards the end of his life visited him in prison. The 'William oge Hurley' to whom a royal pardon was extended on 6 November 1581[3] may have been an elder brother. He had a much younger brother named Andrew who in 1642 was over eighty years of age, blind and paralysed, and living in exile in Portugal.[4] The family later moved to Lickadoon, County Limerick.[5] O'Hurley most probably received his early education at the cathedral school established for secular priests at Emly by his namesake, Thomas O'Hurley, bishop of Emly.[6] Nothing further is known of his early life. His parents' choice of the University of Louvain rather than either of the two English universities, or the inns of court at London, was to be the decisive factor in the shaping of his career.[7]

At Louvain, Dermot O'Hurley qualified as Master of Arts in the *Paedagogium Lilii* in the year 1551, coming thirteenth in his class. Eight years later he became professor of philosophy in this college, having acquired a reputation for his commentaries on Aristotle.[8] At the same time he

---

1 According to Rothe, *De Processu Martyriali*, 48, O'Hurley was born at Lycadoon, a few miles from Limerick and within the diocese of Limerick. But when he entered the Collège du Lis at Louvain, O'Hurley described himself as 'Imolacensis' (Jean-Louis Bax, *Historia Universitatis Lovaniensis, c.1790*. BR, MS 22172, vol. vii, 1254). As he was not a clerical student or a priest, he was not describing his diocese of incardination. 'Imolacensis' must therefore refer to his place of birth. **2** Rothe, *De Processu Martyriali.*, 48–71; reprinted in Moran, *Analecta*, 423–37. **3** *Fiants Ire., Eliz.*, no. 3767. **4** M. Gonçalves da Costa (ed.), *Fontes inéditas Portuguesas para a história de Irlanda* (Braga, 1981), 281. **5** Rothe, *De Processu Martyriali*. **6** Lynch, *De Praesulibus Hib.*, ii, 64. **7** Rothe, *De Processu Martyriali*. **8** Jean-Louis Bax, *Historia Universitatis Lovaniensis, c. 1790*. BR, MS 22172, vol. vii, 1254. Sir James Ware, *The history of the writers of Ireland*, ed. Walter Harris (Dublin, 1764), 98; E.H.J. Reusens (ed.), *Documents relatifs à l'histoire de l'Univerité de Louvain ... 1425–1797*, v (Louvain, 1892), 369.

embarked upon an arduous course of legal studies, leading to the distinguished degree of *doctor iuris utriusque* through which he acquired the high office of dean of the university's law school.[9] Dermot O'Hurley's stay in Louvain, both as student and professor, lasted fifteen years. It was succeeded by a term of four years in the University of Reims as professor of laws, a position to which he had been appointed by the archbishop of Reims and founder of the university, Louis de Guise.[10] We know nothing of his activities there, for the records are no longer available.[11] After a stay at Reims he departed for Rome,[12] probably in or before 1570.[13]

No trace of O'Hurley at Rome is to be found. It is most probable that he continued his academic career. That this was so is confirmed by a line in the valedictory verses in which his appointment to the see of Cashel was commemorated.[14] The later allegation[15] that, while at Rome, he was a member of the Holy Office is not sustained by any other evidence.

In 1581, however, Gregory XIII, presumably on curial advice, decided to provide him as archbishop to Cashel. He agreed to this, though still a layman, and, in virtue of a special papal brief issued in his favour, he received clerical tonsure and was advanced to the four minor and three major orders in sixteen days, between 29 July and 13 August.[16] At the Secret Consistory held on 11 September 1581, he was provided to the metropolitan church of Cashel,[17] and on 27 November was granted the *pallium* in person.[18] The new archbishop is next heard of on 5 August 1582. He had arrived once again at Reims. He had brought much-needed money from the English College at Rome to Dr William Allen's seminary.[19]

At Reims, O'Hurley began preparations for his mission to Ireland. Le Croisic, a port at the mouth of the Loire, was chosen as a point of departure as it was more secluded than Nantes. Holmpatrick, a harbour in the vicinity of Skerries, County Dublin, was chosen as a safe place of disembarkation as it was exempt from the jurisdiction of Dublin corporation and was privately owned. A papal receipt and other documents were entrusted to a Wexford merchant, while O'Hurley himself was to be transported in a ship from Drogheda whose captain would have been familiar with

---

9 Verstegan, *Theatrum*, 80. Valerius Andreas, *Fasti academici studii generalis Lovaniensis* (2nd ed., Louvain, 1650), 214. **10** Verstegan, *Theatrum*. **11** Unfortunately most of the archives of the University of Reims and of the Collège des Bons-Enfants had disappeared some time between the compilation in 1757 of an inventory of documents belonging to these institutions and 1885, when Cauly wrote his history. Inquiries at the Archives Départementales in Châlons-sur-Marne failed to elicit any further information other than the statement of the Abbé E. Cauly, kindly pointed out by M. l'Archiviste (see E. Cauly, *Histoire du Collège des Bons-Enfants de l'Université de Reims* (Reims, 1885), preface, xii). **12** Verstegan, *Theatrum*.

Holmpatrick. Misfortune struck from the outset. The Wexford ship was intercepted by pirates, and the bundle of letters and other testimonials of his consecration was handed over to the lords justices in Dublin.[20] Awareness of O'Hurley's departure seems to have preceded his arrival, owing to the combination of the pirates' haul and the spies' reports.[21] But, most seriously, O'Hurley was returning to Ireland at a time of particular danger of which he was not aware.

In the latter half of 1583 Ireland remained gripped in crisis. The Munster rebellion which had raged since 1579 was at length on the point of suppression, but the troubles begun in Munster had already spread to every other province in Ireland. In Ulster, Turlough Luineach, the powerful chief of the O'Neills, had renounced his earlier agreements with the other Ulster chiefs, and daily threatened the borders of the English Pale. In Connacht, the brittle peace established by the English lord president, Sir Nicholas Malby, was becoming increasingly unstable, and the province was again engulfed in war. In the Pale itself, the insurrection of a senior peer of the realm, Viscount Baltinglass, in 1580 brought rebellion to the very gates of Dublin, while the discovery of a widespread conspiracy among the gentry of County Meath generated an acute anxiety among the administrators in Dublin that treason was rampant; and though the viscount's revolt and conspiracy were soon suppressed, the Gaelic septs of Wicklow and Offaly, and minor Gaelicized Geraldine families of Kildare, continued in rebellion. Thus, as O'Hurley

13 Verstegan says that O'Hurley's stay in Louvain, both as student and professor, lasted fifteen years. He was four years at Reims. This would seem to indicate that he departed thence to Rome *c.*1567.   **14** '*Postquam Rhemorum veneranda Doctor in Urbe / Voce sua Legum pulpita personuit …*' This poem of thirty lines is preserved in Rome, Biblioteca Vallicelliana MS H 48, f. 69rv, and has been printed in Moran, *Spicil. Ossor.*, i, 80.   **15** Lords Justices Loftus and Wallop to Sir Francis Walsingham, chief secretary, Dublin, 20 October 1583. London, PRO, S.P., 63/105/29; printed in Brady, *Ir. Ch. Eliz.*, 69–72; calendared in *Cal. S.P. Ire., 1574–85*, 475.   **16** Cf. Registrum Ordinationum ab anno 1580 ad annum 1588 of the diocese of Rome (Rome, Archives of the Vicariate); printed in *Collect. Hib.* 25 (1983), 12–19.   **17** Minutes of the Secret Consistory held on 11 September 1581. BV, MSS Barb. Lat., 2929, f. 38r (copy); printed, with some omissions, in W.M. Brady, *Ep. Succ.*, ii, 10, and in *Collect. Hib.* 25 (1983), 19–20.   **18** Minutes of the Secret Consistory held on 27 November 1581. AV, Acta Camerarii, 11, f. 366v; AV, Fondo Conamerarii, Acta Miscellanea, 13, f. 266r (copy); BV, MSS Barb. Lat., 2929, f. 41r (copy); Rome, Biblioteca Corsini, Cors. MS 48, f. 458r (copy); printed (from a copy of the longer version preserved in Paris, Bibliothèque Nationale, MSS Latins, 12,2, 12, f. 563) in Brady, *Ep. Succ.*, ii, 10, and in *Collect. Hib.* 25 (1983), 20–1.   **19** See *The letters and memorials of William Cardinal Allen* (1532–1594), ed. by the Fathers of the Congregation of the London Oratory (London, 1882), 151, 155–6, 160, 162.   **20** This is mentioned by them in their letter of 7 March 1584 to Walsingham: London, PRO, S.P., 63/108/8 (modern copy); printed in Brady (ed.), *Ir. Ch. Eliz.*, 74–6; calendared in *Cal. S.P. Ire., 1574–85*, 498.   **21** Loftus and Wallop to Robert Beale, acting secretary of the English privy council, Dublin, 8 October 1583. London, PRO, S.P., 63/105/10; printed in Brady (ed.), *Ir. Ch. Eliz.*, 68–9; calendared in *Cal. S.P. Ire., 1574–85*, 472.

prepared to return to Ireland the administrators in Dublin believed themselves to be confronted by an unprecedented and vigorous display of dissidence. Isolated in Dublin, plagued by suspicion, and in fear of their imminent overthrow, they regarded the arrival of this papal appointed archbishop with extraordinary concern.

On landing at Skerries, O'Hurley was met by a priest, John Dillon, and he and his companion went to Drogheda,[22] where they lodged in a hostelry. His appearance there seems to have attracted some attention, and the authorities at Dublin were notified. On the advice of a resident of Drogheda, O'Hurley and his companion left for Slane.[23] Though resident there, with the cognisance of the baron of Slane, he appears to have extended his activities into the O'Reilly's country.[24]

ARREST AND IMPRISONMENT

O'Hurley's presence in Meath beccame known to the authorities through a visit of Sir Robert Dillon, chief justice of the common pleas, to his first cousin, the baron of Slane, with whom the archbishop had stayed. On learning of O'Hurley's whereabouts, Dillon informed the Dublin government, and the Baron was summoned to attend upon the lords justices, Adam Loftus and Sir Henry Wallop.[25] After some pressure, Slane at length agreed to procure O'Hurley's arrest. By this time the archbishop had moved to Carrick-on-Suir, County Tipperary, where he hoped to arrange a meeting with the queen's archbishop of Cashel, Miler Magrath.[26] Slane sent to him there, urging him to come to Dublin to purge the baron himself from any taint of treason. O'Hurley agreed to accompany Slane to Dublin, and on his arrival there shortly before 8 October 1583 he was immediately arrested and imprisoned in Dublin Castle.[27]

---

22 '... itineris socium seu ducem Ioannem Dillonum Presbyterum' (Rothe, *De Processu Martyriali*.). **23** Rothe, *De Processu Martyriali*. **24** Loftus and Wallop to Walsingham, 20 October 1583 (note 15). **25** Manuscript entitled 'Out of Romish collections of annals of Ireland', an eclectic collection for the years 1460–1591, compiled *c*.1591. Bodl., MS Rawl. B. 479, ff 98v–101v; printed in *Anal. Hib.* 1 (1930), 125–8. Rothe, *De Processu Martyriali*. **26** See Rothe, *De Processu Martyriali*; for the connection between O'Hurley and Magrath, see Dermot O'Hurley to Miler Magrath, the queen's archbishop of Cashel, 20 September 1583. Bodl., Carte MSS, 55, f. 546. The role of the baron of Slane is further revealed in Wallop's accounts for the period 1579–84, which contain a record of a payment made to 'the Lorde Barron of Slane for his chardges travellinge into Mounster for the apprehensyon of one Doctor Hurley late come from beyonde the Seas whom he broughte to the Castle of Dublyn' (PRO, E. 351/230). **27** Loftus and Wallop to Beale, Dublin, 8 October 1583 (note 21).

An initial interrogation of the archbishop by Edward Waterhouse, a senior member of the Irish privy council, was conducted under instructions from Lords Justices Loftus and Wallop between 8 and 20 October. The results of this interrogation were unsatisfactory, and the lords justices wrote on 20 October to Sir Francis Walsingham, secretary of state to Queen Elizabeth, seeking further advice.[28] Walsingham replied, instructing them to use 'Torture or any other severe manner of proceedinge' against O'Hurley so as 'to gaine his knowledge of all forraigne practises against her Majesty States'. Loftus and Wallop, however, seem to have been reluctant to proceed with the torture of O'Hurley, and they wrote to Walsingham on 10 December suggesting that he be despatched to the Tower of London for interrogation, as they lacked the necessary instruments of torture.[29] But Walsingham, convinced of the seriousness and urgency of the matter, was adamant. At some date before 7 March 1584 the lords justices were directed to extract information from O'Hurley 'not only of any practise of disturbance pretended against the Land [Ireland] in particular, but also of any other forrigne Conspiracy against her Majesty for England or any other parts of her Dominions'. They were, it seems, instructed to try gentle persuasion, but, if that failed, to 'put him to the Torture ... which was to Toaste his Feet against the Fyer with hot Bootes'.[30]

After this letter was received O'Hurley was once more interrogated, and, his answers being considered insufficient and evasive when only gentle persuasion was used, the lords justices authorized (probably by a written commission) the use of torture against O'Hurley by his interrogator, Waterhouse, and the principal secretary of the Irish privy council, Geoffrey Fenton. The results of the interrogation under torture of O'Hurley were sent to Walsingham on 7 March 1584.[31] Despite his ordeal, O'Hurley revealed no information other than that he had nothing to say. No further examination of the archbishop under torture is known to have taken place, and, on 28 April, Queen Elizabeth expressly forbade its use.[32]

28 Loftus and Wallop to Walsingham, Dublin, 20 October 1583 (note 15).   29 Loftus and Wallop to Walsingham, Dublin, 10 December 1583. London, PRO, S.P., 63/106/7 (modern copy); printed in Brady, *Ir. Ch. Eliz.*, 72–3; calendared in *Cal. S.P. Ire.*, 1574–85, 482.   30 See note 20.   31 Ibid.   32 Cf. Walsingham to Loftus and Wallop, London, 28 April 1584. London, PRO, S.P., 63/109/66 (draft); printed in Brady, *Ir. Ch. Eliz.*, 79–80; calendared in *Cal. S.P. Ire. 1574–85*, 509.

TRIAL

The lords justices' anxiety to arrest and interrogate O'Hurley was based upon their conviction that he was deeply implicated not only in the rebellion in Munster but also in the conspiracies of Viscount Baltinglass and William Nugent, the ramifications of which continued to trouble the Dublin administration.[33] Walsingham's insistence upon the most thorough investigation was equally due to the certainty on the State's part that an international conspiracy led from Rome was still operating effectively against England and was continuing to use Ireland as its principal base.[34] The failure of the interrogation and torture of O'Hurley did little to assuage their fears, but rather deepened the government's embarrassment. While on the one hand it was clear that O'Hurley knew little, and had little to reveal, about militant Counter-Reformation activities in Ireland or elsewhere, on the other hand it was patently obvious that the authorities had acted with extreme brutality against an individual, innocent of any such implication, whose blamelessness would be publicly revealed by a trial at common law.

The idea of proceeding by martial law was first mooted by the lords justices in a letter to Walsingham dated 7 March 1584,[35] and they advanced two main reasons for adopting this course. It would mean that the archbishop would not have to be tried in public, and so would not be in a position to make an 'Impudent and Clamarous' denial of the charges against him or 'exclaim to the people that he was troubled for some Noble men of this country' with all the publicity which a trial at common law would give such claims. It would also avoid the danger for the government of his being acquitted on the grounds that 'his Treasons were committed in forreigne partes'. Walsingham, after consulting the queen, communicated to the Lords Justices Loftus and Wallop her preference for a trial at common law, but also her consent to his trial by martial law, if there was any real chance that he would be acquitted in a common-law trial either 'by reason of the affections of such as shall be of the Jurie' or because it was doubtful if under common law he could be convicted of 'treasons comitted in foraine partes agaynst hir Majestie'.[36] On 19 June 1584, Loftus and Wallop, acting with the

---

33 See, e.g., Loftus and Wallop to Walsingham, Dublin, 7 March 1584 (note 20), where the lords justices report to Walsingham that O'Hurley 'would not confesse that he brought from Rome the popes Lettres of Comfort addressed to the Earle of Desmond, viscount of Baltinglass and other Rebels'. **34** See, e.g., Loftus and Wallop to Walsingham, Dublin, 10 December 1583 (note 29), in which the lords justices imply that they have been charged with extracting from O'Hurley his knowledge 'of all forraigne practises against her Majesty States'. **35** See note 20. **36** See note 32.

consent of Sir John Perrot, shortly to be sworn in as lord deputy to replace them, authorized a special commission to the knight marshal to 'do execucon' upon Dermot O'Hurley.[37]

MARTYRDOM

In keeping with their concern for secrecy, the authorities determined on O'Hurley's execution at a very early hour of the morning of 20 June 1584.[38] The archbishop was conveyed out of Dublin Castle by the postern gate and taken to Hoggin Green to be hanged on a gibbet. According to a contemporary account, the execution party was taken by surprise by a number of city worthies who had come to the Green to shoot an archery match. O'Hurley was allowed to make his last and only speech, in which he protested his innocence of any 'cause ... that might in the least degree deserve the paines of death' and asserted that he was being put to death by martial law 'for my function and profession of the holy Catholick Faith'.[39]

Dermot O'Hurley ended his life 'most patiently', 'recommending his soule to God his maker and redeemer'. The reliable account by a contemporary chronicler[40] makes no mention of his having been drawn and quartered. Howlin also merely refers to his having been hanged from a gibbet.[41] The earliest known references to the martyrdom in contemporary letters[42] and the first printed account[43] state that the Archbishop was hanged. So too does David Rothe,[44] who was in a position to check with O'Hurley's relatives and friends. John Coppinger says that the Archbishop was 'strangled with a wyth'.[45]

In their letter of 9 July 1584, the lords justices informed Walsingham that two days before they handed over government to the new lord deputy, John Perrot, 'beinge the 19th of the last [month]', they 'gave warrant to the knight Martiall in her Majesties name to do execucon upon him, which accord-

---

37 Loftus and Wallop to Walsingham, Dublin, 9 July 1584. London, PRO, S.P., 63/111/12; printed in Brady, *Ir. Ch. Eliz.*, 84–5; calendared in *Cal. S.P. Ire. 1574–85*, 517.   **38** See note 25.   **39** Ibid.   **40** Ibid.   **41** Howlin, *Perbreve Compend.*; printed, with some inaccuracies, in Moran, *Spicil. Ossor.*, i, 87–8.   **42** Robert Parsons, SJ, to [Pedro de Ribadeneira, SJ], Paris, 15 [*recte* 10?] September 1584. AV, A.A., Arm. I–XVIII, 4062, f. 3r (contemporary copy); printed in *Cath. Rec. Soc. Publ.* 39 (1942), 232–3. Conor O'Mulryan, OFM, Bishop of Killaloe, to Tolomeo Cardinal Galli, Lisbon, 29 October 1584. AV, Segretario di Stato, Portogallo, 4, f. 462r; printed in *IER* 1 (1864–5), 475–6, in *Archiv. Hib.* 7 (1918–21), 331, and in M. Gonçalves da Costa (ed.), *Fontes inéditas portuguesas para a história de Irlanda*, 196.   **43** Verstegan, *Theatrum*.   **44** Rothe, *De Processu Martyriali*.   **45** Coppinger, *Theatre*, 574–5; reprinted, with some inaccuracies in Moran, *Spicil. Ossor.*, iii, 38.

ingly was performed'.[46] The swearing-in of Perrot took place on Sunday 21 June. The lords justices signed the writ for O'Hurley's execution on Friday 19 June. In their letter to Walsingham, they do not specify Friday as the day of execution. But the contemporary chronicler is specific, stating that 'this execution was don on Saturday morning and the next Sunday the Lords Justices yealded their place and Government unto Sir John Perrot'.[47] Coppinger, who is a much later source, says that the archbishop was killed 'upon fridaie morning in the dawning'. He also says that the death occurred in May, which is manifestly incorrect.

Again according to the contemporary chronicler, when the news of Dermot O'Hurley's execution spread in the city certain women recovered his body to bury it in a nearby oratory, St Kevin's. They kept his clothes as relics. Rothe and Mooney[48] also mention St Kevin's as the place of interment. Philip O'Sullivan Beare[49] states that a citizen of Dublin named William Fitzsimon arranged for the martyr's body to be taken from the grave where the officials had placed it and transferred in a wooden casket to a secret burial place. It is possible to reconcile these accounts, for Fitzsimon may have been urged by the women to exhume the body and helped by them in preparing it for Catholic burial.

MOTIVE FOR MARTYRDOM

While Dermot O'Hurley was still alive, news of the severe torture inflicted on him was brought to Paris. This information was transmitted to Rome to Cardinal Galli by William Nugent and Barnaby Geoghegan in their letter of 4 June 1584.[50] The torture was designed, they said, to compel the archbishop to confess to matters of conspiracy or to renounce the Catholic faith, but in spite of the hideous suffering which he underwent, O'Hurley neither gave the crown officials any information nor denied the faith. The lords justices in Dublin, at the insistent persuasion of the queen's secretary

---

46 See note 37.   47 See note 25.   48 Donagh Mooney, *De Provincia Hiberniae S. Francisci.* BR, MS 3195, 69; printed in *Anal. Hib.* 6 (1934), 91.   49 Philip O'Sullivan Beare, *Hist. Cath. Ibern.* (Lisbon, 1621), ff 102v–104v; reprinted, with critical editing, in Philip O'Sullivan Beare, *Historiae Catholicae Iberniae compendium*, ed. Matthew Kelly (Dublin, 1850), 123–6. 50 William Nugent and Barnaby Geoghegan, Irish laymen, to Tolomeo Cardinal Galli, Paris, 4 June 1584. AV, Segretario di Stato, Francia, 17, f. 439v; printed in Augustine Theiner, *Annales Ecclesiastici quos post Caesarem S.R.E. Cardinalem Baronium ... continuat Augustinas Theiner*, iii (Rome, 1856), 818–19; English translation in Denis Murphy, *Our martyrs* (Dublin, 1896), 142.

of state, went to extraordinary lengths to discover from this papal arch-bishop what he knew about any Counter-Reformation plots at home or abroad against the queen and her realms. In due course they began to accept that O'Hurley had no knowledge of any papal plans for an invasion of Ireland and no connection with any foreign crusade to liberate Ireland. He was what he claimed to be, a scholar who had been appointed archbishop by the pope and had come home to do the work of an archbishop. As there is no evidence to show that Dermot O'Hurley intended to foment revolt, but on the contrary came seeking peace, as he wrote to Miler Magrath,[51] the lords justices were courting the queen's favour by their protestations of loyalty to her person and sense of vigilance in her interests.

Very early in the interrogation they learned that O'Hurley was a man of integrity. He admitted, as they reported on 20 October 1583,[52] that he had been asked to carry to Ireland letters from the cardinal protector of Ireland to the earl of Desmond and others, but also insisted that he had left them in France, for 'he woulde not medle with them'. He further admitted that he had been present at a meeting in Rome of Cardinal Galli with Viscount Baltinglass, his brother Richard, and Christopher Barnewall, but firmly denied seeing any letters from Irish rebels which Barnewall claimed[53] the cardinal had displayed. The contemporary chronicle[54] tells us that before the lords justice resorted to torture 'many ways were sought with the bishop to charge the lord of Slane with somewhat, but he denying to chardge him or any man else, was in the end tortured many waies', and that they then discovered that the brutal torture did not force him 'to accuse the Lord of Slane or any other against his conscience'. It explicitly records the reaction of Lord Justice Wallop, who was 'much incensed against him for his constancy in the Catholick faith'.

From the beginning of their dealings with him Dermot O'Hurley's true identity was known to the lord justices. The day after he was imprisoned in Dublin Castle they notified London, describing their prisoner as 'nomi-nated by the Pope to be Archbisshope of Cashell',[55] and two weeks later, in a letter to Walsingham, they referred to him as Doctor Hurley 'by creacon of the Pope Archbishopp of Cashell'.[56] O'Hurley, who was wearing secular garb, readily acknowledged his episcopal character. Within a few months, after much questioning and threatening, it was obvious to Loftus and Wallop

51 See note 26. **52** See note 15. **53** 'The examination of Christofer barnewall at dundalke the 12 of August 1583', London, PRO, S.P., 63/104/38 I; printed in Brady, *Ir. Ch. Eliz.*, 65–7; calendared in *Cal. S.P. Ire. 1574–85, 465*. **54** See note 25. **55** See note 27. **56** See note 15.

that they had made a political miscalculation in arresting an innocent man who was much revered and had influential friends, and that they had now to face the danger that their plan would rebound upon themselves. They did not admit this to Walsingham. To save themselves further embarrassment and political risk they proposed that O'Hurley be transferred to the Tower of London and that Barnewall, whose confession they now doubted, be also summoned thither 'to justifie his former deposition and other matter against Hurley'.[57] When Walsingham rejected this proposal Loftus and Wallop continued to interrogate their prisoner, and failing to discover any involvement with foreign conspiracies, they had the archbishop tortured.[58]

When reporting this to Walsingham they subtly shifted the emphasis to the other great source of worry for the crown officials at London and Dublin, the return to the realm of newly-trained seminary priests and prelates that might stiffen the opposition of the queen's Catholic subjects:

> wee doubt not but your Honour will discerne how many wayes Hurley is to be overtaken with Treason in his owne person and with what bad minde he came into Ireland instructed from Rome to poyson the Hearts of the people with disobedience to her Majesties Government.[59]

Anti-papal feeling had been strong among the crown officials in England and Ireland since 1578. Many of them in both countries regarded the pope as the arch-enemy, who was sending into Elizabeth's kingdom highly trained priests, Jesuits and friars – and, in the case of Ireland, bishops also – who would lead the people in stiff opposition to the queen's laws about religion. Accordingly, the lords justices were on safe ground when they revealed to Walsingham their latest plan to rid themselves of this undesirable Catholic archbishop. It was their plan and they were asking Walsingham to adopt it as his own when they wrote:

> wee desire your Honour to consider, how he may speedily receive his deserts, so as not only his owne evile may dye with himselfe, and thereby the Realme delivered of a perilous member but also his punishment to serve for an example, ad terrorem to many others, who wee finde by his owne Confessions are prepared at Rome to runn the same course both here and for England.

57 See note 29.   **58** See note 20.   **59** Ibid.

They had decided to put Dermot O'Hurley to death because he was a Catholic archbishop and because they hoped that his execution would deter other bishops and priests from entering the kingdom. They felt confident that Walsingham and those close to him would agree that Catholic bishops and priests were a special danger to the realm. To execute a papal archbishop would help the anti-Catholic propaganda of government officials in both kingdoms. And the lords justices hoped it would confirm the queen's Irish subjects in their obedience and loyalty. They shrewdly reminded the queen's secretary of state of their own loyal service and asked him to remember 'in how little Safety wee live here for the like Services wee have already done to her Majesty'.

The following day, in another letter to Walsingham,[60] Loftus and Wallop reveal that something akin to panic greatly disturbed these officials when they came to consider the support with which seminary priests and bishops could readily muster in Ireland. From his prison, Archbishop O'Hurley had written to the earl of Ormond and to a relative in Dublin. The letters were intercepted and were forwarded to Walsingham so that he could see 'what favour this Romish Runagates have with our good Potentates here'. This development, they were convinced, justified their own anti-papal stance and their proceedings against the archbishop. They wished Walsingham to advise them how to proceed legally against O'Hurley 'and not further to stir those Coalles to scorch our selves'. In his reply Walsingham said that it was the queen's pleasure that Archbishop O'Hurley, 'beyng so notoriouse and ill a subject', should be executed.[61]

Dermot O'Hurley was sentenced to death because he was a Catholic archbishop and adamantly refused to take the Oath of Supremacy. Most of the relevant Catholic sources state this clearly[62] or imply it.[63] But in the letters of Loftus and Wallop, who sentenced the Archbishop to death, the true story slowly emerges. In his address from the scaffold to the Dublin merchants, which is recorded in the contemporary chronicle,[64] the archbishop himself gave the motive for his killing:

> Be it therefore known unto you . . . that I am a priest anointed and also a Bishop, although unworthy of soe sacred dignities, and noe cause

60 Loftus and Wallop to Walsingham, Dublin, 8 March 1584. London, PRO, S.P., 63/108/9 (modern copy); printed in Brady, *Ir. Ch. Eliz.*, 76–8; calendared in *Cal. S.P. Ire., 1574–85*, 499. 61 See note 32.   62 Verstegan, *Theatrum*; Howlin, *Perbreve Compend.*; see note 25; Rothe, *De Processu Martyriali*; Coppinger, *Theatre*; O'Sullivan Beare, *Hist. Cath. Ibern.*   63 See note 42 (Parsons; O'Mulryan).   64 See note 25.

could they find against me that might in the least degree deserve the paines of death, but merely for my funcon of priesthood wherein they have proceeded against me in all pointes cruelly contrarie to their own lawes ... and I doe injoin you (Deere Christian Bretheren) to manifest the same unto the world and also to beare witness at the day of Judgement of my Innocent death, which I indure for my function and profession of the holy Catholick Faith.

David Rothe says that when Archbishop O'Hurley had recovered somewhat from the appalling shock of the extensive burns inflicted during torture he was tempted with the offer of high position if he would 'resign the office of archbishop which he held, renounce the primacy of Rome and acknowledge the Queen's supremacy, both ecclesiastical and secular'. One of those sent to deal with him and tempt him was an Englishman, Thomas Jones, who in 1584 became the queen's bishop of Meath. Rothe alone records that the archbishop's only sister Honora was sent to him with some new temptation, imploring him to yield. It was not unusual for senior officials of the crown to tempt a captured bishop or priest with offers of rich benefices and good preferment in the Established Church on condition that he formally admit the queen's supremacy in all matters of religion. Verstegan, Howlin, and O'Sullivan Beare state that such offers were many times made to O'Hurley in an unsuccessful attempt to persuade him to renounce the Pope's authority. Coppinger speaks of 'alluring promises of uncertaine and decitfull promotion' made to the Archbishop to get him 'to relent or to faint in the profession of the catholique religion, or to embrace the protestant negative religion'.

FAMA MARTYRII

In a deliberate attempt to keep the Catholics from learning of the harsh treatment being given to Dermot O'Hurley and from making a public outcry in his favour, the lords justices kept the archbishop in close confinement. But the efforts of Loftus and Wallop were unsuccessful, and news of the savage torture inflicted on him spread quickly. It was brought to Paris at the beginning of June 1584 by two young Irishmen.[65]

The archbishop of Cashel was put to death on Saturday 20 June 1584, the

65 See note 50.

day before the swearing-in as lord deputy of John Perrot, who took over power from the lords justices. These two crown officials, with the consent of the new lord deputy, sentenced O'Hurley to death on 19 June.[66] Their warrant instructed the constable of Dublin Castle to execute him early in the morning, when there would be very few, if any, spectators. But the contemporary chronicle which records the time of the execution also reports that there were present a number of Dublin merchants who had gone into the fields to practise archery and that the archbishop addressed them. It must have been these men who gave the news to the Catholics of Dublin, for the same source says that 'the report of the execution was spread abroad in the City'.[67] The *fama martyrii* appears to have been instant. This source then reports that pious women brought the body to St Kevin's for burial and that the clothes the archbishop was wearing were kept as relics. Rothe reports that pilgrimages were made to his grave and that miracles were worked there. O'Sullivan Beare records a tradition that a noble woman who had been possessed of an evil spirit for a long time was cured at the place of execution.

News of the execution spread quickly, at first in Dublin and then throughout the country. The Catholics reacted by regarding Dermot O'Hurley as a martyr for the faith. In September the news was known in Paris, and Robert Parsons, SJ,[68] reported it to Pedro de Ribadeneira in that month. In the following month, if not earlier, it was known in Portugal, and Bishop Conor O'Mulryan reported the martyrdom to Tolomeo Cardinal Galli in his letter of 29 October 1584.[69] The bishop – and those who had informed him – had no doubt that Archbishop O'Hurley was a martyr. He told the cardinal that the archbishop of Cashel '*gloriosissime et constantissime martirium perpessus est*'.

The recusant scholar and publisher Richard Verstegen was also a skilled engraver. He was the first to record O'Hurley's martyrdom in print, in 1587, in his *Theatrum Crudelitatum*. He enhanced his account with an engraving which was a composite representation of the three Irish martyrs, Dermot O'Hurley, Patrick O'Healy, and Conn O'Rourke. The printed word helped considerably to propagate and preserve the reputation of martyrdom. There were at least eight editions of Verstegen's *Theatrum* up to 1607, and these contributed in no small way to maintaining the *fama martyrii* overseas. Moreover, John Bridgewater, an English priest, reprinted word for word Verstegen's account of the martyrdom in 1588.[70] Tommaso Bozio, an Italian

---

66 See note 37. **67** See note 25. **68** See note 42. **69** Ibid. **70** Bridgewater (*alias*

Oratorian, published a short account of the torture and death of O'Hurley three years later.[71]

In 1590, or about that year, the Irish Jesuit John Howlin, who was living in Lisbon, compiled his *Perbreve Compendium*, in which he gave a succinct account of the martyrdom. The Franciscan Donagh Mooney referred briefly to the death of O'Hurley in his history of the Franciscan Province of Ireland written 1617–18.[72] Both these works remained in manuscript form, unprinted for about three hundred years. But they were known to many including the Franciscan historian Luke Wadding, who utilized them. Wadding made reference to the martyred Dermot O'Hurley in his widely read *Annales Minorum*.[73] Wadding also had copies of the publications of his friend David Rothe, including his *De Processu Martyriali*, in which this highly esteemed martyrologist printed a long account of the sufferings and death of Archbishop O'Hurley and thereby helped to spread and strengthen the *fama martyrii*.

A number of Rothe's Irish contemporaries also mentioned the martyrdom in their writings – Richard Stanihurst,[74] John Coppinger, Philip O'Sullivan Beare, and John Mullan.[75] Later, in 1669, Anthony Bruodin published an account of O'Hurley's martyrdom.[76] The exiled archdeacon of Tuam, John Lynch, also penned a record of it in his history of Irish bishops.[77]

In the nineteenth century the reprinting of Rothe's *Analecta Sacra* and O'Sullivan Beare's *Historiae Catholicae Iberniae Compendium* rekindled the memory of the martyrdom among the Irish. The reawakened reputation of martyrdom was further strengthened in the nineteenth and twentieth centuries by the historical works and critical editions of manuscripts published by Patrick F. Moran and others.

O'Hurley's case was dealt with during the Ordinary Process *de fama martyrii* held at Dublin in 1904. Indeed, it was deemed the most prominent of the many cases then discussed, with the result that his name was actually

Aquaepontanus) prepared an enlarged edition of *Concertatio Ecclesiae Catholicae in Anglia adversus Calvino-Papistas et Puritanos sub Elizabetha Regina* (Trier, 1588). His account of Dermot O'Hurley is printed after the conclusion of Part II of the *Concertatio* on f. 212v, at the beginning of a supplement which is not paginated or foliated. **71** Thomas Bozius, *De Signis Ecclesiae Dei* (2 vols, Rome, 1591–2), i, 431. **72** See note 48. **73** *Ann. Min.*, ad an. 1271, no. XVIII. **74** Richard Stanihurst, *Brevis praemunitio pro futuraturaura concertatione cum Jacobo Usserio* (2nd ed., Douai, 1615), 29–30. **75** Mullan, *Epitome Tripartita*, 56–7. **76** Anthony Broudin, *Propugnaculum Catholicae Veritatis* (Prague, 1669), 446–8; see also Anthony Bruodin, *Anatomicum Examen Inchiridii Apologetici* (Prague, 1671), 58–63, where he refers to Coppinger's *Theatre* and prints the relevant passage in English. **77** Lynch, *De Praesulibus Hib.*, ii, 64.

inserted into the title of the cause of the Irish martyrs: *Dublinen.*
Beatificationis seu Declarationis martyrii servorum Dei Dermitii O'Hurley ... et
sociorum. The General Promoter of the Faith was well satisfied with the
evidence, as he outlined it in his *Disquisitio*, 84–8. He began his survey with
the sentence: *De Dermot O'Hurley, archiepiscopi Casseliensis, martyrio et martyrii*
causa, compertum habemus. After surveying the evidence from the various
martyrologists, he refers to the importance of the letter of William Nugent
and Barnaby Geoghegan from Paris, 4 June 1584, and that of Bishop Conor
O'Mulryan from Lisbon, 29 October 1584, to Cardinal Galli. He then states
that the relevant documentation in the Public Record Office, London, is of
the greatest value: *Omnium tamen ea documenta sunt gravissima, quae a publico*
Anglico tabulario eruta fuerunt. This critique by the General Promoter of the
Faith concludes with the favourable verdict:

> *Quare nihil dubii est, quin praeclara haec causa sacrae Congregationis iudicio*
> *subiici queat.*

Accordingly the decree *In Hibernia, heroum nutrice*, approved by Benedict
XV on 12 February 1915, formally authorized the introduction of
O'Hurley's cause. Therefore, during the Apostolic Process held at Dublin
between 1917 and 1930 for 260 cases of reputed martyrdom, the evidence
for Dermot O'Hurley's martyrdom was examined. The findings were then
presented to the Holy See.

CHAPTER 5

Margaret Ball (née Bermingham)

Ciarán Brady

EARLY LIFE

The chief sources for the consideration of Margaret Bermingham as a martyr are Howlin's *Perbreve Compendium*[1] and Rothe's *De Processu Martyriali*.[2] Howlin is the earlier of the two, writing before 1599, and appears to have observed personally the events which he describes. Rothe has little to add to Howlin other than a few circumstantial details. The accounts given by Howlin and Rothe can be authenticated at a number of crucial points by a variety of contemporary independent sources.

Margaret Bermingham, daughter of Nicholas Bermingham of Corballis in the barony of Skreen, County Meath, and Catherine, daughter of Richard De La Hide of Drogheda, was born *c.*1515. In 1530, she married Bartholomew Ball, a native of Balrothery, County Dublin, and a leading figure in the merchant community of Dublin city.[3] Ball was bailiff of Dublin from October 1541 to October 1542 and mayor of the city in 1553–4.[4] He appears to have died around the beginning of 1568.[5] Bartholomew and Margaret had issue of twenty children, of whom five appear to have survived. These were Walter, Nicholas, Thomas, Katherine and Eleanor.[6]

As a respected matron of the city of Dublin, Widow Ball appears to have established a school for the instruction of the youth of the recusant community of the Pale. According to Howlin, 'the maids and young people who left her house ... profited by becoming accomplished scholars at length and very often heirs and followers of Christ', and 'hence it was',

---

1 Howlin, *Perbreve Compend.*; printed, with some inaccuracies, in Moran, *Spicil. Ossor.*, i, 105–106. **2** Rothe, *De Processu Martyriali*, 182–9; reprinted in Moran, *Analecta*, 505–9. **3** 'A visitation begonne in the cittie of Dublin by Daniell Molyneux, Esquire, otherwise called Ulster King of Arms and Principall Herald of all Ireland, in the yeare of grace one thousand six hundreth and seven'. Dublin, Genealogical Office, MS 47, 17, 25 [hereafter, 'Visitation by Molyneux']. **4** *Anc. Rec. Dublin*, i, 409, 433. **5** Ibid., ii, 50; see also Margaret Bermingham's suit as a widow, in PROI, Chancery Decrees, R.C. 6/1, no. 260. **6** 'Visitation by Molyneux'.

wrote Rothe, 'that noble ladies, who were anxious to have their children brought up in piety and virtue, used to send them from a great distance to be educated in her household, as being the home of piety and school of virtue'.

Howlin and Rothe also attest to her frequently having given refuge to Catholic priests, and it is this which appears to have caused her first serious encounter with the authorities. Some time in the late 1570s, she was arrested in the company of a priest, who was actually saying Mass in her house, and briefly imprisoned, until released 'by money and with the aid of noble persons'.[7]

These accounts of Margaret Bermingham's fidelity to Catholicism are supported by independent evidence. In the mid-sixteenth century, the Berminghams of Corballis were prominent in the Palesmen's opposition to the Tudor government. William Bermingham, a close relative and probably a brother, was the chief agent sent to court by the Palesmen in 1562 to complain of the harshness of the earl of Sussex's administration.[8] His son, Patrick Bermingham, also of Corballis, was active on several occasions as the Palesmen opposed particular governors, and was generally regarded as one of the most dangerous recusants in the Pale.[9] It is clear, therefore, that Margaret Bermingham's own kin were stout defenders of the old religion.

Of her children, at least Nicholas appears to have been a recusant. He was mayor of Dublin in 1582–3 and member of parliament for the city in the assembly of 1585.[10] His will, dated 1610, indicates that he died a Catholic, and his family continued in the same faith.[11] Nothing definite can be discerned about the dispositions of the remainder of Margaret's family, with the exception of her eldest son, Walter, who, according to the evidence, was the source of his mother's difficulties.

ARREST AND IMPRISONMENT

According to Howlin and Rothe, Walter alone of the children conformed to Protestantism, and his mother's attempts to persuade him to recant

---

7 Howlin, *Perbreve Compend*; Rothe, *De Processu Martyriali.* **8** Sir William Fitzwilliam to Cecil, 13 June 1562, in PRO, S.P., 63/6/24 (*Cal. S.P. Ire., 1509–73*, 196); 'Bermyngham's memorial ... for the government of Ireland', 24 Sept. 1563, in PRO, S.P., 63/9/27 (*Cal. S.P. Ire., 1509–73*, 223). **9** PRO, S.P., 63/149/32 (*Cal. S.P. Ire., 1588–92*, 278). **10** *Anc. Rec. Dublin*, ii, 165; Edmund Hogan (ed.), *The description of Ireland in ... anno 1598* (Dublin, 1878), 351. **11** PROI, Thrift abstracts, no. 1472.

proved to be unavailing. Howlin, who claims to have been an eye-witness on such occasions, asserts that she would 'invite her son to dine' with many Catholic divines 'in order to recover him from heresy by their conversation'. But Walter was not susceptible to persuasion. Indeed, his embarrassment at his mother's activities may have compelled this prominent alderman during his mayoralty (1580–81) to take the drastic action which Howlin, Rothe, and Christopher Holywood, SJ, the author of the *Supplicia Magna*,[12] relate. Ball, according to these sources, had his mother arrested, dragged through the city streets on a hurdle, and thrown into prison.

MARTYRDOM

This time Margaret Bermingham was not released. Conditions in prison were such as to constitute a sentence of slow death, especially for an old woman of gentle birth. She endured these conditions for three years, when she died 'worn out by the squalor of the prison and the afflictions of hardship and illness'.[13]

MOTIVE FOR MARTYRDOM

No clear indication survives as to the statute under which Margaret Bermingham was penalized. It seems unlikely that the Oath of Supremacy was proffered to her: the oath was not usually tendered to any native-born citizens, let alone non-office-holders. It is more likely, then, that the Act of Uniformity was invoked against her, but even this unusual step could not have been taken with such a prominent and well-respected citizen without at least the passive collaboration of the Mayor. She may have been brought before the court of high commission, a tribunal which investigated causes of religious dissent and of which Walter Ball had been appointed a member.[14]

Why Walter Ball elected to act in such a perverse manner remains uncertain. But external evidence casts some light on the matter. The period of Ball's mayoralty coincided both with the exposure of the Nugent

---

12 Christopher Holywood, *Supplicia Magna a Persecutoribus aliquot Catholicorum in Ibernia sumpta*, early seventeenth century: BR, MS 2158–67, f. 43v.; printed in Moran, *Spicil. Ossor.*, iii, 27. **13** Howlin, *Perbreve Compend.* **14** Ball was a member of the commission for ecclesiastical causes from 1577 onwards; cf. *Fiants Ire. Eliz.*, no. 3698.

conspiracy in Meath and the actual rebellion of Viscount Baltinglass. These events excited great alarm within the Dublin administration, and for many months English officials feared that the entire Pale might rise up in rebellion.[15] In such a state of emergency, Ball may have felt it necessary to act publicly against so obvious a non-conformist within his own family.

These circumstances apart, however, independent sources would seem to support the depiction of Walter Ball's religious disposition given in Howlin, Rothe, and Christopher Holywood's *Supplicia Magna*. An avid promoter of a Protestant university in Dublin, he was one of the collectors for the building fund and was congratulated by Queen Elizabeth for his efforts on its behalf.[16] In his will, he bequeathed £26 13s. 4d. for the maintenance of four scholars at the college.[17] Two of his sons were among the first students.[18] According to Holywood, Ball remained implacable in his opposition to Catholicism up to the time of his death, and his will, proved in December 1598, which asserts his belief in justification by faith alone and repudiates 'superstitious charges', confirms this.[19]

Thus the intolerant behaviour of Walter Ball towards his mother, which resulted directly in her death, is seen to be in character. The key details supplied by Howlin, a direct witness of Walter's intransigence, and Rothe are borne out fully by outside records. Margaret Bermingham suffered imprisonment and death because of her deep commitment to Catholicism.

FAMA MARTYRII

The memory of Margaret Bermingham was alive when Henry Fitzsimon, SJ, came to Dublin in 1598, and her sufferings and death were referred to by Christopher Holywood, SJ.[20] Thereafter her *fama martyrii* was enshrined in the martyrological writings of the seventeenth century.

When the Ordinary Process *de fama martyrii* was held in Dublin in 1904 for the Irish martyrs of the sixteenth and seventeenth centuries, the evidence for Margaret Bermingham's reputation of martyrdom was examined and approved. It was then forwarded, with the other findings of the

15 Viscount Gormanstown to Sir William Gerrard, Naas, 28 July 1580, in PRO, S.P., 63/75/12 (*Cal. S.P. Ire., 1574–85*, 240); Archbishop Loftus' report of the Earl of Kildare's speeches, Dec. 1580, in PRO, S.P., 63/79/26 (*Cal. S.P. Ire. 1574–85*, 275–6). 16 Cited in J.W. Stubbs, *A history of the University of Dublin* (Dublin, 1889), 350–6. 17 W. Ball Wright, *Ball family memoirs* (York, 1908), 21. 18 G.D. Burtchaell and T.U. Sadleir (ed.), *Alumni Dublinienses* (Dublin, 1935), 36. 19 Ball Wright, op. cit., app. vi, x. 20 Holywood, *Supplicia Magna*.

tribunal, to the Holy See. In due course the General Promoter of the Faith gave his verdict on her case, in his *Disquisitio*, 90–1. After reviewing the evidence, he stated:

> *Cuius causa martyrii sacrae Congregationi per me licet subiiciatur, quae iudicet, an illa in carceris duritie incommodisque mortem invenerit.*

Because the General Promoter of the Faith listed her case among those in Class V, i.e. those who had died in prison, the Advocate in his *Responsio ad Disquisitionem*, 221–3, examined the evidence again and at the end of his reply wrote:

> *Quae cum ita sint, non est dubium quin haec causa favorabile Eminentissimorum Iudicum suffragium obtineat.*

This assessment was correct. In February 1915, Margaret Bermingham was one of the 257 named martyrs for the introduction of whose cause authorization was granted. Accordingly her case was examined during the Apostolic Process held at Dublin 1917–30. The findings were then presented to the Holy See.

CHAPTER 6

Maurice MacKenraghty

James Coombes

EARLY LIFE

The date of birth of Maurice MacKenraghty[1] is unknown. Howlin,[2] Rothe[3] and Coppinger[4] give his place of origin, and also the information that he had a degree in theology. He was born in Kilmallock, a prosperous walled town in the Desmond lands in County Limerick. According to O'Sullivan Beare,[5] his father was a goldsmith and silversmith and a native of Irraghticonnor. This barony, in the neighbouring county of Kerry, is bordered on the north by the estuary of the river Shannon and extends inland for up to thirty miles. The father is almost certainly to be identified with the 'Thomas Enryckty, burgess of Kyllmalock' and 'Thomas Kinraght, goldsmith ... of Kilmallocke' mentioned in the fiants of Elizabeth, which show that he sought and was granted a pardon in April 1566 and January 1570.[6]

Thomas MacKenraghty was a full citizen of Kilmallock and probably enjoyed the patronage of the earl of Desmond. But he and his son Maurice lived in unsettled times. Between the years 1569 and 1573, and again between 1579 and 1583, Munster was devastated by the first and second Desmond wars.[7] The roots of conflict were complex. The Tudor monarchy was determined to extend its authority to all parts of Ireland. The threat to religious liberty was also growing. The fifteenth earl of Desmond was an indecisive character who was unable to cope with these changing patterns. He was also in financial straits and found it increasingly difficult to obtain

---

1 This is the correct form of his surname. The form O'Kenraghty was used in the Apostolic Process. The surname occurs in many forms. 2 Howlin, *Perbreve Compend.*; printed, with some inaccuracies, in Moran, *Spicil. Ossor.,* i, 89–91. 3 Rothe, *De Processu Martyriali,* 147–60; reprinted in Moran, *Analecta,* 482–91. 4 Coppinger, *Theatre,* 580. Reprinted, with some inaccuracies, in Moran, *Spicil. Ossor.,* iii, 40. 5 Philip O'Sullivan Beare, *Patritiana Decas* (Madrid, 1629), 165. 6 *Fiants Ire. Eliz.*, nos. 840, 1470. 7 For further information on the resistance to the Tudor policy, see G.A. Hayes-McCoy in *NHI,* iii, 94–141; Ciarán Brady, 'Faction and the origins of the Desmond rebellion of 1579', in *IHS* 22 (1981), 289–312.

either rents or services from his tenants or to maintain his footing against his powerful rivals, in particular the earl of Ormond.

On 18 July 1579, Desmond's first cousin, James Fitzmaurice Fitzgerald, landed in County Kerry with a tiny force of less than a hundred men. This expedition was financed by Pope Gregory XIII, and included the noted English priest Nicholas Sanders. Fitzmaurice was killed on 18 August. In the words of a modern historian, 'success, which never seemed likely, was now impossible; the death of the one real leader, a man of the highest principle and religious integrity, meant failure for the whole movement'.[8] Desmond's brothers, James and John, continued the war. The earl himself vacillated for months, but he was finally committed on 15 November 1579, when he captured and sacked the town of Youghal.

Maurice MacKenraghty had become chaplain and confessor to the earl of Desmond and, according to Mullan, had engaged in a zealous pastoral mission in Kilmallock and its vicinity.[9] He accompanied the earl to war and remained with him through all vicissitudes until his capture in 1583. In this he was not merely following his lord, as the old traditions would have dictated, but, as sources[10] make clear, was active and zealous in a priestly ministry. Rothe's emphasis on his lack of 'intention of rebelling' reflects the concerns of the early seventeenth century rather than those of the 1580s. What is clear beyond question is that he was put to death because he was a Catholic priest.

ARREST AND IMPRISONMENT

By the autumn of 1583, the earl of Desmond was a hunted fugitive with only about ten followers in the area near the boundary of Counties Cork and Kerry. On 17 September, the little party was surprised by soldiers under the command of Maurice Roche, Viscount Fermoy. According to Rothe, this occurred because of treachery by one Murtagh Swiney, who had been a captain in Desmond's army. The earl escaped, but on 11 November he was killed in a petty and accidental skirmish near Tralee, County Kerry.

MacKenraghty was captured on 17 September. On 19 September Roche wrote to the earl of Ormond to tell him that MacKenraghty was in his hands.[11] Ormond in turn wrote to William Cecil, Lord Burghley, stating

8 F.M. Jones, *The Counter Reformation*, 29, in Corish, *Ir. Catholicism*. **9** Mullan, *Epitome Tripartita*, 29. **10** Howlin, *Perbreve Compend.*; Rothe, *De Processu Martyriali.*; Coppinger, *Theatre*. **11** Maurice Roche, Viscount Fermoy, to Thomas Butler, tenth earl of Ormond, that he had sent a Captain Roberts to bring in the captive. He had also sent his servant, Patrick Grant, in Roberts's company, to be chained to the priest, 'that no man may se him, nor speke with him, till he com hither to me ... I wold this chaplen, and I, wear for one owr with you in your chamber, that you may know the secretes of his hart, which by fayr, or fowle means, he must open unto me'.[12] There is no record of any such interrogation.

Ormond sent MacKenraghty to prison in Clonmel. Here, as in other southern towns, Counter-Reformation Catholicism was already beginning to make a real impact; and, as in these other towns, the citizens of Clonmel were beginning to come up against the problem of combining loyalty to the pope with loyalty to the queen.

Maurice MacKenraghty continued his ministry during what proved to be a long imprisonment. In 1585, Victor White, a prominent citizen, approached the principal jailer and asked permission to have the priest in his house overnight, on the eve of Easter Sunday (in this year Easter fell on 11 April), to provide Mass and confession for his family and neighbours. Permission was granted, and the priest spent the night hearing confessions. However, the chief jailer had betrayed them to Sir John Norris, president of Munster, who just at this time had arrived in Clonmel. Norris arranged to have White's house surrounded by soldiers and raided. The raiding party entered it shortly before Mass was due to begin and naturally caused great panic. Some people tried to hide in the basement; others jumped through the windows; one woman broke her arm in an attempt to escape. The priest hid in a heap of straw and was wounded in the thigh by the probing sword of a soldier. Despite the pain, he remained silent and later escaped. The soldiers dismantled the altar and seized the sacred vessels. They arrested Victor White and threatened him with death unless he told them where the priest was hiding. When MacKenraghty heard of White's plight he sent a friend to tell him that he was prepared to surrender so that White's life might be spared. White tried to dissuade him, replying that he would prefer to lose liberty and even life itself rather than that the priest should die. But MacKenraghty gave himself up to save his friend and was again thrown into prison.

Military Governor of Munster, Castletown, 19 September 1583. London, PRO, S.P., 63/104/95 i (contemporary copy). Calendared in *Cal. S.P. Ire., 1574–85*, 470. **12** Butler to Cecil, Carrick-on-Suir, 23 September 1583. London, PRO, S.P., 63/104/95. Calendared in *Cal. S.P. Ire., 1574–85*, 470.

TRIAL

There are three accounts of the trial of Maurice MacKenraghty. He was interrogated by Sir John Norris and his assistants, but there is no suggestion that he was given a formal trial by a process of civil law.

Howlin says that MacKenraghty's constancy was tested by tempting offers of gifts and ecclesiastical dignities. He was offered not merely his freedom but whatever he might ask of the queen's ministers, on condition that he would affirm on oath that the queen was the lawful head of the Church. Because he repeatedly denied this but confessed the Catholic faith and the authority of the pope, he was condemned to death as a traitor.

According to Rochford,[13] Norris 'after much invective', condemned the priest to death and then, *after* passing sentence, offered him a pardon if he would renounce the Catholic faith and acknowledge the queen as supreme head of the Church. A Protestant minister also tried unsuccessfully to convert the priest by engaging him in debate. Rochford adds that on no account would MacKenraghty supply the name of any person who had attended his Mass or received the sacraments from him.

Rothe states that sentence of death was pronounced though there was no due process of law: the sentence, he says, was *extra ordinem*. He adds that MacKenraghty could have saved his life had he abjured the true faith and taken the Oath of Supremacy.

There is no essential contradiction between these three accounts. Especially in trials by martial law, there was no fixed procedure or sequence of events. What is made perfectly clear is that Maurice MacKenraghty was condemned to death because he would not take the Oath of Supremacy.

MARTYRDOM

Howlin states that MacKenraghty, after he heard the sentence of death pronounced on him, had a serene countenance, that he gave thanks to God, that he advised the bystanders to confess the Catholic faith and be obedient to the pope, and that while he was being taken to the place of execution he addressed the people so devoutly and learnedly that he moved many to tears. Howlin further says that MacKenraghty was permitted to complete

---

13 Robert Rochford, SJ, to his colleagues, Lisbon, 20 March 1586 – Rothe, *De Processu Martyriali*, 160–2.

the final stage of the journey to the scaffold on his knees and that in this fashion he moved forward praying all the time while the heretics mocked him. Then, at the place of execution, he faced the people and preached to them, asking the Catholics to pray for him and blessing them.

Rochford,[14] in his letter written eleven months after the event, states that MacKenraghty was dragged at the tail of a horse to the place of execution and that there he exhorted the people with much learning and piety to be constant in the faith. Rothe quotes from Howlin's *Perbreve Compendium* the following sentence: 'When he came to the place of execution, he turned to the people and addressed them some pious words as far as time allowed; in the end he asked all the Catholics to pray for him and he gave them his blessing.'

Howlin and Rochford say that MacKenraghty was hanged, that he was taken down from the gallows while still alive and then beheaded. Howlin adds that his body was then divided into four parts, but Rochford states that the local Catholics persuaded the executioners, with the help of bribes, to desist from further mangling the body. Rothe, noting the discrepancy, says that while Howlin reported the carrying out of the sentence (i.e. knowing that the sentence included quartering, he recorded that MacKenraghty had been quartered), Rochford may have reported what actually happened.

Howlin, Rothe, Coppinger, and Mullan state that MacKenraghty died on 30 April 1585. As Sir John Norris, who had condemned him to death, was in attendance at the parliament which opened in Dublin on 26 April, it may be reasonably assumed that the martyrologists here give a new-style dating, and that MacKenraghty suffered on 20 April, old style.

His head was exposed for several days in a prominent place. Then, according to Rochford and Howlin, the Catholics purchased his body and gave it honourable burial. The Franciscan historian Donagh Mooney, who visited Clonmel about thirty years later, tells us that MacKenraghty's remains were laid to rest behind the high altar in the church attached to the suppressed Franciscan friary.[15] They may have been moved about sixty years later.[16]

---

14 Ibid.   **15** Donagh Mooney, *De Provincia Hiberniae S. Francisci*. BR, MS 3195, 58. Printed in *Anal. Hib.* 6 (1934), 80.   **16** A modern historian states that in 1647 his body was taken to the Franciscan friary in Askeaton, in County Limerick, but he cites no authority for this statement (W.P. Burke, *History of Clonmel*, Waterford, 1907, 40).

MOTIVE FOR MARTYRDOM

There is no ambiguity about the motive for MacKenraghty's martyrdom. When captured in September 1583, he was not condemned to death. Eighteen months later sentence of death was passed on him after his brief parole, escape, and recapture. The occasion of these latter events was completely spiritual. His condemnation to death was occasioned by his hearing confessions, and by preparing to celebrate Mass and preach the gospel. The cause was his open denial of the royal supremacy in matters spiritual. Moreover, there is no reason to believe other than that his congregation consisted of people who were loyal to the crown.

The issue on which he was condemned after interrogation by Sir John Norris, president of Munster, was clear cut. He refused to acknowledge Queen Elizabeth as head of the Church but emphatically reiterated his loyalty to the Catholic faith and his obedience to the pope.

It is totally incorrect to claim that MacKenraghty was condemned to death because he was a rebel. When captured in September 1583, he was known to the authorities for what he was, i.e. a Catholic priest who was acting as chaplain to the earl of Desmond.[17] He was imprisoned but not sentenced to death. The queen, when appointing Ormond to be lord general and governor of Munster by letters patent bearing the dates 8 November 1582 and 6 January 1583, had also commissioned him to hunt down all notorious rebels and traitors, to levy her subjects in Munster for purposes of war, and to execute martial law.[18] It was apparently the queen's intention that her prisons be used, when necessary, and that due processes of law be observed. These letters patent make no mention whatever of bishops, seminary priests and Jesuits, or of religion. By further letters patent, dated at Dublin on 6 March 1585, the queen, with the consent of Sir John Perrot, lord deputy, commissioned the earl of Ormond to execute martial law within the counties of Kilkenny and Tipperary.[19] Again, there is no reference to Catholic priests or the Catholic religion. There is one passage which reads:

> That you shall likewise have full power and authority to take all such persons as do willingly or otherwise are known to provide, aid, support or maintain any outlaws, open thieves, murderers or rebels, and to send

---

17 Maurice Roche to Thomas Butler, Castletown, 19 September 1583 (note 11). Thomas Butler to William Cecil, Carrick-on-Suir, 23 September 1583 (note 12). **18** *Calendar of Ormond deeds*, ed. Edmund Curtis (6 vols, Dublin, 1932–43), v, 319–20. **19** Ibid., vi, 16–17.

them so offending unto the queen's common gaol of any of these
counties, with certificate of the demeanour of the offenders.

Such offenders, if apprehended, were to be imprisoned but not put to
death. An earlier clause in these letters patent authorized the earl to put to
death certain specified classes of 'felon' or criminal; but again there is no
mention of priests or of religion. In March and April 1585, Maurice
MacKenraghty had already been in prison for a year and a half. It could be
claimed that Ormond was authorised to imprison him because as chaplain
to the earl of Desmond he could be regarded as one who willingly assisted
a rebel. But the letters patent did not give any legal justification for putting
such supporters to death. MacKenraghty therefore was not condemned to
death in virtue of this special commission to execute martial law in County
Tipperary. It is important to note that it was Sir John Norris, the military
commander who had become president of Munster, and not Ormond, who
sentenced MacKenraghty to death. By September 1583 three years had
elapsed since Ormond had become military governor of the province.
Wallop and other crown officials in Ireland were jealous of his influence.
Rumours circulated in England that his loyalty was suspect, that he was
either unwilling or unable to overcome the earl of Desmond. Ormond had
good reason to fear for himself, because he had actually been removed from
his command in June 1581 and had not been restored until December 1582.
Persistent criticism forced him in May 1583 to intensify the military
campaign and to attack all the known adherents of Desmond.

The capture of MacKenraghty and the escape of Desmond on 17
September 1583 placed Maurice Roche in a predicament also. Crown officials did not trust him. His part in the rebellion was too fresh in their
memories, and he was a Catholic. Now he had allowed the arch-rebel
Desmond, who was his wife's first cousin, to escape. It was Ormond who
in the first place had insisted, in the face of opposition, on admitting Roche
into the queen's service on 15 July 1581. He might not now be able to dispel
suspicions that he himself had connived at Desmond's escape. Ormond,
as has been seen, had no authority to put MacKenraghty to death. There
is no reason to believe that he would want to do so even if he had any
such authority. But he was prompt to turn the priest's capture to his own
advantage.

Because of Desmond's escape it was important to emphasize the value of
MacKenraghty as a prisoner, especially as a source of information: 'I wold
this chaplen, and I, wear for one owr with you in your chamber, that you

might know the secretes of his hart, which by fayr, or fowle meanes, he must open to me.' Ormond was obviously playing for time. His assessment of the situation was correct. On 15 November he informed the privy council in London that Desmond had been killed by a Donal MacMoriarty, 'of whom, at my last being in Kerry, I took assurance to serve against Desmond'.[20] Ormond was now satisfied that he had pacified Munster. He asked for a pardon for all who had taken part in the revolt, and in letters to Burghley he spoke harshly of those English officers who advocated further rigorous measures. There was no further mention of interrogating MacKenraghty. There is no firm evidence as to why the priest was detained in Clonmel for over eighteen months. But nobody ever suggested that he had been a rebel against the civil authority. He continued his pastoral work in jail. And it was precisely because he continued to function as a priest that he was sentenced to death.

He was executed under martial law. To proceed against him as a Catholic priest in accordance with the common law would have demanded a long process. There might have been a public outcry and even the possibility of an acquittal by a local jury. In addition, Norris had his own personal reasons for seeking a speedy process. He was a brilliant commander who hankered after more important theatres of operation and regarded any tour of duty in Ireland as an irritation.

FAMA MARTYRII

Maurice MacKenraghty was executed in public. The Catholics who witnessed his death were favourably impressed. Undoubtedly it was they who were responsible for the almost instant reputation of martyrdom. This *fama martyrii* persisted in Clonmel and its environs for at least a century. It was still a vivid memory when Rothe and Mooney were collecting material on the Irish martyrs in the second decade of the seventeenth. The court off Lough Street in Clonmel, where Victor White had his residence, was known as Martyr Lane down to Cromwellian times.[21] However, it was the written or printed word which contributed most to the *fama martyrii*. Howlin based his written account of the martyrdom on the testimony of three eye-witnesses who told him what had occurred in Clonmel in 1585.

---

20 *Cal. S.P. Ire., 1574–85*, 478–9.   **21** Burke cites an inquisition held at Clonmel on 20 March 1622 which refers to 'Marter Lane in Lough Street' (op. cit., 57).

And Rothe succeeded in getting a copy – perhaps even the original – of the letter written by Rochford.

MacKenraghty's reputation of martyrdom was very probably a contributing factor to the extraordinary growth of vocations to the priesthood in Clonmel and its vicinity which began very shortly afterwards.[22] His name was firmly established in the canon of the Irish martyrs. He is listed by the nineteenth-century hagiographers O'Reilly and Murphy.

When the Ordinary Process *de fama martyrii* was held at Dublin in 1904 for the Irish martyrs of the sixteenth and seventeenth centuries the evidence for his reputation of martyrdom was examined and approved. It was then forwarded, with the other findings of the tribunal, to the Holy See. In due course the General Promoter of the Faith gave his verdict on his case. Having reviewed the evidence, he stated in his *Disquisitio*, 99–100:

> *Quum igitur, quin sit Mauritius, propter fidei Catholicae professionem morte mulctatus, dubitari non posse videatur, nullum superest impedimentum, quominus de eius martyrii causa apud sacrorum rituum Congregationem agatur.*

In February 1915 Maurice MacKenraghty was included in the 257 named martyrs for the introduction of whose cause authorization was granted. Accordingly his case was examined at the Apostolic Process held at Dublin 1919–30. The findings were then presented to the Holy See.

---

22 The Jesuit recruits included Andrew Mulroney, Nicholas Leynach, Thomas Shine, and Thomas White (see Hogan, *Distinguished Irishmen*, 48–51, 107–8, 353). Among those who studied to become diocesan priests were John Barron and Denis Shine: see *Archiv. Hib.* 2 (1913), 16, 20.

CHAPTER 7

Dominic Collins, SJ

*Proinsias Ó Fionnagáin**

EARLY LIFE

Dominic Collins was born *c.*1566[1] in the walled seaport of Youghal, in the county of Cork, on the south coast of Ireland. His father was named John, and his mother Felicity O'Dril or O'Dula.[2] The family was evidently of good standing in the community, as both John Collins and one of his sons served as mayor of Youghal.

At the time of Dominic Collins's birth and early youth, the people of Youghal were experiencing a conflict of loyalties: loyalty to the crown of England and loyalty to the Catholic faith. The arrival of new English colonists also added to the tension of everyday life in Youghal and other Irish towns in this period. The Act of Supremacy and the Act of Uniformity were the law of the land since 1560, but the passing of the law was one thing, its observance another. The crown had to secure its power in the secular life of the country before it could impose effectively its new religious policy. Enforcement of the Acts of Supremacy and Uniformity in the first two decades of Elizabeth's reign was limited to the area within the Pale, that is, Louth, Meath, parts of Dublin and Kildare, where the authorities could prohibit the public celebration of the Mass. But in towns such as Waterford and Youghal, where garrisons were established on a temporary basis, priests were only driven out for a time and were able to return on the departure of the soldiers to other fields of activity.

When Collins was about ten years old, two Jesuits arrived in Youghal and set up a school there. Of this school, Bishop Tanner of Cork and Cloyne reported to the Father General of the Society on 11 October 1577 that Fathers Charles [Lea] and Robert Rochford were spreading everywhere the

---

* The writer gratefully acknowledges the splendid pioneering work of John MacErlean, SJ (1870–1950), for the beatification of the Irish Martyrs. **1** 'Catalogos publicos de la provincia de Castilla del ano 1600'. Rome, ARSI, MSS Castell, 14, ff 393v, 423v. **2** This information comes from Nieremberg, *Ideas*, 635–7, and Alegambe, *Mortes Illustres*, 240–2. It is quite possible they derived it from Irishmen living on the Continent.

good odour of the Jesuit institute. Not only were the two Jesuits instructing youth, but they were also teaching Christian doctrine to adults.[3] The young Collins may have attended this school, for he had studied Latin as a boy,[4] but in any event he could have profited directly, or indirectly through his family, from the religious teaching imparted by the Jesuits.

In 1579, James Fitzmaurice Fitzgerald landed with a small force in Kerry in the hope of strengthening the Catholic magnates, both Anglo-Irish and Gaelic, in defence of their religion and possessions, but he met with an untimely death that same year. His kinsman, the earl of Desmond soon afterwards became leader of the rebellion. Desmond, hereditary overlord of Youghal, now seized the town, which had stood aloof from him, and sacked the houses and property of those loyal to Elizabeth.[5] In the following February, a government force under a Captain White entered the town, but was soon afterwards routed. When the earl of Ormond finally came to relieve the town, he found it deserted, but he invited the refugee townsfolk to return and ordered the walls to be rebuilt. The Jesuit school at Youghal disappeared in the turmoil.

About 1586, Collins set sail for France. He probably hoped to find there the opportunity of entering on an honourable career such as would now be out of his reach in his own country. He landed at Les Sables d'Olonne and travelled overland to Nantes, where he found work as an inn servant for the next three years.[6] This humble occupation would have given him both the money he needed to enter on a military career and a good working knowledge of the French language.

He then enlisted in the army of Philip Emanuel de Vaudemont, duke of Mercoeur, who was fighting in the Catholic League against the Huguenots in Brittany. His term of military service lasted some nine years, during which he attained the rank of captain and was known to the French as 'Capitaine de la Branche'.[7]

Dominic Collins proved himself a very successful soldier. According to Thomas White, who must have heard the story from Collins himself, he

3 Edmund Tanner, bishop of Cork and Cloyne, to Everard Mercurian, SJ, Father General, 11 Oct. 1577, in Dublin, Jesuit Provincial Archives, MS A 1. 4 A Life of Dominic Collins by Thomas White, SJ, Rome, 29 March 1604. Rome, ARSI, MSS Hist. Soc., 177, ff 169rv, 172rv. [hereafter, *Life of Collins*]. 5 *Cal. Carew MSS, 1575–88*, 304, 309. 6 Sir George Carew, lord president of Munster, to the English privy council, Cork, 13 July 1602, enclosing the deposition of Dominic Collins, taken before him at Cork, 9 July 1602. London, PRO, S.P., 63/211/83 [hereafter, Letter of Carew]. Calendared in *Cal. S.P. Ire., 1601–3*, 437, 439–42; deposition printed in Edmund Hogan, *Ibernia Ignatiana: seu Ibernorum Societatis Jesu patrum monumenta collecta*, i (Dublin, 1880), 98–102.

recovered the territory and château of Lapena from the Huguenots, and the duke of Mercoeur made him military governor of the place.[8] When Henry Navarre, at that time still a Calvinist, had offered him 2,000 ducats if he would hand over the castle, he refused. Later, when he realized that the League was falling apart, he handed over the castle to the Spanish general, Don Juan del Águila, who gave him letters of recommendation to present to the king of Spain.

In his deposition taken before Sir George Carew, Collins mentioned that, having landed in Spain near San Sebastian and having set out from there with the letters of del Águila for the Spanish court, he was accorded by the king, through the influence of Bishop Thady Farrell, OP, of Clonfert, a pension of twenty-five crowns a month. This pension he held for 'a twelve-month or thereabouts'. At the end of this period he met Thomas White, SJ, with whom he discussed his future and his hopes of entering the religious life.[9]

Collins' association with White brought him under the influence of a sure spiritual guide. They had met for the first time in Lent 1598, when White came to Coruña to hear the confessions of the Irishmen serving in the Spanish navy at that port.[10] Collins was convinced that their meeting was providential, and White has recorded at length the story of the soldier's call to the Society of Jesus. His admission to the novitiate was delayed for several months, but the provincial finally relented in the face of Collins' repeated requests, and he was received as a brother-novice on 8 December 1598. The annals of the Jesuit college at Compostella[11] record that in the 1598 Dominic Collins, an Irishman of distinguished parentage, comely appearance and stature was co-opted as a member of the Society, that he had passed thirty-two years of age, and that he had been a captain of Duke Philip's cavalry in Brittany.

Collins' first test in the novitiate soon presented itself when a plague struck the college. Four priests and three brothers were stricken with the fever and others fled from the scene. For two months he nursed his sick colleagues devotedly. On 4 February 1601, he made his first religious profession. He was only seven months a professed religious when his Spanish superiors appointed him to an unexpected post in his native land.

7 Cf. ibid.; also *Pacata Hibernia*, 317. **8** White, *Life of Collins* (see note 4). **9** Letter of Carew (see note 6). **10** White, *Life of Collins* (see note 4). White says that this meeting took place during Lent 1599, but this must be a lapse of memory, for Collins had been received into the Society on 8 December 1598. **11** Annual letter written by Alfonso Ferrer, SJ, Provincial of the Jesuit province of Castile, Compostella, 3 July 1604. Rome, ARSI, MSS Castell., 32, ff 91v-92r.

A Spanish expedition sailed for Ireland on 3 September 1601. Collins was assigned as *socius* to James Archer, SJ, chaplain to the Spanish forces. This expedition, which sailed from Belem near Lisbon on 3 September, was under the joint command of Don Juan del Águila and Don Diego de Brochero y Anaya as naval commander. On board the flagship were Mateo de Oviedo, OFM, Spanish-born archbishop of Dublin, Thady O'Farrell, OP, bishop of Clonfert, and Archer, to whom Collins had been appointed *socius*. Archer was long known to the English authorities and was pursued relentlessly by their spies.[12]

For a man with so short an experience of religious life as Dominic Collins, it was certainly a surprising decision on the part of his superiors to send him back to his own country so soon. However, an appraisal of his character made during his noviciate may provide some explanation of the reasons for this decision. The catalogues of the Jesuit province of Castile for 1600[13] state that he was a man of good physical strength, that he had good judgement, was mature and prudent, and naturally agreeable in disposition although irascible and stubborn. He was thus well qualified for his unexpected assignment as *socius* to Archer.

As events proved, he was to be Archer's *socius* for only a short time in Ireland. In his examination before Carew,[14] he stated that he met Archer for the first time in February 1602 at the castle of Gortnacloghy, near Castlehaven, and that they remained together at Dunboy until Archer's departure just before the arrival of the English forces to besiege the castle there.

The Spanish expedition had proved ill-fated. The fleet was scattered by storm, and Archer was with the larger squadron which reached Kinsale on 23 September. Collins was with the smaller squadron, under de Zubiar, which was forced back to Coruña. It arrived later at Castlehaven, where it joined O'Sullivan Beare. O'Neill and O'Donnell had marched south to join them, but this involved their taking the offensive, which was a new departure for them. When they tried to co-operate with the besieged Spaniards their efforts met with disaster.

Collins – who had gone from Castlehaven to O'Neill's camp, no doubt in search of Archer, to whom he was accredited *socius* – was present when the Irish army was routed on 24 December 1601. He remained in the area, however, and it was only in the following month that he met Archer for the

12 Nicholas Leynach to George Duras, 25 Sept. 1598, in Dublin, Jesuit Provincial Archives, MS A 5. 13 'Catalogos publicos de la provincia de Castilla del ano 1600'. Spanish and Latin. – Rome, ARSI, MSS Castell., 14, ff 393v, 423v. 14 Letter of Carew (see note 6).

first time at Gortnacloghy. Both Jesuits now accompanied O'Sullivan Beare, who was preparing to defend his patrimony. It was a desperate venture, bearing in mind that del Águila had surrendered Kinsale without making any terms for the Irish chieftains, that O'Donnell had taken ship for Spain, and that O'Neill had returned to Ulster to defend his own principality. Nevertheless, the defenders of Dunboy were to make a heroic and memorable resistance.

Archer stayed at Dunboy until the arrival of the English in early June 1602. His name was still feared and hated by the English notwithstanding the victory at Kinsale and the dispersal of the Irish chiefs. Writing to Sir Robert Cecil, Carew could not forbear voicing his almost superstitious fear of Archer:

> Archer the priest conjures the foul weather, which I do partly believe, for the old men have never seen the like in May. If he remains in Dunboy I hope to conjure his head in a halter. He hath a fellow devil with him, one Dominic Collins, a friar, who in his youth was a scholar and brother to him that was last year mayor of Youghal. Every week that traitorly priest administers the sacrament to them; yet I hope to sow such sedition amongst them that they will break.[15]

ARREST AND IMPRISONMENT

For an account of the arrest and imprisonment of Collins we depend on the reports contained in *Pacata Hibernia*.[16] This work (Book III, chapters vi–ix) presents a day-to-day narrative of the last days of Dunboy Castle, from 6 to 22 June 1602, that is from the landing of the English near Dunboy and their first engagement with the Irish until the fall of the castle, its destruction, the fate of the garrison, and Collins' detention in the prison of Cork.

Archer and Collins saw one another for the last time on 6 June, when

---

15 *Cal. Carew MSS, 1575–88*, 304, 309. **16** The work entitled *Pacata Hibernia* was published in 1633. No author's name appears on the title-page, but the prefatory matter is signed by Thomas Stafford, who had served as an officer under Sir George Carew. The book is an account of affairs in Munster between Carew's appointment in 1600 and the end of the wars there in 1603. Stafford asserts that it was found in Carew's papers shortly after his death in 1629, and asserts further that it had been composed 'by his direction'. It has a vivid quality, which suggests it may well have been composed shortly after 1603, and most probably by Thomas Stafford himself. Whoever composed it had access to Carew's papers. Many of these have survived only as printed in *Pacata Hibernia*.

the English landed near Dunboy to begin their siege of the castle. The final assault began at five o'clock in the morning on 17 June. According to *Pacata Hibernia*, the defence of the Irish was weakening, as their numbers became smaller. Profiting by this, the English renewed the assault at the top of the vault and after some hours gained all the superstructure of the castle, where they mounted their colours. The surviving seventy-seven defenders were now forced to retire into the cellars, which were reached by a winding stone staircase. Here the Irish were able to hold the English at bay and 'upon promise of their lives, they offered to come forth, but not to stand to mercy'. Immediately afterwards, the narrator states, Dominic Collins came forth and 'rendred himselfe'. This was after sunset.[17]

The assault of Dunboy castle was resumed next day. All the survivors, except Collins and two others named Taylor and MacSwiney, were summarily executed. The three prisoners were taken to Cork, where Taylor and MacSwiney were shortly afterwards executed.[18] But Collins was detained in prison in Cork until he was brought to Youghal to be executed there on the last day of October.[19]

TRIAL

Collins spent more than four months in prison at Cork before his sentence of death was finally confirmed. On 9 July 1602, he was examined before Carew, president of Munster.[20] Two authorities, Rothe[21] and Mullan,[22] state that he was condemned to death '*absque iudicii forma*'. This simply means that he did not get the benefit of a trial by jury in a court of common law but was tried by court martial. There is no extant account of the process of Collins' trial. The deposition of Collins before Carew and *Pacata Hibernia* contain all that can be known concerning his arrest, trial, condemnation and execution.

The deposition of Collins taken before Carew consists simply of the answers of the prisoner to the questions put to him concerning his past career as a soldier in France and Spain, his entry into the Society of Jesus,

---

17 *Pacata Hibernia*, 317.   **18** Thomas Taylor, son of an Englishman, was chosen chief of the defenders of Dunboy after the commander of the garrison, Richard MacGeoghegan, had been seriously wounded. For accounts of the charges against him and of his execution, see *Pacata Hibernia*, 318, and *Cal. S.P. Ire., 1601–3*, 437.   **19** *Pacata Hibernia*, 320.   **20** Letter of Carew (see note 6).   **21** Rothe, *De Processu Martyriali*, unpaginated section following the preface. Reprinted in Moran, *Analecta*, 385.   **22** Mullan, *Epitome Tripartita*, 80–1.

his reason for coming to Ireland, namely to be Archer's *socius*, his where-abouts since his arrival in Ireland, and his knowledge of persons and of correspondence between Spain and Ireland. In all this lengthy document there is no suggestion of any specific charge preferred against him or of any sentence passed upon him. From his answers we learn that he was succes-sively at O'Neill's camp, then with O'Sullivan Beare, and lastly among 'his frends', i.e. with Archer and the garrison at Dunboy.

Pacata Hibernia records summarily the sentence and execution of Collins:

> ... the Fryer, in whom no penitence appeared for his detestable trea-sons, nor yet would endeavour to merite his life, either by discovering the Rebells intention, (which was in his power) or by doing some service that might deserve favour, was hanged at Youghall, the Towne wherein he was borne.

The phrase 'detestable treasons' is the nearest we can get to any specific charge. This phrase probably implies a plurality of actions or activities disap-proved of by the authorities. In the case of Dominic Collins 'detestable treasons' may be taken to mean (1) his arrival with the Spaniards, (2) his association with the much-wanted James Archer, and (3) his presence among the defenders of Dunboy castle.

The summary account of the sentence can be reconstructed as follows: Dominic Collins was the companion of the traitor James Archer, and by his presence at the castle of Dunboy aided the enemies of the crown. He was therefore guilty of rebellion and must suffer death. But the life of the pris-oner would be spared if he gave information concerning the rebels' intentions and if he undertook to do some service that merited favour.

In fact there was no need to try Collins at all for his association with the defenders of Dunboy. He might have been sent at once to the gallows as was done with the other survivors of the siege. In the case of Collins, there-fore, the authorities were more interested in the alternative to a summary execution for treason. The double alternative, useful information and future useful service, can be regarded as a desirable objective from the viewpoint of Carew. It is unlikely that Collins could have had any useful information to give, now that his companions at Dunboy were all dead, while his acquaintances, if he had any among the officers in the armies of O'Neill and del Águila, had disappeared from the battlefield of Kinsale. His life, then, in the reasoning of his judges, depended on his willingness to undertake service that might win the royal favour. But such service could only mean readiness on his part to engage in military activity or other pursuits against his Catholic fellow-countrymen and renunciation of his Jesuit vocation. This he refused to consider, and so he chose death.

The 'detestable treasons' of Collins, or his association with Archer and the defenders of Dunboy, should be considered as the *occasion* but not the reason for his condemnation. As an apostate Jesuit he would have proved more useful to Carew than as a mere victim sharing the common grave of the hanged survivors of Dunboy. It is not true, therefore, that Collins suffered death for treason. Four months were spent in determining his fate, whereas the other defenders of the castle were hanged immediately.

The annual letter from the Jesuit province of Castile[23] states clearly that he was tortured. No other early source mentions torture, and references in later sources[24] need not imply more than a general ill treatment. However, nearly all the sources mention a different kind of suffering he had to endure: the promises and threats repeatedly made to him. Tempting offers were made of rapid promotion to honourable rank in the crown forces on condition that he renounced the Catholic faith. According to O'Sullivan Beare,[25] he was visited by Protestant ministers who advanced arguments in support of their religion, holding out at the same time to him promises of ecclesiastical preferment in their Church. D'Outreman[26] and Tanner[27] mention a form of blackmail which added to his sufferings in prison: his relatives urged him to spare his own life and to spare themselves from the infamy of his execution, but outwardly renouncing his faith while remaining at heart a Catholic.

MARTYRDOM

Dominic Collins was put to death on 31 October 1602. This is the date given by both Irish and continental sources. Despite the fact that according to the old style this date falls on a Sunday, it seems probable that the martyrdom did in fact take place then. The early sources state or imply that he was executed by hanging only, but O'Sullivan Beare[28] and historians

---

23 Annual letter, Alfonso Ferrer, SJ, 3 July 1604 (see note 11).   24 E.g. the Necrology of the Jesuit province of Castile, *c*.1604, Rome, ARSI, MSS Castell., 38, f. 179v.; Mullan, *Epitome Tripartita*.   25 O'Sullivan Beare, *Hist. Cath. Ibern.* (Lisbon, 1621), ff 184v-185r. Reprinted, with critical editing, in Philip O'Sullivan Beare, *Historiae Catholicae Iberniae compendium*, ed. Matthew Kelly (Dublin, 1850), 238–9.   26 Pierre D'Outreman, *Tableaux des personnages signalés de la Compagnie de Iésus* (Douai, 1623), 479–80 [hereafter, *Tableaux*].   27 Tanner, *Societas Iesu*, 57.   28 O'Sullivan Beare, *Hist. Cath. Ibern.*

writing after 1643 speak of the execution as having been carried out by hanging and quartering. Yet the authority of Leynach and Mulroney in particular[29] cannot be easily dismissed. According to them, it was an execution by hanging. The eye-witness who described the execution to Haries[30] declared that it was carried out by a poor fisherman acting under duress. Such a person would be unable to carry out the operation of quartering.

Pacata Hibernia alone mentions Youghal as the place of Collins' execution. Two of the earliest sources[31] do not name any place. Field[32] is the first to say that Collins was executed in Cork. In this he appears to be wrong, but his error was taken up by Jesuit sources and soon became widespread. There can be little doubt that *Pacata Hibernia* gives the correct location. Its author may well have been a witness of the execution. In the expression 'was hanged at Youghall, the Towne where he was borne' he goes out of his way to lay emphasis on the place of Collins' death. It is reasonable to assume that the authorities decided he should be executed in his native Youghal in order to spread fear among the Catholics of the place where his family and relatives were well known.

According to the report from Leynach and Mulroney,[33] Dominic Collins went to his execution clad in his Jesuit cassock and from the scaffold he addressed the bystanders. Haries[34] said that his last words were that he had come to Ireland to preach the Catholic faith. The same source records that Collins went to the scaffold cheerfully and that he told an English captain who was present that he would most willingly undergo not one but a thousand deaths for the same cause. That he gave up his life willingly for his faith is the theme of nearly all the sources.

The earliest account of the execution, which was supplied by an eye-witness to Richard Haries, states that the dead man remained on the gallows for three or four hours until the cord broke and the body fell to the ground. It was stripped of its clothes and left naked on the ground, but during the night it was taken away for burial by some devout people. The version of the execution recorded by Leynach and Mulroney mentions also that the rope snapped and that the body fell to the ground to a kneeling position.

29 Nicholas Leynach, SJ, and Andrew Mulroney, SJ, to Thomas White, SJ, Clonmel, 30 March 1605. Rome, ARSI, MSS Anglia, 31, II, f. 166rv. [hereafter, Letter of Leynach and Mulroney]. **30** Account of the Martyrdom of Dominic Collins, from a letter of Richard Haries to James Archer, SJ, Lisbon, 19 January 1603. Rome, ARSI, MSS Castell., 33, f. 94 [hereafter, Letter of Haries]. **31** Ibid.; Letter of Leynach and Mulroney. **32** Richard Field, SJ, to Claudio Aquaviva, SJ, Dublin, 25 February 1603. Dublin, Provincial Archives of the Society of Jesus, MS A 13 (MacErlean transcript). **33** Letter of Leynach and Mulroney (see note 29). **34** Letter of Haries (see note 30).

Apart from Haries, the earlier sources pass over in silence the fate of the remains, but later historians claim that the Catholics gave the body religious burial near the place of execution.

MOTIVE FOR EXECUTION

Dominic Collins, according to *Pacata Hibernia*, was condemned to death for 'detestable treasons'. This is certainly not how Collins himself would have seen it. He had returned to Ireland as part of a Spanish expedition to help O'Neill and O'Donnell in what they claimed was a war for the Catholic faith. Despite the political complexities to which he was so sensitive, Pope Clement VIII had granted these Irish leaders the crusade indulgence, had nominated Ludovico Mansoni as papal nuncio, and had named O'Neill as captain-general of 'the Catholic army'. He had not acceded to O'Neill's request that the Irish Catholics who refused to join his cause should be excommunicated, because most of the Anglo-Irish were unwilling to take up arms against the crown.[35] Archer and Collins were exceptions here. Though both were citizens of the traditionally loyal towns, Archer of Kilkenny and Collins of Youghal, they had sailed with the Spanish fleet as part of a war for the Catholic faith, a war that had the papal blessing. This would have been particularly true of Collins. Archer was both an intellectual and politically astute, but Collins was neither. The motives of this soldier turned Jesuit would have been quite uncomplicated and altogether religious.

As has been seen, during his imprisonment and at his trial he was offered life and preferment if he would deny his faith and serve the crown. He refused even to consider such offers. He went to the scaffold wearing his Jesuit soutane,[36] and in his last few words he declared that the reason he had returned to Ireland was to preach the Catholic faith.[37] There can be no doubt he was completely certain that this was the reason he was being put to death.

35 For full details of the complexities see J.J. Silke, 'Hugh O'Neill, the Catholic question and the papacy', in *IER*, 5th series, 104 (1965), 65–79. **36** Letter of Leynach and Mulroney (see note 29). **37** Letter of Haries (see note 30).

FAMA MARTYRII

From the very beginning all the Catholic sources refer to Dominic Collins as a martyr. Because of the international character of the Jesuit order, his reputation as such was widespread in Portugal, Spain, and Italy within a matter of months.[38] Annual letters in particular would have a wide circulation among Jesuits everywhere. It was an Irish Jesuit, Henry Fitzsimon, who first put Collins' name in print as a martyr in 1628, but the only information he gave was his name and the fact and date of his execution.[39]

D'Outreman[40] (1623) gives further testimony to the spread of Dominic Collins' reputation for martyrdom in the Low Countries. In 1640, the *Imago primi saeculi Societatis Iesu*[41] coupled his name with that of the Scottish Jesuit martyr St John Ogilvie. This firmly established him in the canon of Jesuit martyrs. He is included by Nieremberg[42] (1643), Alegambe[43] (1657), Nadasi[44] (1665), Tanner[45] (1675), Jouvancy (1710), Drews (1723) and Patrignani (1730).

Richard Haries, chronologically the earliest witness,[46] was not a Jesuit. Soon a number of Irish writers who were not Jesuits were bearing witness in print to Collins' martyrdom. The earliest was David Rothe[47] (1619), followed by Philip O'Sullivan Beare[48] (1621) and John Mullan[49] (1629). With the restoration of the Jesuit order in 1814 and the revival of interest in the martyrs in Ireland in the nineteenth century, his name always figures in the lists. To this day he is commemorated in his native town of Youghal and in the cathedral of the diocese at Cóbh.

No relics of Dominic Collins are known to have existed. Nieremberg, writing in 1643, and Nadasi, writing in 1665, claimed that miracles were attributed to his intercession. It is known that a portrait of him existed in Douai in the early 1620s,[50] and a portrait in oils, possibly of the same date, is now in St Patrick's College, Maynooth, to which it was brought from the Irish College, Salamanca. It is unlikely that there is any question in either case of an exact likeness, but at least an idealized depiction of the martyred

---

38 Ludovico Mansoni, SJ, Nuncio to Ireland, to Claudio Aquaviva, SJ, Father General, Valladolid, 19 February 1603. Rome, ARSI, MSS Castell., 33, ff 92r-93v. White, *Life of Collins* (see note 4).   **39** Henry Fitzsimon, *Catalogus praecipuorum sanctorum Hiberniae* (Liège, 1619), 93.   **40** D'Outreman, *Tableaux* (see note 26).   **41** Jean Bolland, *Imago primi saeculi Societatis Iesu* (Antwerp, 1640), 535–6.   **42** Nieremberg, *Ideas*.   **43** Alegambe, *Mortes Illustres*.   **44** Ioannes Nadasi, *Annus dierum memorabilium Societatis Iesu* (2 pts, Antwerp, 1665), 252.   **45** Tanner, *Societas Iesu*.   **46** Letter of Haries (see note 30).   **47** Rothe, *De Processu Martyriali*.   **48** O'Sullivan Beare, *Hist. Cath. Ibern.*   **49** Mullan, *Epitome Tripartita*.   **50** D'Outreman, *Tableaux* (see note 26).

Jesuit was set before the Irish seminarians at Douai and Salamanca. The illustration of the execution printed by Tanner is certainly idealized.[51]

During the Ordinary Process *de fama martyrii* held in Dublin in 1904 the case of Dominic Collins was examined in detail, and the findings were presented to the Holy See. In due course the General Promoter of the Faith (*Disquisitio*, 138) reviewed the evidence and concluded:

> *Igitur, cum spes sit, hanc causam sententia sua sacram Congregationem fore comprobaturam, actorum petitioni, de ea ineunda, concedo*

In consequence of this verdict, his case was among those examined during the Apostolic Process held at Dublin between 1917 and 1930. The findings were then presented to the Holy See.

---

51 Tanner, *Societas Iesu.*

CHAPTER 8

Conor O'Devany, OFM
and Patrick O'Loughran

*Kieran Devlin**

EARLY LIFE

Conor O'Devany and Patrick O'Loughran were natives of the province of Ulster. This northernmost part of Ireland preserved longest the institutions of the traditional Irish way of life, but in their lifetimes it came under the influence of potent sixteenth-century forces: the Catholic Counter-Reformation and the authority of the central government in Dublin.

Traditional Irish society was based on kin-groups. The greatest dynastic group in Ulster was that of O'Neill. Several branches of this family domi-nated most of the province. The power base of the principal grouping was centred on modern County Tyrone. They were continually trying to exer-cise authority over other branches of the family, and indeed over the other Ulster dynasts. The only dynastic family to resist them consistently and successfully was that of O'Donnell, based in modern County Donegal.

The Church in Ireland had been given a diocesan structure in the reforms of the twelfth century. Parish organization followed, though in this society of shifting kin-groups it was always to some extent untidy. The key figure in this parish organization in the later Middle Ages was the *'erenagh'* (in Irish, *aircheannach*).[1] He was a layman, but occupied a quasi-ecclesiastical position. He farmed the church lands. In return he paid a tithe to the bishop, and, with the clergy, was responsible for the upkeep of the church buildings. He was responsible for entertaining the bishop on visitation and

* The author wishes to acknowledge that, although according to the conventions of the series (cf. *ITQ*, 64 [1999] 55) the article is now attributed to him, much of the content was provided by Fr Benignus Millett, OFM, while Monsignior P.J. Corish drew the whole thing together in his inimitable way.   1 For a description of the office of *erenagh* see *Inq. Cancell. Hib. Repert.*, ii, app. III, Coleraine; see also Canice Mooney, *The Church in Gaelic Ireland: thir-teenth to fifteenth centuries*, in Corish, *Ir. Catholicism*, ii, V, 10–15; Kenneth Nicholls, *Gaelic and gaelicised Ireland in the Middle Ages* (Dublin, 1972), 111; P. Ó Gallachair, 'Coarbs and Erenaghs of Co. Donegal', in *Donegal Annual* 4 (1958–60), 276–7.

providing general hospitality for travellers. He was usually a man of some education, and frequently kept some kind of school, with special responsibility for the education of the clergy. In these circumstances it was natural that most of the clergy should come of *erenagh* families, and the clergy of each parish tended to come from the *erenagh* family of that parish.

A striking feature of fifteenth-century Gaelic Ireland was the introduction and rapid spread of reform in the mendicant orders, especially the Observant reform among the Franciscans. Before this, the friars had been mainly concentrated in the towns in the culturally English part of Ireland. In the fifteenth century, when the pastoral mission of the Church was facing serious problems everywhere, these reformed friars enjoyed great authority and respect in Gaelic Ireland, both because of their genuine spiritual commitment and because of the deficiencies of the parish system. From the beginning they put up an organized resistance to the Anglican Reformation.

Conor O'Devany

Conor O'Devany's name appears in many forms in the documents illustrating his life and martyrdom, but there is no doubt that the authentic form is that given by the Four Masters,[2] who like him were natives of north-west Ireland, the principal figures being from his own county of Donegal. They write his name *O Duibheanaigh*. The Ui Duibheanaigh or O'Devanys were the *erenagh* family in the parish of Raphoe, diocese of Raphoe, County Donegal.

In 1609, inquisitions were taken concerning landownership in connection with the plantation of Ulster. In investigating the church lands of the bishop of Raphoe, the inquisitors testified that 'the half-quarter of Tollohedeveny was auncientlie in the sept of the Veneis'.[3] 'Tollohedeveny' is *Tulach Uí Dhuibheanaigh* (O'Devany's Hill), and 'the Veneis' appears clearly to be a scribal error for 'Deveneis'. The modern placename has been shortened to 'Tully'. Here in the parish of Raphoe the O'Devanys were the *erenagh* family.[4] The published papal letters and annate bonds[5] indicate that many of the name were priests in the diocese of Raphoe and in neigh-

2 *Annála Ríoghachta Éireann*, ad an. 1611 [1612 N.S.], compiled between 1632 and 1636: Dublin, RIA, MS 23 P7, f. 292. Printed in *AFM*, vi, 2370, 2372; English translation, ibid., 2371, 2373. 3 *Inq. Cancell. Hib. Repert.*, ii, app. V, Donagall. 4 O'Sullivan Beare's 'haud obscuro genere natus' is no more than conventional. In his edition of Rothe's *Analecta*, Moran conjectures an original 'O Dubheamha' (xciii), but this was only in an attempt to identify him with a family known to have been located near his diocese of Down and Connor. 5 *Cal. Papal Letters*, and *Annates, Ulster*, passim.

bouring parishes of the diocese of Derry during the fifteenth and sixteenth centuries.

It was therefore natural that Conor O'Devany should become a priest, and that he should opt to become a Franciscan was very understandable, if a little unusual. He took this step when he was a very young man, that is, shortly after 1550, for all the sources agree that he was nearly eighty when he was martyred in 1612. He became a Franciscan in the friary of Donegal. This friary had been founded as a house of Observant Franciscans in 1474 by the ruling O'Donnell family.[6] What little has been preserved of his life as a Franciscan is in very general terms,[7] but it indicates that he led the normal life of a dedicated Observant friar.

During the reign of Elizabeth I, the Dublin government extended its political control in Ireland, and with political control it proposed to impose the Anglican Reformation. After 1570, the policies of the queen and of the popes were in direct confrontation. For Pope Gregory XIII (1572–85), the Counter-Reformation mission and the religious crusade went hand in hand. He nominated a considerable number of bishops in Ireland, among them Conor O'Devany, who was appointed bishop of Down and Connor on 27 April 1582.[8] The record of his appointment states that he was dispensed *super defectu natalium*. This may mean that his father was a priest – not uncommon in many places at the time, and probably more than usually common in Gaelic Ireland because priests tended to come from the *erenagh* kin-groups. It may also mean that his parents' marriage was canonically invalid because they were related within the forbidden degrees of kindred. This again was not uncommon, and probably more than usually common in the closely knit kin-society of Gaelic Ireland.

Conor O'Devany was one of three Irish bishops consecrated together on 13 May 1582[9] in the church of Santa Maria dell'Anima in Rome,[10] the consecrating prelate being Cardinal Nicholas de Pellevé, archbishop of Sens, who as cardinal protector of Ireland had formally postulated their

---

6 See Aubrey Gwynn and R. Nevill Hadcock, *Medieval religious houses: Ireland* (London, 1970), 247; Canice Mooney, 'The Friars and Friary of Donegal, 1474–1840', in Terence O'Donnell (ed.), *Franciscan Donegal* (Rosnowlagh, 1952), 3–20. **7** Rothe, *De Processu Martyriali*, 102–44. Reprinted in Moran, *Analecta*, 456–81. O'Sullivan Beare, *Hist. Cath. Ibern.*, ff 230r-236r. Reprinted, with critical editing, in Philip O'Sullivan Beare, *Historiae Catholicae Iberniae Compendium*, ed. Matthew Kelly (Dublin, 1850), 298–305. **8** Minutes of the Secret Consistory held on 27 April 1582. AV, Acta Camerarii, 11, f. 377v. Printed in *Archiv. Hib.* 5 (1916), 175–6. **9** Rothe's statement that the consecration took place on the Feast of the Purification is chronologically impossible and is clearly no more than an attempt to associate the dates of consecration and martyrdom. **10** *Avvisi di Roma* issued on 16 May 1582: BV, MSS Urb. Lat., 1050, f. 162r.

provision in Consistory. This consecration of three Irish bishops in Rome at the same time indicates the close links now being forged between Ireland and the Counter-Reformation papacy.

The *Avvisi di Roma*[11] note that the pope ordered them to return to Ireland. There was still some need for such a formal command, but not in the case of Conor O'Devany, who returned to his diocese of Down and Connor. This was situated in the eastern part of Ulster, the modern County Antrim and most of County Down. He was the third Franciscan in succession to be bishop of that see, Franciscans being frequently appointed in Gaelic Ireland because they were the most suitable candidates. In 1587 he was one of six bishops and a large number of priests who met in synod somewhere in the diocese of Clogher in Ulster to promulgate the decrees of the Council of Trent.[12]

By this date the Dublin government had extended its authority over all of Ireland except Ulster, and Ulster was now under threat. Pressure was stepped up as the danger of a Spanish invasion mounted, and it was increased even after the failure of the Armada in 1588. The tensions can be seen in the letter from the bishop of Derry, Redmund O'Gallagher, to Conor O'Devany, dated 2 July 1588.[13] O'Gallagher as senior suffragen had been appointed to exercise jurisdiction in the province of Armagh *in loco primatis* by apostolic brief dated 13 April 1575, because Archbishop Creagh of Armagh was in prison. This authority O'Gallagher now delegated to O'Devany for one year because he fears he cannot exercise it everywhere on account of increasing harassment.

Both bishops were in fact in equal danger. If, as O'Devany claimed shortly afterwards,[14] he had been imprisoned by the lord deputy, Sir John Perrot, he had already been captured by the time this letter was written, for Perrot's successor, Sir William Fitzwilliam, took his oath of office on 30 June 1588. In fact, the bishop had managed to escape the first time he was captured,[15] but was recaptured and lodged in Dublin Castle. On this second occasion his captors must have found on him Bishop O'Gallagher's letter,

11 Ibid.   12 Renehan, *Collections*, i, 435.   13 Redmund O'Gallagher, Bishop of Derry, to Conor O'Devany, 'Tamlat', 2 July 1588: London, PRO, S.P., 63/137/38 I; calendared in *Cal. S.P. Ire., 1588–92*, 63; Printed in Moran, *Analecta*, xcv, and in O'Laverty, *Dioc. Down and Connor*, v, 365.   14 Petition of Conor O'Devany to Lord Deputy Fitzwilliam, 11 November 1590: London, PRO, S.P. 63/166/59 i; calendared in *Cal. S.P. Ire., 1588–92*, 587–8; printed in O'Laverty, *Dioc. Down and Connor*, v, 367–8.   15 Postscript to a letter of Sir William Fitzwilliam, lord deputy of Ireland, to William Cecil, Lord Burghley, lord high treasurer, 26 October 1588: London, PRO, S.P., 63/137/83 (modern copy); calendered in *Cal. S.P. Ire., 1588–92*, 63; printed in Moran, *Analecta*, xciv-xcv, and in O'Laverty, *Dioc. Down and Connor*, v, 364–5.

proof that he was exercising jurisdiction derived from the papacy. On 26 October 1588, Fitzwilliam wrote to William Cecil, Lord Burghley, lord high treasurer in England,[16] enclosing the captured letter and seeking advice on how to proceed against the bishop on a capital charge (the exercise of papal jurisdiction provided a charge of *praemunire*, but this capital only on a third offence). Fitzwilliam had been in government service in Ireland since 1554. Personally he tended to take a harsh line in civil and ecclesiastical affairs, but his long service had taught him caution in acting without the full sanction of his superiors in London. No reply to his letter has survived. In the late summer the Armada had come and failed, and Conor O'Devany remained in prison.

Here he suffered the hardships usual at the time, and the details supplied by Rothe are probably in the large part accurate. Prisoners had to pay for their own food, and the bishop, far from home, was ill equipped to do this. At the beginning of his imprisonment he was in some danger of death from hunger and thirst, and was saved only by the charity of fellow-prisoners and his own ingenuity. Later he managed at least to avoid starvation either because someone supplied him with money or because the jailer gave him food on credit. This latter seems unlikely, all the more so because the jailer in question, Stephen Segar, was later dismissed for corruption. When the warrant for the bishop's release was issued,[17] it noted Segar's claim that £20 was due to him. Though O'Devany denied this, he had to give sureties that he would pay what was proved to be due as a condition of his release.

On 11 November 1590 he petitioned to be released.[18] The petition was naturally couched in careful language. He described himself as a priest, not a bishop. He did state that he had been imprisoned during the deputyship of Sir John Perrot 'concerning matters of Religion'. He admitted to having committed 'divers faults worthy of condigne punishment' in the past, but he did not specify them. He claimed to have expiated them by his imprisonment. He did promise to be of good behaviour in the future 'in all causes of religion'.

The reference to Perrot was astute, for Perrot's enemies in the Dublin administration, not content with his dismissal from the office of lord deputy in 1588, were building up a charge of treason against him. O'Devany's petition was referred to three commissioners for ecclesiastical causes: Adam Loftus, lord chancellor and archbishop of Dublin, the archbishop of

---

16 Ibid. 17 Warrants to John Maplesden, Constable of Dublin Castle, 16–17 November 1590: London, BL, Additional MSS 19831, ff 1r–2r; printed in O'Laverty, *Dioc. Down and Connor*, v, 366. 18 See note 14.

Armagh, and the bishop of Meath. Loftus was prominent among Perrot's enemies. This may have had something to do with the fact that the decision to release O'Devany was taken in a few days, on 16 November.[19] This warrant for his release stated merely that he had undertaken to behave himself as a dutiful subject and had given sureties that he would appear before the commissioners for ecclesiastical causes if required to do so.

Meanwhile the charges against Perrot built up. He was sent to the Tower in March 1591, put on trial in April 1592, and found guilty in June. It was rumoured the queen would pardon him, but he resolved the question by dying in the Tower in September. The infighting in the Dublin administration continued, and charges were brought against Loftus, one of them being that he had released a Romish bishop without good warrant. In his reply, dated 17 September 1592,[20] Loftus declared that he had released the bishop only after he had taken both the Oath of Supremacy and an oath to be a dutiful subject and to reveal all conspiracies against the crown. There is no suggestion of either oath in his petition for release, and no mention was made at his trial of his having taken an oath to reveal conspiracies. There is no confirmation of Loftus's claim that he took the Oath of Supremacy, and it may be safely rejected.

When he returned to his diocese in east Ulster, resentment against English pressure was hardening into resistance. The two chief families in his diocese, the Scottish McDonnells in north Antrim and the powerful O'Neills of Clandeboye, had mounting grievances, as had all the Ulster leaders. The most powerful of them, O'Neill of Tyrone, was a cautious man and the last to decide on armed resistance. But when the war came, it was chiefly his ability to persuade or force the other leaders to make common cause that made the war such a threat to the government, though, when in the end things began to turn against him, many of these leaders broke with him and sought their own salvation.

A crucial event leading to war was an appeal from some Irish bishops to Philip II of Spain in 1593. The decision to make this appeal had been taken at a meeting of bishops held in west Ulster, probably in Donegal, late in 1592. Their leader was certainly Edmund Magauran, appointed archbishop of Armagh in 1587. It is impossible to be certain exactly how many other bishops were present or who they were.[21] At his trial, Bishop O'Devany

---

19 See note 17.   **20** Answer of Adam Loftus, archbishop of Dublin and lord chancellor of Ireland, to the accusation of Barnaby Rich and Robert Legge, 17 September 1592: London, PRO, S.P., 63/116/59; calendared in *Cal. S.P. Ire., 1588–92*, 582; printed in O'Laverty, *Dioc. Down and Connor*, v, 367.   **21** See J.J. Silke, 'The Irish appeal of 1593 to Spain', in *IER* 92

asserted that he had taken no active part in the war. A memorial on the Irish dioceses, undated and unsigned,[22] but which may with good credibility be attributed to Peter Lombard and dated *c.*1600, refers to him as 'a good man, but ingenuous (*simplicior*) from whom no great help can be expected'. Peter Lombard, a priest from Waterford, was at this time O'Neill's agent in Rome, and on 9 July 1601 was appointed archbishop of Armagh at O'Neill's request. While the reference is so laconic that it is impossible to be certain if the little help to be expected was of a religious or political nature, the latter cannot be ruled out in the circumstances. A fellow Franciscan, who was familiar with the affairs of east Ulster, where Conor O'Devany's diocese was situated, writing within a few months of the martyrdom, mentions, in a passing way as if referring to a well-known fact, that O'Neill had asked the bishop to join in his political and military struggle, but that he had refused.[23]

In his indictment in 1612,[24] Conor O'Devany was accused of assisting Hugh O'Neill and Brian MacArt O'Neill in their treasons. Brian MacArt was Hugh's nephew, to whom he entrusted the conduct of the war in east Ulster, in the territory of O'Neill of Clandeboye. This appointment of relatives to positions of command was Hugh O'Neill's normal method of ensuring centralized control and it was much resented by the other Ulster leaders. The special mention of Brian MacArt O'Neill in the indictment probably reflects the fact that O'Devany lived under his protection during the war, because he was in control of military operations in the bishop's diocese.

The war ended with the surrender of the Ulster leaders in the spring of 1603. They received better terms than they might have expected, largely because Queen Elizabeth was dead. She died on 24 March, six days before O'Neill surrendered. The leaders were allowed to keep their lands, but now they had to hold them under English law.

Catholic hopes had been raised by the ascension of the new king, James I. These hopes were based in large measure on the fact that he was the son of Mary, queen of Scots, but they were to be disappointed. On 4 July 1605, a royal proclamation ordered all Jesuits and seminary priests to leave the kingdom, and all laity to attend the services of the Established Church.

(1959), 279–90, 362–71. **22** Report on the state of the Irish dioceses, *c.* 1600: A.V., Fondo Borghese, series III, 124C, f. 78. Printed in *Archiv. Hib.* 2 (1913), 301. **23** Thomas Fleming, OFM, Dundalk, 25 April 1612: BR, MS 2158–67, ff 198r–199r; printed in Moran, *Analecta*, cxviii–cxxi, in Moran, *Spicil. Ossor.*, iii, 32–3, and in O'Laverty, *Dioc. Down and Connor*, v, 383–6. **24** Indictment and record of the attainder of Conor O'Devany, [1612]: Sir Richard Bolton, *A Justice of Peace for Ireland* (Dublin, 1638), bk 2, pt iii, 3–6; reprinted, with critical editing, in *Archiv. Hib.* 6 (1917), 77–80.

Conor O'Devany was now dependent on what diminished protection the Ulster magnates could afford him. Both he and they were subjected to increasing harassment. A surviving report of a spy from 1606[25] says that O'Neill planned to send O'Devany to Rome and Spain to seek help. It need be given little credence. Such accusations were then commonplace; there is no real indication that O'Neill had any such plans at this time; the bishop, now in his seventies, was an unlikely emissary; and no mention of the alleged mission was made at the time of his trial. Later that same year the attorney general, Sir John Davies, reported seeing him in Ulster, dressed as a friar and living under the protection of Cormac MacBaron O'Neill, brother of Hugh O'Neill, earl of Tyrone.[26] A letter of March 1607, written by George Montgomery, appointed by the king to the united dioceses of Derry, Raphoe and Clogher in 1605,[27] provides clear evidence that the net was tightening. Bishop O'Devany was now protected by Rory O'Donnell, earl of Tyrconnell, who must have been humiliated by the fact that he had to resort to trickery to protect the Catholic bishop from the Anglican one, and indeed seems to have been unable to continue his protection, if the report given to Montgomery was true, that O'Devany had left Ulster and gone to the Pale.

On 4 September 1607, most of the Ulster leaders, including Hugh O'Neill, took ship and sailed from Ireland. With their departure, Conor O'Devany, now in his seventies, became a fugitive. The fact that he had become vice-primate in the same month, because the senior suffragen had died and Archbishop Peter Lombard of Armagh was in Rome, was of little significance. Neither was it of great significance that in August 1608 the Roman datary conferred on him the monastery of Derry,[28] probably at the request of Hugh O'Neill, who had arrived in Rome on 28 April. It was stated to be valued at thirty marks; but, whatever its revenues, they were now in the hands of Bishop Montgomery.

We catch a fleeting glimpse of him in 1610, when he visited the

---

25 Enclosure written by Sir Richard Greames in a letter of Sir Arthur Chichester, Lord Deputy of Ireland, to the earl of Devonshire, 23 April 1606: London, PRO, S.P., 63/218/45 i (modern copy); calendared in *Cal. S.P. Ire., 1603–6*, 453; printed in Moran, *Analecta*, c, and in O'Laverty, *Dioc. Down and Connor*, v, 368–9. 26 Sir John Davies, attorney general for Ireland, to Lord Deputy Chichester, 12 November 1606: London, PRO, S.P., 63/219/132; calendared in *Cal. S.P. Ire., 1606–8*, 17–18. 27 George Montgomery, bishop of Derry, Raphoe and Clogher, to Lord Deputy Chichester, 4 March 1607: Bodl., Carte MSS, 61, f. 344; calendared in *Cal. S.P. Ire., 1606–8*, 126; printed in Moran, *Analecta*, cii, and in O'Laverty, *Dioc. Down and Connor*, v, 369–70. 28 Provision of Conor O'Devany as commendatory abbot of the Monastery of *Cella Nigra*, Derry diocese, August 1608: AV, Per Obitum 1608, f. 82r.

pilgrimage centre of *Insula Viventium* near Roscrea in north Munster. In or about 1607, Pope Paul V had indulgenced a number of traditional Irish pilgrimage centres.[29] In the previous year about 15,000 people were reported to have gathered there on Palm Sunday. Despite his age the bishop made the pilgrim-round barefoot and, it may be reasonably conjectured, administered the sacrament of confirmation to several people.[30]

Some time during these years he compiled his *Index Martyrialis*, or list of those who suffered for the faith in Ireland. There were possibly two copies in existence, neither of which has survived. David Rothe had a copy when writing his *De Processu Martyriali*,[31] and O'Devany sent a copy to the Jesuits shortly before he was captured. This final capture and imprisonment came in the early summer of 1611.

Patrick O'Loughran

The priest Patrick O'Loughran was also of an *erenagh* family, and one that had special links with the senior branch of the O'Neills, whose head during his lifetime was Hugh O'Neill, earl of Tyrone. Part of an Irish chief's revenue was derived from lands set aside for this purpose: these were in addition to the lands he personally owned. These lands were called in English O'Neill's 'mensal' or 'demesne' lands: the Irish term was *lucht tighe Uí Néill*.[32] They were coterminous with the parish of Donaghmore, County Tyrone, where the O'Loughran family were *erenaghs*. As is clear from the papal registers, the annate bonds, and the register of the archbishops of Armagh,[33] many of that name served as priests in the latter Middle Ages in the parish of Donaghmore and its annexed perpetual vicarage, and held other benefices in the diocese of Armagh.

---

29 The papal brief is printed in *Archiv. Hib.* 3 (1914), 261–4. **30** This information occurs only in David Rothe's *Epistola paraenetica* (Moran, *Analecta*, 297–8). The passage runs as follows: 'Quid si ... aut videres trepidam fugam, aut audires moestam vociferationem ululantium foeminarum, quae proximis diebus, stimulatae spiritu poenitudinis quo sibi propitiarent Deum, sordesque animorum fletu diluerent, profectae ad Insulam quam vocant viventium, dum inibi, ut fit, sua nudipedalia sacrosque circuitus conficerent in multo planctu et carnis maceratione, nonne toto corpore perhorresceres, si te inspectante, grex ille innocuus ovicularum Christi, invaderetur ab infesto luporum agmine, e proxima militum barbarorum statione ... Discruciarent utique animum tuum afflictarum spectacula foeminarum, et collium istorum compugnantium strepitus te magis offenderet, quam tota pedum ac plantarum tuarum laceratio, et frigidus ille sudor quem largiter emisisti, cum ipse anno praeterito laboriosam illam peregrinationem obires, et poene deficeres in ipsa geniculatione, quae quam acerba sit in locis arenosis et asperis sanctae stationis, praesertim cum nuda, diuturna, et multiplex fuerit, nemo qui Insulam ipsam adivit id ignoraverit.' **31** See Moran, *Analecta*, 385, 386. **32** See Eamon Ó Doibhlin, *Domhnach Mór* (Omagh, 1969), 1–62; 'O'Neill's "Own Country" and its Families', in *Seanchas Ardmhacha* 6 (1971–2), 3–23; 'The Deanery of Tulach Óg', ibid., 150–4, 159. **33** *Cal. papal letters* and *annates*, Ulster, passim. For the Armagh registers, see Aubrey Gwynn, *The medieval province of Armagh* (Dundalk, 1946), iii–xi.

Quite a number of these priests were called Patrick. The exact style of the present Patrick is given in *Annála Ríoghaghta Éireann*.[34] He was called *Giolla Phádraig*, 'the servant of Patrick', a common Irish variation on a saint's name. He was about thirty-five at the time of his martyrdom,[35] and so would have been born about 1577. There is no record of his ordination to the priesthood, but it may be assigned to about the year 1600, that is, towards the end of the war. Statements that he was a Franciscan tertiary[36] or Bishop O'Devany's chaplain[37] are probably misunderstandings arising from the fact that they were tried and martyred together: there are no indications that they had even met beforehand. In a list compiled in Flanders two months after the 'Flight of the Earls', in 1607, 'Patricio Lurcano' is identified as the chaplain to O'Neill's wife, the countess of Tyrone.[38] A memorandum submitted to Pope Paul V by Archbishop Peter Lombard in Rome states that he was O'Neill's chaplain;[39] this memorandum is undated, but on internal evidence might well date from 1612, when accounts of the martyrdom had already gained wide circulation. At his trial,[40] he made no attempt to conceal the fact of his close association with O'Neill, and it may be taken as certain that he was a chaplain in O'Neill's household.

The war ended when Hugh O'Neill surrendered on 30 March 1603. The terms granted by the new king, James I, were not ungenerous. O'Neill and the other Irish leaders were restored to their estates. It was soon made clear, as mentioned above, that henceforth they must hold these estates under the provisions of English law. O'Neill had some success in coming to terms with the situation, but O'Donnell and Maguire, younger and less experienced men, were soon under great pressure, so much so that they began to consider leaving Ireland to make a career in the Spanish army in the

34 See note 2. **35** Account of the martyrdom entitled *La Morte Gloriosa d'un Vescovo Zoccolante, e d'un sacerdote martirizati in Ibernia el primo Febraro 1612*, 1612: Milan, Biblioteca Ambrosiana, MS H. 71. Inf., ff 137r-139v [hereafter, *La Morte Gloriosa*]. **36** O'Mahony, *Brevis Synopsis*, 70–1, 74 (contemporary copy); printed in *Anal. Hib.*, 6 (1934), 177, 178. **37** Report on the state of Ireland by Archbishop David Kearney and others, 1612: Salamanca MSS, item in unclassified bundle; English translation in Moran, *Spicil. Ossor.*, i, 122–3. See also Donagh Mooney, *De Provincia Hiberniae S. Francisci*, 1617–18: BR, MS 3195, 7, 68, 75, 89; printed in *Anal. Hib.* 6 (1934), 22, 91, 98, 112. **38** A.G. Sim., Secretaria de Estado: Negociaciones de Roma, leg. 625; printed in M.K. Walsh, *Destruction by Peace: Hugh O'Neill after Kinsale* (Armagh, 1986), 184. **39** Memorandum presented by Peter Lombard, archbishop of Armagh, to Pope Paul V, c. 1612: AV, Fondo Borghese, series II, 23, f. 210; printed in Archiv. Hib. 3 (1914), 297–8. **40** [Francis Fay], *Martyrium Reverendissimi D. F. Cornelii Dovenii, Dunensis at Connerensis episcopi, ex Seraphica D. Francisci Reg. Observant. familia assumpti, et R. D. Patritii Luchrani presbyteri Dublinii in Hybernia, sub Arthuro Chichestriensi prorege anno M.D.CXII. 1 Februarii Dublinii faeliciter consummatum* (Cologne, 1614). See O'Sullivan Beare, *Hist. Cath. Ibern.*

Netherlands. Maguire travelled there secretly in the summer of 1607, probably to make firmer arrangements. He returned, unexpectedly quickly, at
the end of August. On 4 September, the ship sailed again from Ireland
carrying the Irish leaders and their dependants, to a total of ninety-nine.
O'Neill sailed with them, having at the last moment decided to join what
has come to be known as the 'Flight of the Earls'. Historians have not
succeeded in unravelling his motives. He had been more successful than the
younger men in maintaining his position in Ireland, and he could have little
prospect of a career abroad, for he was now nearly sixty years of age.

According to one account of his trial,[41] Patrick O'Loughran stated that
as O'Neill's chaplain he had gone with his lord into exile. However, another
account[42] makes him say quite explicitly that he had indeed travelled from
Ireland to the Netherlands, and on the same ship that had carried the earls
into exile, but on its first voyage, not with the earls on its second, and that
his reason for going was to pursue his studies (*se quidem ea navi fuisse in
Belgium traductum navatum operam litteris, prius tamen, quam O'Nellus, et
O'Donnellus*). These two accounts are not necessarily incompatible, if one
makes the reasonable assumption that neither sets out to give a full account
of Patrick O'Loughran's reply to the charges against him.

Of the ninety-nine persons who sailed from Ireland on 4 September
1607, we know the names of sixty-six in all,[43] and the name of Patrick
O'Loughran is not among them. However, 'Patricio Lurcano' is included in
a list, dated 8 November 1607, of those accompanying the countess of
Tyrone in Flanders, while a further list, dated 28 May 1608, of eleven priests
and students wishing to remain in Flanders to study contains the name of
'Patricio Lucherano, sacerdote'.[44] On the other hand, he may have travelled
on to Rome to join O'Neill, who had arrived there in April. At his trial he
stated that he had been to Rome and knelt before the pope.[45] That this was
in 1608, possibly as early as June, may be suggested by documents in the
archives of the datary[46] conferring two Irish benefices on him, though, as

41 [Francis Fay], ibid.   **42** O'Sullivan Beare, *Hist. Cath. Ibern.*   **43** For the identification
of those persons, see Tadhg Ó Cianain, *The Flight of the Earls*, ed. and trans. Paul Walsh
(Maynooth/Dublin, 1916), pp. x, 16–19.   **44** List of those remaining with the Countess of
Tyrone: A.G. Sim., Secretaria de Estado: Negociaciones de Roma, leg. 625; printed in Walsh,
op. cit., 184. List of priests and students: A.G. Sim., Secretaria de Estado: Negociaciones de
Roma, leg. 1749; printed ibid., 212, and in *Ir. Sword* 2 (1954–6), 201; see also Ó Doibhlin,
Domhnach Mór, 67.   **45** [Francis Fay], *Martyrium Reverendissimi*.   **46** Provision of Patrick
O'Loughran to the vicarage with cure and the rectory without cure of souls of the parochial
church of St Nicholas at Manfieldstown, Armagh diocese, June 1608: AV, Per Obitum 1608,
f. 82r. Provision of Patrick O'Loughran to the rectory of the parochial church at
Desertcreight, Armagh diocese, April 1609: AV, Per Obitum 1609, f. 4v.

noted already in connection with Conor O'Devany, an Irish benefice was conferred at the same time on the bishop, who certainly was not then in Rome. However, the conferring of these parochial benefices on the priest Patrick O'Loughran does give some indication that he had close links with Hugh O'Neill and helps to confirm that he was a chaplain in his household.

At some stage, however, he had some connection with the Irish College at Douai in the Low Countries. In a list of students of this college, printed in 1622, there is a hand-written addendum of ten names in one of the two surviving copies. It includes 'D. Patr. Lorcanus Martir',[47] who must be identified with Patrick O'Loughran.

In 1611 he decided to return to Ireland, and was arrested immediately he landed. Why he took the decision to return is unknown, but at this time priests were regularly returning from the continental seminaries.

ARREST AND IMPRISONMENT

The government faced many problems in its efforts to impose political and religious conformity after success in the war had in theory established its sovereignty over the whole island. The 'Flight of the Earls' had given it the opportunity for large-scale confiscation and plantation in Ulster. This, however, only increased the resentments of the Old Irish, and the government had real but exaggerated fears of foreign plots and possible invasion. The Old Irish were, of course, Catholic. So were the Old English as a body, and though they had been loyal during the war and wished to continue so, their Catholicism posed a political problem. Because they still had great economic power, and in consequence political power, they could be expected to have a majority in the Parliament, which for many reasons it was desirable to call.

A proclamation of 11 March 1605 had declared all Irishmen to be immediately subject to the king. With it went a declaration of amnesty 'against reviving questions and challenges committed in the late rebellion'.[48] In England, parliament met after the Gunpowder Plot (5 November 1605) and inevitably passed further penal legislation against Catholics. This legislation embodied a new Oath of Allegiance. It was less demanding than the Oath

---

47 John Brady (ed.), 'The Irish Colleges in the Low Countries', in *Archiv. Hib.* 14 (1949), 67.
48 *Cal. S.P. Ire., 1603–6*, 266.

of Supremacy, but in addition to requiring Catholics to swear that they accepted James as their lawful king they had to swear further that the pope had no power to depose him.[49] This oath seriously divided the English Catholics, despite a formal condemnation by Pope Paul V on 22 September 1606.

In Ireland, the government tried to establish the position that the declaration of amnesty applied only to those who took an oath of allegiance, and justified tendering the English oath by an appeal to the royal prerogative. This was considered to be preferable to the more rigorous Oath of Supremacy, as the government wished to produce obedient citizens rather than make martyrs. However, there were many skilled lawyers among the Old English, who were able not merely to question the claim that the benefits of the general amnesty applied only to those who took an oath, but also to point out that the English Oath of Allegiance could not be lawfully tendered in Ireland because it had not been passed in an Irish parliament. The government was thus forced from one inadequate expedient to another.

This unsatisfactory situation nurtured its fears. Lord Deputy Chichester and the bishops of the Established Church would have preferred to take a stern line with Catholics. From London, however, the problem was seen with a different emphasis. The king and his council there wished to give priority to a political settlement. They felt that the religious issue demanded a longer-term solution, to be brought about by evangelization rather than by pressure. The dilemma arose from the fact that the religious and political issues were inseparable.

Matters came to a head when, in 1610, it was decided that the parliament could be postponed no longer. A choice had to be made between conciliating the anticipated Catholic majority or reducing it to a minority by creating new parliamentary seats, especially in the planted counties of Ulster. The second option was taken, and pressure on the Catholics was stepped up. On 26 April 1611, the king commanded Chichester, among other things, to ensure that 'there must be a uniform order set down for the suppression of papistry'.[50] Chichester reissued the 1605 proclamation in July, but he naturally sought more detailed instructions from London as to what other steps he should take. They came in a letter dated 20 August,[51] and must have given him only mixed satisfaction. The Oath of Supremacy

---

49 For an analysis of the implications of the oath, see Philip Hughes, *Rome and the Counter-Reformation in England* (London, 1944), 308–11. **50** *Cal. S.P. Ire. 1611–14*, 31–2. **51** Ibid., 96–7.

was to be tendered as hitherto, that is sporadically and as opportunity offered. The tendering of the Oath of Allegiance should be suspended, since it was doubtful if its refusal could be legally punished. However, the letter went on to say that it would be well if some titular bishops could be punished in an exemplary manner, provided it could be made clear that they were not being punished for strictly religious activities. When this letter arrived, Bishop Conor O'Devany was already in prison. There was only one other Catholic bishop in Ireland, Archbishop Kearney of Cashel.

It has been necessary to set out the complexities of the situation in some detail in order to understand the accounts of the trial of Conor O'Devany and of his companion, Patrick O'Loughran. In particular, it must be noted that there were two oaths in question, the Oath of Supremacy and the Oath of Allegiance. The documentation makes it clear that, both during his imprisonment and when actually at the gallows, the bishop was offered not only pardon but preferment if he would take the Oath of Supremacy. Naturally the Oath of Supremacy was not mentioned at his trial. The Oath of Allegiance was, but as part of his harassment by a judge who must have known that refusal of this oath could not be legally punished in Ireland. The charge on which Conor O'Devany was tried was treason. No other charge would permit a death sentence.

Bishop O'Devany was arrested in May or June 1611 at the house of Brian McHugh Óg MacMahon, described as being 'on an island in a great lake'.[52] MacMahon had married Hugh O'Neill's daughter and had supported him during the war, though he had refused to leave with him in 1607. He was now one of the few people left in Ireland to whom the bishop could turn with any hope of protection. Rothe says he had gone to MacMahon to settle family quarrels. These were indeed common among Irish noble families. One account[53] says the band of soldiers who arrested him came upon him by chance, and this is probably what happened. Statements that he was arrested on orders from Dominic Sarsfield[54] or Lord Deputy Chichester[55] are probably rationalizations designed to show that his known enemies had been personally involved in his arrest. He was brought to Dublin and imprisoned in the Castle.

Patrick O'Loughran was arrested immediately he landed in Cork in

52 Memorandum by Richard Conway, SJ, *c.* 1612: Salamanca MSS, item in unclassified bundle; English translation in Moran, *Spicil. Ossor.*, i, 123–6; reprinted in O'Laverty, *Dioc. Down and Connor*, v, 379–82; *La Morte Gloriosa* (see note 35); Rothe, *De Processu Martyriali*; O'Sullivan Beare, *Hist. Cath. Ibern.* **53** O'Sullivan Beare, *Hist. Cath. Ibern.* **54** [Francis Fay], *Martyrium Reverendissimi* (see note 40). **55** *La Morte Gloriosa* (see note 35).

June.[56] When questioned by the lord president of Munster, he freely admitted that he was a Catholic priest. Rothe says that he added that he had travelled with the earls and ministered to them, but he may be confusing what O'Loughran may have said at Cork with what he may have said later at his trial. Two sources[57] say or imply that he was imprisoned with the bishop at the Castle, while three others[58] say it was in the common criminal jail. It is impossible to be certain, but it is more likely that he was imprisoned in the common jail.

Some sources[59] stress the hardships and miseries of their imprisonment, while others speak of their being visited and relieved by Catholic citizens of Dublin[60] and by Franciscans, who brought them the means of saying Mass in prison.[61] These accounts are not incompatible. The statement[62] that government officials tried by threats and promises to induce them to abandon the Catholic religion may be safely accepted.

As threats and promises proved unavailing, the question of what to do with them posed itself. In July, Chichester reissued the proclamation of 1605, but this had only threatened Catholic priests with imprisonment, and it seems to have been widely believed, even by Protestants, that they and other priests then in prison would simply be kept there.[63] By the beginning of October, Chichester had decided to 'proceed against the titularie Bishop of Downe and six of the preistes now in prison ... nexte Term in the kinges Bench'.[64] He did not specify on what charges he intended to proceed, and it is possible that at this date he had not finally decided, despite the fact that on 20 August he had received clearance from London to make an example of a Catholic bishop. Given the legal position, it was much more difficult in Ireland than in England to convict a priest or bishop on a capital charge of treason: refusal to take the Oath of Supremacy was subject to the penalties

---

56 Memorandum by Richard Conway (see note 52); *La Morte Gloriosa*; [Francis Fay], *Martyrium Reverendissimi*; Rothe, *De Processu Martyriali*; O'Sullivan Beare, *Hist. Cath. Ibern.* 57 Memorandum by Richard Conway; *La Morte Gloriosa*. 58 [Francis Fay], *Martyrium Reverendissimi*; Rothe, *De Processu Martyriali*; O'Sullivan Beare, *Hist. Cath. Ibern.* 59 *Martyrium Reverendissimi*; O'Sullivan Beare, *Hist. Cath. Ibern.* 60 Account of the martyrdom entitled *Compendium Martyrii Reverendissimi Domini D. fratris Cornelii O Duveany ex Ordine Minorum Dunensis Conorensis episcopi suique sacellani ex litteris ad Minoritas Hybernos ex Hybernia Lovanium missis extractum*, compiled by the Irish Franciscans at Louvain, 1612: BR, MS 2158–67, ff 201r-204v; printed in *Collect. Hib.* 26 (1984), 13–19 [hereafter, *Compendium martyrii*]; brief extracts in English translation in O'Laverty, *Dioc. Down and Connor*, v, 382–3; *La Morte Gloriosa* (see note 35). 61 *Compendium Martyrii*, ibid. 62 Memorandum by Richard Conway (see note 52). 63 O'Sullivan Beare, *Hist. Cath. Ibern.* 64 Lord Deputy Chichester to Robert Cecil, Earl of Salisbury, lord high treasurer, 7 October 1611: London, Lambeth Palace Library, Carew MS 629, f. 171r; calendared in *Cal. S.P. Ire., 1611–14*, 142–3, and in *Cal. Carew MSS, 1603–24*, 127–9.

of treason only on a third offence, and in any case Chichester's instructions would not allow him to arraign Catholic ecclesiastics on this charge. It is quite possible that the final decision was taken only shortly before 16 December, when a commission was issued to empanel a grand jury to find charges of treason against Bishop O'Devany.[65] The decision to proceed on a charge of treason would also explain why Patrick O'Loughran, a confessed associate of O'Neill, was singled out from the priests in prison to face the same charge with the bishop on 28 January 1612.

TRIAL

The trial of the prisoners is well documented. The details of the legal process appear from the chance preservation of the indictment of Bishop O'Devany by its inclusion in a book of precedents for lawyers.[66] There are many accounts of the trial from Catholic sources, no less than six from the actual year of the trial,[67] and three others written by 1621.[68] Yet a reading of these accounts suggests a certain confusion over the actual sequence of events. None of the authors claims to be an eyewitness. Only two[69] explicitly claim to be based on the testimony of eyewitnesses. It is unlikely that any of them were particularly well informed on the legal processes of a trial for treason. This particular trial was a highly emotional occasion, conducted in a crowded courtroom. Especially dramatic moments tended to be best remembered, though not always, it would appear, in the correct context. Fortunately, the processes of indictment and trial have recently been thoroughly studied for sixteenth-century England,[70] and these were the same as the processes in early seventeenth-century Ireland. A comparison of these known processes with the Catholic documentation on this particular trial leaves no doubt that the most coherent account is *Martyrium Reverendissimi Cornelii Dovenii et Patritii Luchrani*,[71] which also advances the most convincing evidence of its credibility, claiming to the based on the oral

---

65 Indictment of Conor O'Devany (see note 24).   **66** Ibid.   **67** Thomas Fleming, 25 April 1612 (see note 23); Report on the state of Ireland (see note 37); Thomas White Lombard, SJ, to Mafeo Cardinal Barberini, Rome, 7 June 1612: BV, MSS Barb. Lat., 8928, f. 32r; calendared in *Archiv. Hib.* 18 (1955), 142; Memorandum by Richard Conway (see note 52); *Compendium Martyrii* (see note 60); *La Morte Gloriosa* (see note 35).   **68** [Francis Fay], *Martyrium Reverendissimi* (see note 40); Rothe, *De Processu Martyriali*; O'Sullivan Beare, *Hist. Cath. Ibern.*   **69** Memorandum by Richard Conway (see note 52); [Francis Fay], *Martyrium Reverendissimi* (see note 40).   **70** John Bellamy, *The Tudor law of treason* (Henley-on-Thames, 1979); see also Penry Williams, *The Tudor regime* (Oxford, 1979), 378–89.   **71** See note 40.

testimony of many eye-witnesses, letters received 'daily' from Catholics, and two printed books, which it has not been possible to locate. It seems reasonable, then, to use this as the basic account, supplemented, and in one respect probably corrected, by others.

It may help to clarify the situation if the normal conduct of a treason trial is first briefly described. In important respects, trials for treason were 'show-trials'. The government prepared its case and expected a conviction, though acquittals were not unknown. The process began by summoning a 'grand jury' in the place where the treason was alleged to have been committed, to consider if the evidence warranted committing the prisoner for trial. The government usually provided much of the evidence and directed the jury what to find: it might even name the jurors. The trial jury, or 'petty jury', was to decide if the evidence produced in court warranted conviction, but the distinction between the functions of the two juries was not altogether clear, and the findings of the grand jury in its indictment might be produced as evidence in court.

When the trial opened the court was usually crowded. The authorities were not averse to this, because they wished the conviction of a traitor to be witnessed by as many people as possible. The accused were brought into court, and the indictment was formally handed to the justices. Each prisoner was then called separately to the bar. His indictment was read to him, and he was asked to plead. Sometimes the accused responded by trying to discuss the charges with the judges, but this was not allowed. If he pleaded not guilty, he elected to be tried 'by God and my country' (the legal phrase for trial by jury). A jury was then empanelled, though at this stage, especially in trials involving the question of allegiance to the pope, the accused might argue that such matters could not be properly evaluated by lay jurors and ask to be tried by judge alone. Again, this was not allowed. In theory the accused could object to each juryman as he was named, but in practice this right was heavily curtailed, and a strict statutory right to object to jurors in treason trials was introduced only later. The indictment was recited to the jury, and the trial began. The court crier might invite anyone who might testify as a witness to come forward, but witnesses, while desirable, were not considered essential. The accused was not allowed to call witnesses. The best evidence was a confession, failing which the indictment of the grand jury might be used. The accused was not allowed the help of counsel, though counsel were present for the crown. Though the accused might have succeeded in getting advice from lawyers while in prison awaiting trial, he was handicapped by the fact that he did not know the exact terms of his indictment until it was read to him in court. The proceedings normally concluded by a summation by crown counsel, to which the accused was sometimes allowed to reply. The jury then retired to consider their verdict. If it were a verdict of guilty, the judge pronounced the mandatory sentence: the convicted traitor was to be hanged, drawn and quartered.

The proceedings against Bishop O'Devany began with a commission issued at Dublin on 16 December 1611 to empanel a grand jury in County Down, the place where his treason was alleged to have been committed. It appears to have been a slow task assembling a jury in the depth of winter, and it met in Newry only on 15 January 1612. The government could afford to lose no time if they planned to bring him to trial in the next law term, which in 1612 ran from 14 January to 8 February.[72] The jury found that Conor O'Devany, on the first day of January 1602, and on divers days before that date in the reign of Queen Elizabeth, in the county of Down, had treasonably advised, abetted and comforted the earl of Tyrone, Brian MacArt O'Neill, and other most wicked traitors, that he was present with the traitors when their crimes were committed, and that he advised, adhered to, assisted and maintained the traitors in the execution, commission and perpetration of these treasonable acts against the peace, crown and dignity of Queen Elizabeth, and against the laws in force in the kingdom of Ireland.[73]

On 22 January the bishop was brought before the court of king's bench in Dublin. This was the supreme tribunal for all offences against the crown. According to one source,[74] this session was presided over by Lord Deputy Chichester and the chief justice. This may be accepted as true, for though the lord deputy could not judge in king's bench, this session was only for the purpose of charging the prisoner, and the fact that this court was in origin that in which the king (or in Ireland his representative, the lord deputy) dispensed justice in person was still a residual memory. The bishop was charged with treason. He pleaded not guilty and elected to be tried by jury (*ponit se super patriam*). The trial was fixed for 28 January.[75]

No such detail has been preserved in the case of Patrick O'Loughran, but

---

72 On the fixing of the law terms, see the note in C. R. Cheney, *Handbook of dates for students of English history* (London, 1945), 65–9.   **73** Indictment of Conor O'Devany (see note 24).   **74** *La Morte Gloriosa* (see note 35).   **75** Indictment of Conor O'Devany (see note 24). This document dates the trial as *die Martis prox. Quindenam Sancti Hilarii xxiiii*, etc., but this must be a misprint, presumably for xxviii, for 'the Tuesday after the quindene of St Hilary' was 28 January in 1612. Barnaby Rich (*A Catholicke conference between Syr Tady Mac Mareall a popish priest of Waterford, and Patricke Plaine a young student in Trinity College by Dublin in Ireland* (London, 1612), ff 3v–6r) confirms that this was in fact the date.

it may be assumed his indictment followed a similar course. Both appeared before the court of king's bench on the appointed day.

Rothe gives the names of two judges, Dominic Sarsfield and Christopher Sibthorp, and the civil records confirm that both were judges of king's bench at this time.[76] The Catholic sources[77] show a special hostility to Sarsfield, one of them[78] even saying that the 'heretical judge', who is not named, had feigned illness and absented himself to avoid having to condemn a man he knew to be innocent. This seems very unlikely, but the special hostility to Sarsfield was real. The reason for it was that he was of Old English stock, and while Sibthorp as New English might be forgiven for actively supporting the government's religious policy, Sarsfield would not be similarly forgiven. He had in 1610 received a rather extraordinary patent promising him promotion to the post of chief justice of the court of common pleas on the death of the current incumbent as a reward for his services in supporting the political and religious programme of the crown,[79] and he did in fact get his appointment, though he had to wait until 1625.

All the Catholic sources agree that Sarsfield took the leading part in the trial, bullying and hectoring the accused in a way judges sometimes did in treason trials. Sibthorp by comparison is allotted a muted and minor role. This may reflect the special hostility to Sarsfield, but it may in fact be true, if only because Sarsfield was by appointment the senior of the two judges. All the sources are agreed on the substance of the proceedings, but are not in full agreement on the order of events. Because, as has been seen, the order of events in a treason trial was not rigidly fixed, it is impossible to establish it definitively in the case of this particular trial. It has already been suggested that *Martyrium Reverendissimi Cornelii Dovenii et Patritii Luchrani*[80] provides the most plausible framework, with perhaps one exception. This is the placing of the single most dramatic incident in the trial, when, in response to a claim, apparently by the priest, that ecclesiastics could not be judged by laymen, Sarsfield caustically commented that Pilate judged Christ, and the bishop replied that he was content to play the role Christ had played before Pilate. The above document places this incident *after* both the bishop and the priest, in that order, had responded to the charges against them, and says it was the occasion for the introduction of a new charge against the bishop.

76 *Liber Munerum Publicorum Hiberniae*, ed. Rowley Lascelles (2 vols, London, 1852), pt ii, 33. **77** *Martyrium Reverendissimi* (see note 40); O'Sullivan Beare, *Hist. Cath. Ibern.* **78** O'Sullivan Beare, *Hist. Cath. Ibern.* **79** *Liber Munerum Publicorum Hiberniae* (see note 76), pt ii, 36. **80** *Martyrium Reverendissimi* (see note 40).

However, three other accounts[81] present this exchange as arising out of the *bishop's* interrogation. O'Sullivan Beare, further, sets it in a framework in which the trials of the bishop and priest are conducted quite separately. Although cases are known of persons accused of treason being tried together even though they had asked to be tried separately, it seems on the whole more likely that in this case two separate trials were held, with a verdict given after each, possibly followed in each case by sentence, though both sentences may have been withheld until the end. In any case, the death sentence was mandatory after a conviction for treason.

The accounts of the trial make it clear that the central thrust of Conor O'Devany's defence was to insist that the real reason he was on trial was not because he had committed treason but because he was a Catholic bishop. In addition, he handled the details of the treason charge so skilfully that it is a reasonable inference that a good lawyer had been among those who had visited him in prison. While he would not have known the details of his indictment until it was read out in court, these details could be reasonably anticipated, and advice on the main lines of defence could be given even more easily. He began to show his legal skill when faced with the proposed jury.

It seems certain that both accused were brought into court together and both indictments read – sixteen counts of treason against the bishop, according to Rich,[82] though here he may be elaborating. The bishop, according to Fleming,[83] refused to answer unless he was addressed by his proper title, and the court agreed. This may have been so, or it may be a Catholic elaboration. The bishop formally pleaded not guilty. As he had already elected to be tried by jury, a jury was now proposed. It consisted of eleven English and Scots and one Irishman (twelve English and Scots, according to two accounts,[84] but this appears to be less likely). The bishop objected: such a jury was hostile; it was illegal, because an Irish jury had to be composed of Irish natives; and the proposed jurors had no competence to judge matters of religious allegiance. He further demanded to be tried in an ecclesiastical court because he was an ecclesiastic. When his objections were not allowed, he asked Sarsfield to try the case without a jury, once again arguing that this jury was incapable of assessing the facts. Sarsfield replied that if he were to judge the case his verdict would be guilty. The trial proceeded by jury.[85]

81 *Compendium Martyrii* (see note 60); *La Morte Gloriosa* (see note 35); O'Sullivan Beare, *Hist. Cath. Ibern.* 82 Barnaby Rich, *A Catholicke Conference* (see note 75). 83 Thomas Fleming, OFM, Dundalk, 25 April 1612 (see note 23). 84 *Compendium Martyrii* (see note 60); *La Morte Gloriosa* (see note 35). 85 *Compendium Martyrii*; *La Morte Gloriosa*; *Martyrium*

Rothe has a passing reference to a witness being called to prove the charges in the indictment, but the main part of the trial revolved on the bishop's answer to these charges. Some of the sources[86] place his answers before the empanelling of the jury, but two[87] place them after. Either is possible; it is also possible, and indeed quite likely, that he spoke twice in much the same sense. He admitted he had lived in the war zone during the war, but he had done so because it was the area of his pastoral care, which it was his strict duty to discharge, and he had confined himself to this duty. Even if what he had done could be construed as treason, all such offences had been pardoned by the general amnesty issued by James I. Sarsfield interjected that the benefits of this amnesty extended only to those who had taken the required oath and had got a certificate to show they had done so. The bishop replied that not one in ten of the laity had such a certificate. He added that it was unlawful for a Catholic to take the oath and that an ecclesiastic should not be required to appear in a secular court to take any oath. He repeated that all this showed was that he was being prosecuted not for treason but for his faith.

It was probably at this stage that Sarsfield made his caustic remark that Christ had appeared before a lay judge, Pilate. A new charge was now introduced, either by Sarsfield[88] or by a newly produced witness,[89] to the effect that the bishop had been a party to the 'Flight of the Earls'. Both sources strongly imply that the bishop made no answer to this charge and go to some pains to show that he could have rebutted it, having been many days' journey from the earls at the time of their flight. Rothe develops an argument that it was no treason to have been privy to the 'Flight of the Earls'. While this may in fact have been so, the new charge against the bishop was perilously close to the charge hanging over Patrick O'Loughran. One can only surmise about some compulsion on the part of the writers to show the bishop innocent of this charge which he himself seems not to have felt. In any case, he could prove his innocence only by calling witnesses, and this he was not allowed to do. The charge was not in his indictment, and the outcome of his trial could now be reasonably predicted. By far the most likely explanation of why he remained silent in the circumstances is that he deliberately chose to be silent, as Christ was silent before Pilate on the charge brought against him.

Reverendissimi (see note 40); Rothe, *De Processu Martyriali*; O'Sullivan Beare, *Hist. Cath. Ibern.* **86** *La Morte Gloriosa*; Rothe, *De Processu Martyriali*; O'Sullivan Beare, *Hist. Cath. Ibern.* **87** *Compendium Martyrii*; [Francis Fay], *Martyrium Reverendissimi.* **88** *Martyrium Reverendissimi.* **89** Rothe, *De Processu Martyriali*.

The jury retired briefly and returned with a verdict of guilty. Three sources agree that the one Irish juror did not consent to the verdict.[90] If this was so, the verdict was legally null, for the law required that it be unanimous.

Only two sources[91] give any real detail on the trial of Patrick O'Loughran. The charge against him, as is clear from their accounts of what happened in court, was that he had committed treason by joining O'Neill in his flight from Ireland. The sources do not agree on his response. One[92] simply states that he was not allowed to reply to the charge. The earliest detailed account[93] says he admitted that he went with O'Neill, because as his chaplain he could not desert his prince, and added that he had been to Rome and had knelt before the pope. He had never been involved in politics, he claimed: he had been no more than O'Neill's chaplain. This was no crime in Ireland, for O'Neill's right to the services of a chaplain had been recognized even after his surrender in 1603; and if it was no crime to be his chaplain in Ireland, it was certainly no crime to be his chaplain abroad. Neither was it a crime for a Catholic priest to leave Ireland. If he were to be executed, it would be for his religion. Sarsfield again intervened, saying that accompanying O'Neill in his flight was incompatible with the Oath of Allegiance. The priest replied by saying that ecclesiastics could not be bound by an oath administered in a civil court. The second detailed account of his reply to the charge[94] claims that he said he had gone abroad to pursue his studies. As already noted, these two accounts are not necessarily incompatible.

Whatever Patrick O'Loughran said must have been before he was confronted with the jury, clearly the same jury which had just found the bishop guilty. He refused to be tried by any jury, saying that the present jury would certainly find him guilty, while even a Catholic jury would be afraid to acquit him. Sarsfield then pronounced a verdict of guilty.

The mandatory sentence followed: the two convicted traitors were to be hanged, drawn, and quartered. Rothe records a tradition to the effect either that Sarsfield sentenced the bishop and Sibthorp the priest, or the other way around – which he does not know. It is most likely the Sarsfield as the senior judge pronounced both sentences, and this is implied in the other sources which advert to the matter.

---

90 Report on the state of Ireland (see note 37); Rothe, *De Processu Martyriali*; O'Sullivan Beare, *Hist. Cath. Ibern.* **91** *Martyrium Reverendissimi*; O'Sullivan Beare, *Hist. Cath. Ibern.* **92** *Compendium Martyrii* (see note 60). **93** *Martyrium Reverendissimi.* **94** O'Sullivan Beare, *Hist. Cath. Ibern.*

MARTYRDOM

Ten sources in all give details of the actual martyrdom.[95] They are in substantial agreement to an even greater extent than the accounts of the trial, with the exception of the account by the Protestant, Barnaby Rich. Rich, however, is manifestly trying to discredit Bishop O'Devany. Four Catholic sources may be singled out as presenting a particularly vivid and immediate picture. Two[96] have already been noted as claiming to be based on the testimony of eye-witnesses. The third[97] was written within three months of the executions by an Irish Franciscan. It was written from Dundalk, which is only fifty miles from Dublin. He does not claim explicitly to have his information from eyewitnesses, but he could have scarcely avoided meeting one or more who were. The fourth[98] was compiled by Irish Franciscans at Louvain from letters received from Ireland a short time after the martyrdom. The following account, then, will cite individual documents only when there is special reason to do so.

Execution normally followed swiftly on conviction, and the date appointed was 1 February. Both prisoners were taken to Dublin Castle and lodged in separate cells. Further attempts were made to get them to take the Oaths of Supremacy and Allegiance by offers of pardon and preferment: this would not have been unusual in the circumstances. It was still possible for brave and determined people to visit and comfort them. O'Sullivan Beare records what the bishop said to a woman visitor: that he had not felt better for ten years, and that his only concern had been that he would have been confined to prison to wear out in feebleness and old age. He asked her to see to it that he would be buried in his Franciscan habit, saying he esteemed it more than the insignia of a bishop.

The day of execution was dark and cloudy, as is common in Ireland at the beginning of February. Early in the afternoon the constable of the castle delivered the prisoners to the sheriff. Three sources[99] say or imply that this took place at about 4 p.m., but two others[1] more plausibly give 4 p.m. as

---

95 Barnaby Rich, *A Catholicke conference* (see note 75); Fleming, 25 April 1612 (see note 23); Report on the State of Ireland (see note 37); Memorandum by Richard Conway (see note 52); Annual letter for 1612 written by Christopher Holywood, SJ: Rome, ARSI, MSS Anglia, 41, f. 53v; *Compendium Martyrii* (see note 60); *La Morte Gloriosa* (see note 35); *Martyrium Reverendissimi* (see note 40); Rothe, *De Processu Martyriali*; O'Sullivan Beare, *Hist. Cath. Ibern.* **96** Memorandum by Richard Conway (see note 52); *Martyrium Reverendissimi* (see note 40). **97** Fleming, 25 April 1612 (see note 23). **98** *Compendium Martyrii* (see note 60). **99** *Martyrium Reverendissimi* (see note 40); Rothe, *De Processu Martyriali*; O'Sullivan Beare, *Hist. Cath. Ibern.* **1** *Compendium Martyrii* (see note 60); *La Morte Gloriosa* (see note 35).

the hour of the execution itself, 'one hour before sunset', which in Ireland at this time of year is about 5 p.m.

As was customary, the victims were drawn on carts to the place of execution, prone and face upwards. The bishop asked to make his last journey in his Franciscan habit, but was forced to wear other clothing over it.[2] Most of the sources recall his remark that he was being carried to his execution, while Christ had had to carry his cross.

The place of execution was across the river to the north of the city, on a little hill that Moran has plausibly identified with the place now called George's Hill.[3] It is rather less than a mile from Dublin Castle. As the procession went its way, ministers of the Established Church continued to urge the condemned men to change their minds. Huge crowds of Catholics accompanied them. They came from the city and elsewhere, and included some who up to this had been afraid to confess their faith. Some of the sources give estimates of actual numbers. Such estimates are by nature unreliable and prone to exaggeration, but it may be accepted that at least by the time the gallows was reached the crowd numbered several thousand. At one stage, it looked as if they might try to rescue the prisoners from soldiers guarding them, but the bishop begged them not to. He blessed them with his bound hands, and exhorted them and his fellow-prisoner to be constant in the Catholic faith (Rich[4] says he remained silent, but this is contradicted by all the other sources).

The procession made its way to the gallows. The public executioner, an Irishman, had fled rather than carry out the sentence, and only an Englishman in jail for murder could be induced to act as executioner, in return for a promise that his life would be spared. Three sources[5] agree that this substitution had to be made on the very day of the execution, and one[6] asserts that the discovery that there was no hangman was made only when the gallows was reached.

When they arrived at the gallows the prisoners dismounted from their carts and knelt to pray. The crowd may have again threatened a rescue,[7] but the sheriff, backed by soldiers, ordered the prisoners to approach the gallows. The bishop had now taken off his cloak, and appeared in his Franciscan habit. It was probably at this stage that he gave his Franciscan cowl to the woman who had comforted him in prison a day or two

2 *Compendium Martyrii*; *Martyrium Reverendissimi*; O'Sullivan Beare, *Hist. Cath. Ibern.*
3 Moran, *Analecta*, cv. 4 See note 75. 5 *Martyrium Reverendissimi* (see note 40); Rothe, *De Processu Martyriali*; O'Sullivan Beare, *Hist. Cath. Ibern.* 6 *Martyrium Reverendissimi*.
7 Report on the state of Ireland (see note 37).

before.[8] He asked that the priest be executed first, fearing that the horror of the scene might shake his resolution but this was refused. The priest urged the bishop to go first, promising to follow him, and saying that it was unfitting for a bishop to die without a chaplain to attend him.

The bishop began to mount the steps of the scaffold, praying as he did so, and a great cry arose from the crowd. Even at this stage he was still being offered pardon and preferment if he would confess his treason and take the prescribed oaths. Promises of preferment were made by Protestant ministers; one of them, named Luke Chalenor,[9] asked him, in the name of the lord deputy, to confess his treason. The bishop replied that he was being put to death for his faith and not for treason, and recalled the rewards he had already been offered if he would take the Oath of Supremacy. He refused to pray with Chalenor. These exchanges took place in Latin. He attempted to address the crowd in Irish, but was not allowed to do so.

It was when he reached the top step of the gallows that his prayers seem to have been turned into a kind of address to the crowd. He prayed for all who were there, for the Catholics of Dublin and Ireland, urging them all to persevere in their faith. He prayed for all heretics and for their reunion with the Church and forgave his persecutors. Some sources say an attempt was made to stop him,[10] and this is quite likely, for speeches from the gallows were only allowed if their content was acceptable.

The hangman asked his pardon for what he was about to do; this was a fairly common gesture of courtesy before the grisly task. The bishop kissed the rope and placed it round his neck; he drew the veil over his face and held out his hands to be bound.[11] At this stage there occurred a dramatic incident recorded by almost all sources. It had been a dark, gloomy day, and it was now near sunset. As the bishop stood on the scaffold the sun broke through the clouds, and the scene was bathed in its red light for a moment until the hanging had taken place, when the clouds closed in again.

After the hanging came the disembowelling. The hangman then cut off the bishop's head and held it up with the ritual words 'Behold the head of a traitor'. He then put it aside while he quartered the body. When he turned back it was gone, and it was not found despite a large reward offered by the lord deputy. The crowd then surged forward seeking relics of the martyr's

8 *Compendium Martyrii* (see note 60); *Martyrium Reverendissimi* (see note 40); O'Sullivan Beare, *Hist. Cath. Ibern.* **9** Lynch, *De Praesulibus Hib.*, i, 230 (written in 1672), is the first Catholic source to give his Christian name. Luke Chalenor, formerly a fellow of a Cambridge college, was one of the first fellows of Trinity College, Dublin, founded in 1592; see Phillips, *Ch. of Ire.*, ii, 449, 451). **10** *Compendium Martyrii*; *Martyrium Reverendissimi*. **11** *Compendium Martyrii* (see note 60).

flesh and clothing, seizing even the cloak he had worn over his Franciscan habit (which a soldier named Robert Dinel had bought from the hangman) with an excess of zeal that the Franciscan Thomas Fleming[12] thought disedifying. Beneath his clothing the bishop had been wearing a hairshirt. The Protestant Rich[13] claimed that they even cut up the executioner's cloak for relics (he would naturally have taken it off beforehand). This may be a sneer at popish superstition, but it may well have happened.

Now it was the turn of the priest Patrick O'Loughran. There had been some fears – and hopes – that he might yield, especially if he had to witness the bishop's execution, for he was temperamentally a timid man, but he was steeled by the bishop's example. He mounted the scaffold reciting the canticle *Nunc dimittis*. He too seems to have tried to address the crowd and to have been prevented, but like the bishop he seems to have been able to deliver from the scaffold a prayer and blessing that turned into something like an address.[14] When his execution was over the crowd again surged forward seeking relics. This time the soldiers were better prepared, and some people were injured, but some did succeed in soaking clothes in his blood.[15]

It was now almost sunset, and it was decided to mount a guard over the remains instead of burying them immediately.[16] Some of the crowd remained to spend the night in prayer and what Rich calls 'heathenish howling' and 'popish ceremonies', no doubt the traditional rites of vigil for the dead. The remains were buried next day at the site of the gallows, where crowds continued to linger.[17] It was the Feast of the Purification and also a Sunday, but Rich's statement that many priests came and said Mass would appear unlikely, or at least exaggerated. The following night twelve young Catholic men disinterred the remains and gave them honourable burial.[18] Where they were buried was naturally a closely guarded secret. Of the accounts which explicitly claim to be based on eyewitnesses, one[19] deliberately does not name the place; the other[20] says cryptically 'with other martyrs' (*con otros marteres*). The eyewitness whose account is embodied in this second document claimed to have been one of the twelve youths who

12 Fleming, 25 April 1612 (see note 23). 13 Barnaby Rich, *A Catholicke Conference* (see note 75). 14 Memorandum by Richard Conway (see note 52); O'Sullivan Beare, *Hist. Cath. Ibern.* 15 Memorandum by Richard Conway; *La Morte Gloriosa* (see note 35). 16 *Compendium Martyrii* (see note 60); *Martyrium Reverendissimi* (see note 40); *La Morte Gloriosa.* 17 Memorandum by Richard Conway. 18 Memorandum by Richard Conway; *La Morte Gloriosa*; *Martyrium Reverendissimi* (see note 40); Mooney, *De Provincia Hiberniae* (see note 37); O'Sullivan Beare, *Hist. Cath. Ibern.* 19 *Martyrium Reverendissimi.* 120 Memorandum by Richard Conway (see note 52).

carried out the re-internment. It may have been in St Kevin's churchyard, where Dermot O'Hurley had been buried.[21] Mooney says it was in the church of St James at Kilmainham near Dublin, while O'Sullivan Beare says it was in a church where Protestant worship had not yet been held, but he does not name it. There were good reasons for keeping their final resting-place secret, and it remains unknown.

MOTIVE FOR MARTYRDOM

Lord Deputy Chichester had been advised from London that in order to terrify Catholics into submission in the coming parliament he might proceed against some Catholic bishops, provided it could be made clear they were not being punished for religious reasons. This inevitably suggested a charge of treason (it was also the only charge which carried the death penalty). Conor O'Devany became the victim because he was a Catholic bishop and a government prisoner. But the unreality of the charge of treason was clear from the time it was made until his death on the scaffold. He was put to death for the Catholic faith. His executioners knew it and he knew it.

One Catholic witness, Peter Lombard, *might* seem to have some reservations, but what he says must be read in context. Lombard was writing about politics, not about martyrs. In 1612, he was trying to convince Pope Paul V that Catholic bishops might be safely appointed in Ireland provided the government could not accuse them of any connection with O'Neill, and he used the news of the martyrdom he had just received as an example to bolster his argument.[22] Ironically, when writing about 1600 in support of O'Neill's war, he had dismissed Conor O'Devany as a good man but too ingenuous to be of any great help.

Patrick O'Loughran was certainly a chaplain in Hugh O'Neill's household. The charge against him, in so far as it can be reconstructed from the accounts of the trial, was that he had committed treason by joining O'Neill in his flight. The substance of his answer was that as O'Neill's chaplain it was his duty to be with his lord.[23]

In any case, the act of leaving Ireland could not in and by itself be construed as treasonous. In mid-December 1607, a few months after the

---

21 *La Morte Gloriosa.*   **22** Memorandum presented by Peter Lombard (see note 39).
23 *Martyrium Reverendissimi.*

Flight of the Earls, judges were sent to Ulster to empanel a grand jury to indict the fugitive nobility on a charge of treason. As was normal, they brought with them the evidence to present to the jury, to the effect that the fugitives had conspired to take Dublin Castle and other forts, to kill the lord deputy and council, to foment a new rebellion, and to bring in foreign forces to help them; and that they had committed 'divers rebellious acts' immediately before their departure, and had departed with the intention of returning with a foreign force to invade the realm.[24] The indictment was duly found, and the fugitives were then proclaimed traitors.

There is no trace of this in the trial of Patrick O'Loughran. Neither is there any reference to his having assisted O'Neill during the war. These things bore no relationship to the real reason for putting him on trial. The purpose of the trial was to cow the Catholic body in preparation for the coming parliament. The bishop was put on trial because he was a bishop and in prison. O'Loughran was singled out from the priests held in prison because his connection with O'Neill gave some plausibility to the necessary charge of treason.

FAMA MARTYRII

The government's plan misfired. As the documentation makes clear, what the martyrdom did was to stiffen the resolve of the Irish Catholics: in the words of the latest historian of the period, 'O'Devany's death was an event of unexpected importance in the Counter-Reformation in Ireland.'[25] Its essential importance lay in the extent to which it brought together the Old Irish and the Old English Catholics, groups of quite different historical experience and with interests other than religion still in many respects widely divergent. Though persecution was stepped up, and though they were reduced to a minority in parliament, the penal legislation finally proposed was much less draconian than the Catholics had feared, and in fact none of it was enacted.

Within a few days of the execution, the lord deputy was writing to Lord High Treasurer Cecil in England that 'a Tytularie Byshope and a priest beinge lately executed here for Treason meerly, are ... thought Marters, and adored for Saynts',[26] and the very anti-Catholic Barnaby Rich confirmed

24 Chichester and council to the king, *Cal. S.P. Ire., 1606–8*, 342. The document is undated, but it states that the judges set out 'about ten days before Christmas'.   25 Aidan Clarke in *NHI*, iii, 209.   26 Lord Deputy Chichester to Lord High Treasurer Cecil, 6 February

this in his book published in 1612. On 5 March 1612, David Rothe was writing of the bishop's death in the context of a general persecution. Accounts of the martyrs written by Irish Catholics multiplied rapidly. The Jesuit Henry Fitzsimon simply lists Conor O'Devany in his *Catalogus Praecipuorum Sanctorum Hiberniae*, published at Liège in 1619. In the consistorial record of the appointment of Edmund Dungan of Down and Connor in 1625, the see is noted as vacant *'per obitum bonae memoriae fratris Cornelii Duensis, ob fidem Catholicam archbishop haereticis obtruncati'*.[27]

Accounts in French and Spanish are known to have been published in 1614, but as these have not been traced it is impossible to say if they were written by Irishmen. It was probably an Irishman, the Franciscan Luke Wadding, who was most instrumental in bringing the martyrdom of Bishop Conor O'Devany to the notice of the Catholic world, and especially to the Franciscan Order.[28] (The priest Patrick O'Loughran rather inevitably tended to be less well remembered.) Later Franciscan martyrologists kept the bishop's memory alive – the Frenchman Arthur Monstier (1638) and the Spaniard Juan de San Antonio (1732).[29]

In the later seventeenth century, O'Devany's martyrdom was recorded by the Irish writers Bruodin (1669) and Lynch (1672).[30] After the papal period of silence the story was taken up again in the nineteenth century by Matthew Kelly, Patrick J. Moran, Myles O'Reilly, James O'Laverty, Denis Murphy and others.[31]

Many people treasured relics of Conor O'Devany; indeed, the Franciscan Thomas Fleming frowned on what he regarded as excessive zeal in this regard. Within six years of the martyrdom, two Irishmen, John Curtis and Malachy O'Shiel, who appear to have been priests, arrived at the Franciscan friary of the Aracoeli in Rome. They brought with them what they claimed was a rib taken from the martyred bishop, towards whom they professed great reverence and devotion. They asked the friars to preserve the relic in the sacristy of the Aracoeli, and they agreed, when the Irishmen had signed a sworn testimony to the facts they had alleged. This document, dated 30

1612: London, PRO, S.P., 63/232/8; printed in O'Laverty, *Dioc. Down and Connor*, v, 375 (see note 13).   **27** Brady, *Ep. Succ.*, i, 269.   **28** *Ann. Min.*, ad an. 1271, no. XV.   **29** Arthur Monstier, *Martyrologium Franciscanum* (Paris, 1638), 40; Juan de San Antonio, *Bibliotheca Universa Franciscana* (3 vols, Madrid, 1732–3), i, 279.   **30** [Anthony Bruodin], *Propugnaculum Catholicae Veritatis* (Prague, 1669), 498.; Lynch, *De Praesulibus Hib.*, i, 228–31.   **31** Kelly edited O'Sullivan Beare's *Hist. Cath. Ibern.* (1850), and Moran edited Rothe's *Analecta* (1884). See also Moran, *Spicil. Ossor.* (1874–84), and *Hist. Cath. Abps.*, i (Dublin, 1864); Myles O'Reilly, *Memorials of those who suffered for the Catholic faith in Ireland* (London, 1868), 163–80; O'Laverty, *Dioc. Down and Connor*, v (1895) (see note 13); Denis Murphy, *Our martyrs* (Dublin, 1896), 238–57.

November 1617, was countersigned by the Guardian, Father Francis, who added a statement to the effect that he had ordered the relic to be kept with due honour in the sacristy of the Aracoeli and that the two Irishmen had said that the bishop had been quartered. This document was preserved in the Franciscan provincial archives in the Aracoeli. It was presented to the Irish Franciscan province in 1983, and is now in the Franciscan Library, Killiney, County Dublin.[32] Ten years later, the Irish Franciscan historian Luke Wadding mentioned in his *Annales Minorum* that he had seen this relic,[33] but an exhaustive search for it in 1983 was unsuccessful. Another relic of the martyred bishop was brought to Rome shortly after his martyrdom, probably by a Jesuit, but it too has been lost. It was preserved at the Gesù, where it was shown to Patrick F. Moran when he was vice-rector of the Irish College, Rome, between 1855 and 1866. It was a piece of linen tinged with blood enclosed in a fold of paper with the inscription '*Ex sanguine Cornelii Episcopi Dunensis et Conorensis*'.[34]

Dionisio Massari, dean of Fermo, later to become the Secretary of the Sacred Congregation *de Propaganda Fide*, wrote an account of the time he spent in Ireland while he was there as auditor to the papal nuncio, Archbishop Rinuccini. It is in the form of a diary covering the years 1645 to 1647. While he does not date the incidents he records, the context allows this one to be placed in the early spring of 1646, probably at the beginning of March. He had spent the night as guest of Robert Nugent and his wife at Carlanstown, County Westmeath. Before he left the following morning they showed him the head of the martyred bishop, with, he wrote, 'the eyes, skin and hair still fresh as if the head been severed from the shoulders that very hour'.[35]

It was soon being claimed that many miracles had been worked through the intercession of the martyrs, and in particular of Conor O'Devany,[36] but only one has been recorded. On the evening of the execution, a gentleman with a paralysed arm bribed the guards to allow him to spend the night in vigil. In the morning his arm was healed. Two accounts[37] also treat as miraculous an event that happened the day after the execution. Two daughters of a Protestant, Edward Brabstone, went in their carriage to the gallows and 'reviled the martyrs and those who were venerating them'. Their horses

32 FLK, MS D 23, no. 3. It refers to the Irishmen as *domini* and to Curtis as *pater*. They have not been further identified.   33 *Ann. Min.*, ad an. 1251, no. LVII.   34 Moran, *Analecta*, cvi.   35 APF, Miscellanee Varie, 9, 127: English translation in *Cath. Bull.* 7 (1917), 114. 36 Memorandum by Richard Conway (see note 52); *Compendium Martyrii* (see note 60); *La Morte Gloriosa* (see note 35); *Martyrium Reverendissimi* (see note 40); O'Sullivan Beare, *Hist. Cath. Ibern.*   37 *Martyrium Reverendissimi*; O'Sullivan Beare, *Hist. Cath. Ibern.*

suddenly bolted and overturned the carriage. The coachman was thrown out and his arm was broken, while the face of the daughter who had been 'more impudent about the saints' was disfigured. Whatever may be thought of this story, of its truth, its miraculous character or even its edifying nature, it certainly reflects contemporary opinion that Conor O'Devany and Patrick O'Loughran had died as martyrs for the Catholic faith.

When the Ordinary Process *de fama martyrii* was held in Dublin in 1904 for the Irish martyrs of the sixteenth and seventeenth centuries, their reputation for martyrdom was examined and approved. It was then forwarded to the Holy See with the other findings of that tribunal. In due course the General Promoter of the Faith gave his verdict on their cause. Having reviewed the evidence, he concluded (*Disquisitio*, 156):

> *Quare, quum, nec de Famulorum Dei caede neque de causa caedis dubitandi esse locus videatur, optimam causam sacrorum rituum Congregationi committi posse existimo.*

In February 1915, Conor O'Devany and Patrick O'Loughran were included among the martyrs for the introduction of whose cause authorization was granted. Accordingly their cause was examined at the Apostolic Process held in Dublin between 1917 and 1930. The findings were then presented to the Holy See.

CHAPTER 9

Francis Taylor

Colm Lennon*

EARLY LIFE

The principal source for the consideration of Francis Taylor as a martyr is the work published in Paris in 1629 by an Irishman, John Mullan (Joannes Molanus). This comprises, firstly, *Idea Togatae Constantiae*, a rhetorical but scantily detailed account of Francis Taylor's life and death;[1] secondly, *Epitome Tripartita Martyrum*, a list of Catholics including Francis Taylor who underwent persecution in Britain and Ireland;[2] and finally (only in some copies), two testimonial letters from leading Catholic clergymen familiar with Irish affairs, giving the established facts about Francis Taylor's imprisonment.[3] The portrait provided by these elements may be developed by reference to external independent records, which also provide a context for the study of Francis Taylor's career.

The family into which Francis Taylor was born c.1550[4] was prominent in the political and economic life of Dublin city and county. The principal seat of the Taylors was at Swords, a town seven miles to the north of the municipality. Their importance among the gentry of north County Dublin is attested to by the fact that Ortelius inscribed the family name at Swords on his map of Ireland in *Additamentum Theatri Orbis Terrarum* (1573). Generations of Francis Taylor's ancestors had been active in administrative and commercial circles in Dublin up to the mid-sixteenth century. They had intermarried with other leading official and mercantile families of the region,[5] and bearers of the Taylor name were to retain the influential position of the family well into the seventeenth century.[6]

---

* I am very grateful to Monsignor Patrick J. Corish for making available to me his commentary on the background to Francis Taylor's imprisonment. **1** Mullan, *Idea Tog.*, 338. **2** Mullan, *Epitome Tripartita*, 96. **3** Thomas Fleming, archbishop of Dublin, and the Reverends Luke Rochford, Patrick Cahill, Dominic Nugent and Henry Cusack, Dublin, 17 August 1630, and from Reverend Thomas Mede, Paris, 4 May 1631, to John Mullan: Mullan, *Idea Tog.*, addendum. **4** While the date of his birth is not recorded, it may be placed around 1550, as later references show that he was an old man at the time of his death in 1621. **5** See John D'Alton, *The history of the county of Dublin* (Dublin, 1838), 136, 146–50. **6** In the

Francis was the second son of Robert Taylor of Swords and his wife, Elizabeth Golding.[7] Mullan refers to the brother of Francis named Walter who became an accomplished scholar and priest on the continent and who was reprieved from sentence of death for his missionary activities in England in the early 1580s.[8] Francis married Gennet, daughter of Thomas Shelton, a leading merchant of Dublin.[9] They had six children: Thomas, who became active like his father in municipal affairs,[10] George, Walter, James, Robert and Mary, wife to Matthew Field of Corduff in County Dublin.[11]

The civic affairs of Dublin may be traced in detail in the 'assembly rolls', i.e. the minutes of the common council of the guilds, the assembly representing the corporation of Dublin.[12] These records show that Francis Taylor followed family traditions in serving the civic community for a period of twenty-seven years. He began by being chosen as one of the two city sheriffs in 1586,[13] occupied the offices of city treasurer and auditor on numerous occasions,[14] and reached the zenith of his career in 1595 with his election as mayor of Dublin.[15] In addition to these appointments, Alderman Taylor was entrusted with many administrative tasks involving the welfare of the citizens. These included his election as one of two city agents who travelled to the English court in 1597 to represent city interests before the monarch and privy council.[16]

During the latter part of Francis Taylor's civic career, the smooth running of the administration of the municipality, the autonomy of which was embodied in the ancient city charters, was threatened. The events which caused this to happen also led directly to Francis Taylor's personal predicament.

By and large, the Dublin merchant aristocracy supported the Reformation in the reign of Henry VIII, from a combination of loyalty to

1630 visitation of Dublin by Archbishop Bulkeley, reference is made to Michael Taylor of Swords as a protector of priests whose house was used for Mass (see M. V. Ronan (ed.), 'Archbishop Bulkeley's Visitation of Dublin, 1630', in *Archiv. Hib* 8 (1941), 63). **7** 'A visitation begonne in the cittie of Dublin by Daniell Molyneux, Esquire, otherwise called Ulster King of Arms and Principall Herald of all Ireland, in the yeare of grace one thousand six hundreth and seven.' Dublin, Genealogical Office, MS 47, 23 [hereafter, Visitation of Molyneux]. **8** Mullan, *Epitome Tripartita*, 75. **9** Visitation of Molyneux. **10** *Anc. Rec. Dublin*, ii, 295. See note 12. **11** Visitation of Molyneux. **12** Sir John T. Gilbert and Lady Gilbert have edited and published the rolls as *Calendar of ancient records of Dublin in the possession of the municipal corporation* (19 vols, Dublin, 1889–1944). The relevant volumes are ii and iii (Dublin, 1891, 1892). **13** *Anc. Rec. Dublin.*, ibid., ii, 202. **14** Ibid., ii, 217, 227, 265, 298, 321, 448, 465, 483, 534; iii, 11, 28. **15** Ibid., ii, 283. **16** Minute Book of the Corporation of Dublin, known as the 'Friday Book', 1567–1611: Dublin, Corporation Archives, MS MR/17, ff 35r, 116r; printed in *RIA Proc.*, sect. C, xxx (1912–13), 490, 513.

the crown and incipient humanist influence.[17] Tensions arose, however, when it became clear that this loyalty might not receive political reward and that the proposed measures for religion involved real changes in belief and worship. These tensions began to manifest themselves as early as the reign of Edward VI (1547–53) and developed considerably during the first deputyship of Sir Henry Sidney (1565–71) in the reign of Elizabeth I (1558–1603).[18] The dilemma of Dubliners and other politically loyal towns-people was aggravated by the papal Bull of Excommunication of Elizabeth in 1570, which released her Catholic subjects from allegiance to her and thereby rendered them liable to be considered traitors in government eyes. In these circumstances the group of newly arrived English officials and settlers, Protestant in religion, came to appear to be the only reliable and loyal element among the Irish population.

Pressure on the towns eased in the last decade of the reign of Elizabeth I because it was necessary to conciliate them while the government was engaged in the last great struggle against Gaelic Ireland, the Nine Years War, in which Hugh O'Neill posed as the champion of Catholic Ireland. Despite the aid given by the townspeople to the war effort against O'Neill, suspicions about their true loyalties abounded, especially as the beginnings of an effective Counter-Reformation mission among them coincided with the later years of the war.[19]

At the end of the war in 1603, the Catholics, or 'recusants' as the government called them, came under pressure from several quarters. There were attempts to limit the powers of self-government contained in the ancient town charters, and to remove Catholics from controlling positions in the town councils, by insisting that holders of public offices take the Oath of Supremacy as prescribed by statute in 1560, and by imposing fines for non-attendance at the services of the Established Church, as laid down by the Act of Uniformity of the same year. As the fine of 12 pence for every Sunday missed did not provide a deterrent for wealthy men, the government devised a method for enforcing the law effectively. In the reign of James I (1603–25), recusants began to be summoned before the prerogative

---

17 See Brendan Bradshaw, *Ir. Const. Rev.*, 154–9. 18 The latest contribution to an under-standing of these developments are Brendan Bradshaw, 'Sword, Word and Strategy in the Reformation in Ireland', in *Hist. Jn.* 21 (1978), 475–502; N. P. Canny, 'Why the Reformation failed in Ireland: *une question mal posée*', in *JEH* 30 (1979), 423–50; Colm Lennon, *Richard Stanihurst the Dubliner, 1547–1618* (Dublin, 1981), 27–34. 19 See, for example, the suspicions expressed by Fynes Moryson, an English official in Ireland during the Nine Years War, in C. Litton Falkiner, *Illustrations of Irish history and topography, mainly of the seventeenth century* (London, 1904), 253–63.

court of castle chamber, an institution not bound by the prescription of statute law or the procedures of common law.[20] It could not impose the death penalty, but could exact more or less what fines the king wished, and condemn men to indefinite imprisonment 'during pleasure'.[21]

The situation in Dublin in the first decade of James' reign was tense as manifestations of widespread recusancy determined the government on a course of more severe repression. It was important that Dublin as the centre of the realm should be seen to be conformable to royal policies in religion.[22] An English observer of the Dublin scene, who had been resident in the city for several years, wrote in 1610 that not more than a tenth of the population there were adherents of the State religion.[23] The recusant majority carried out their worship openly, and in his eyes the civic government was hindered by the fact that the governors of the city were predominantly Catholic and tended to favour their co-religionists in fiscal and other matters. Arguing that political loyalty was incompatible with allegiance to the papacy, this unofficial source was moved to question the operation of the city's charter.[24]

The government's response can be monitored in a number of records, including those of the court of castle chamber, the city assembly, and others emanating from the Catholic side.[25] In a twofold attack, more than twenty aldermen and wealthy citizens of Dublin were fined heavily and condemned to imprisonment during pleasure for recusancy.[26] Francis Taylor was not among them. Also the subscription by civic office-holders to the Oath of Supremacy came to be insisted upon more and more. Several mayors and sheriffs-elect were debarred from taking up office because they refused the oath. These included John Shelton, Francis Taylor's brother-in-law, selected as mayor in 1604.[27] In the crucial year of 1613 several senior recusant aldermen were 'overleaped' by a young and inexperienced councillor who became mayor of the city by default.[28]

---

20 See Herbert Wood, 'The court of castle chamber', in *RIA Proc.*, sect. C, xxxii (1913–16), 152–70. **21** The first volume of the proceedings of the court, covering the years 1573–1620, was preserved by the happy accident of its having been treated as private property and removed by a government official; it is printed in *HMC Rep. Egmont MSS*, i, 1–60. **22** See *Cal. S.P. Ire., 1603–6*, 306. **23** Barnaby Rich, *A new description of Ireland* (London, 1610), 60. **24** Ibid., 62–9. **25** For examples of the latter, see Archbishop Lombard's long report to Cardinal Aldobrandini (*c.* 1617) on the problem of conscience facing recusants in Ireland: AV, Fondo Borghese, series III, 124C, ff 93–113, printed in John Hagan (ed.), 'Miscellanea Vaticano-Hibernica, 1580–1631', in *Archiv. Hib.* 3 (1914), 324–59; Reginald Walsh (ed.), 'Persecution of Catholics in Drogheda, in 1606, 1607 and 1611', in *Archiv. Hib.* 6 (1917), 64–8; John Meagher (ed.), 'Presentments of recusants in Dublin, 1617–18', in *Reportorium Novum* 2 (1957–60), 269–73. **26** *HMC Rep. Egmont MSS*, i, 30–2. **27** *Anc. Rec. Dublin*, ii, 430–2. **28** Lodge, *Desiderata*, i, 285.

ARREST AND IMPRISONMENT

Against this background the government was preparing to summon a parliament. By now the parties in Ireland were clearly defined. One was the 'Old English', Catholic in religion, comprising the townspeople and others who were for the most part descendants of settlers in Ireland in pre-Reformation times. The second was the 'New English', Protestant in religion, and by origin for the most part those who had arrived in Ireland since the Reformation in the 1530s. The third was the 'Old Irish', Catholic in religion, in numbers the greater part of the population but not having political weight commensurate with these numbers. Traditionally the Old English had had a majority in parliament, but the last Irish parliament had been convened as far back as 1585, and much had changed since then. Nevertheless, they still possessed so much property that they seemed to have good assurance of retaining their majority which, in the circumstances of the early seventeenth century, was necessary if they were to be an effective opposition. This the government determined to prevent if at all possible; and if a majority could not be denied them, the government was determined that this majority should be too cowed to offer opposition. Bishop O'Devany had been put to death in order to cow the Old English. In the event, his execution had had precisely the opposite effect.

There was no statutory requirement that members of parliament take the Oath of Supremacy, but at this juncture there were official hints that those elected would be expected to do so. In fact no legislation compelling them to take this oath was introduced. The government instead concentrated on attempting to secure a majority of the members returned. New boroughs were created in planted areas that could be trusted to return Protestants. The persecution of recusant office-holders was stepped up, the government hoping by this to ensure that any Catholics returned to Parliament would be of the compliant type. Inevitably there were a number of bitterly contested elections, leading to a petition to the king alleging many irregularities, the setting up of a royal commission to investigate them, and the report of the commission.[29]

The civic community of Dublin, which was entitled to return two members, made its own preparations for the meeting of parliament. In 1610, a subcommittee of the aldermen was established to discuss what measures needed to be passed in parliament for the good of the city.[30] Francis Taylor

---

29 These documents are printed in *Cal. S.P. Ire., 1611–14*, 359–64, 436–55. **30** See note 16.

was a member of this subcommittee, which met twice weekly. It was intended that eventually parliamentary bills would be drafted and submitted to the English government before the meeting of the full legislative assembly. Obviously, the aldermen knew that an opportunity would be afforded the city's members to speak out on behalf of the citizens who were becoming increasingly conscious of the encroachment of central government on their civic privileges and religious beliefs. A contemporary chronicler was convinced that the Dublin community had no intention of choosing as member of parliament anyone who was not an 'open recusant'.[31]

The writ authorising the holding of the election was directed to the sheriffs of Dublin in 1613.[32] Although of Old Irish stock, the mayor had conformed to the State religion. The majority of the guild freemen, the electors, were Catholic, as were the two sheriffs. The Catholic freemen persuaded the sheriffs to hold an election in the absence of the mayor. Two Catholic aldermen were elected, one of them being Francis Taylor. When the mayor returned to Dublin he declared the election invalid, and held another one, at which he declared two Protestants elected.[33] For the Catholic side it was argued that the first election was valid; that even if it was invalid, the second was also invalid; and that if the second was validly held, the majority there had been for the Catholic candidates.[34] The position in law and in fact was so uncertain that the royal commission inquiring into the electoral malpractice did not pronounce a verdict. By this time the issue had been decided for all practical purposes. The Protestant members were sitting in parliament, and several Catholic citizens had been imprisoned.

At about this time, and quite certainly in connection with these events, Francis Taylor was imprisoned. There is, however, no reference to Francis Taylor in the records of the court of castle chamber – and, as already noted, this record is not a transcript, but the original.[35] An explanation may be sought as follows: he could have been fined and imprisoned by a purely

---

31 William Farmer's 'Chronicle of Lord Chichester's government of Ireland ... for the years 1612–15', in Lodge, *Desiderata*, i, 156. **32** Printed in *Commons' Jn. Ire., 1613–66*, 6. **33** Petition delivered by the recusant party's agents to the king, May 1613: London, PRO, S.P., 63/232/11–12; calendared in *Cal. S.P. Ire., 1611–14*, 360–1, 362. Documents of the Commission to Examine the Abuses in Parliament and Country, August-November 1613; calendared in *Cal. S.P. Ire., 1611–14*, 436–8, 441–2, 445. See also Farmer's 'Chronicle', in Lodge, *Desiderata*, i, 155–8. **34** Documents of the Commission to Examine the Abuses in Parliament and Country, August-November 1613; calendared in *Cal. S.P. Ire., 1611–14*, 436–8, 441–2, 445. **35** See note 21.

administrative act of the lord deputy, something which would have been quite possible, especially in the circumstances of the time. Certainly, prominent citizens were imprisoned by the lord deputy in April 1613. One of these was told to prepare himself for execution.[36] There is no record of these penalties in the published sentences of the court of castle chamber. These entries have a possibly significant gap between 14 May 1613 and 11 February 1614. The recusants' petition was presented in May 1613, and the royal commissioners reported on 12 November. During these months any action considered to be administratively necessary might also have been judged better not recorded even in the files of the court of castle chamber.

There might have been special problems in the case of Francis Taylor because he held no office for which he was legally bound to take the Oath of Supremacy, though the records of castle chamber show that the court was not always strictly scrupulous on this point, and it was always possible to proceed against him under the Act of Uniformity. To sum up, the silence of the court records, especially at this time, is in no way incompatible with Francis Taylor having been heavily fined and imprisoned at the king's pleasure, almost certainly some time between May 1613 and February 1614.

Francis Taylor's arrest and imprisonment are attested to in Mullan's publication of 1629.[37] Although he himself may have had limited information about the events, perhaps no more than is contained in his brief sketch in *Epitome Tripartita Martyrum*, he seems to have sought further information from impeccable Catholic sources in the diocese of Dublin. The two letters from leading clergymen who were in a position to be well informed affirm that Francis Taylor had been in prison for seven years at the time of his death on 30 January 1621.[38] Mullan gives no date for the committal to prison of Francis Taylor in *Idea Togatae Constantiae*, but in the brief entry on Taylor in *Epitome Tripartita Martyrum* he refers vaguely to his death as having taken place *post Olympiadem*. John Lynch, who based his brief account of Francis Taylor on Mullan's *Idea Togatae Constantiae*, relates his arrest to the round-up of recusants in Dublin in 1616 and therefore states that his death took place after five years' captivity.[39] Of all these sources, the testimony of the Catholic clergy to whom Mullan applied for information is probably the most authoritative.

---

36 Petition to the King (see note 33). 37 Mullan, *Epitome Tripartita*. 38 See note 3.
39 John Lynch, *Alithinologia sive veridica responsio ad invectivam mendaciis, falaciis, calumniis, et imposturis foetam in plurimos antistites, proceres, et omnis ordinis Hibernos a R.P.R. ... F. ... C. ... Congregationi de Propaganda Fide, Anno Domini 1659 exhibitam* (Saint-Malo, 1664), 13.

MARTYRDOM

Conditions in prison were such as to constitute a sentence of slow death for an old man of gentle birth. Francis Taylor endured them for at least five years, possibly seven, until he died on 30 January 1621[40] 'from old age and the distresses and hardships of imprisonment'.[41] His will was drawn up on 4 January 1621 and witnessed by his sons George and Robert.[42] In it he expressed his wish that he be buried in the parish church of St Audoen, Dublin, in the place where his parents had been interred. He provided that his wife would have an income and accommodation, and made his son Thomas his heir and principal legatee of his lands and tenements. The sum of 40 shillings was to be laid aside for 'poor people', 'in way of devotion for my soules health'.[43] After his death, according to Mullan, Francis Taylor's sons were granted permission after long importunity to take their father's body and bury it with suitable funeral rites.[44]

MOTIVE FOR MARTYRDOM

It is universally agreed by all the commentators referred to that Francis Taylor suffered imprisonment and death because of his strong attachment to the Catholic faith. Mullan's *Idea Togatae Constantiae* contains in its very title the notion of the destruction of a patrician figure because of his defence of Catholicism.[45] In the text, Mullan indicates that Francis Taylor was well known as a protector of priests and that this was one of the reasons for his being persecuted.[46] Both he and the clerical testators assert that he was put into prison *pro fidei confessione*,[47] having suffered much at the hands of 'the enemies of the Catholic church'.[48] John Lynch associates Francis Taylor with the large group of recusants imprisoned for refusing the Oath of Supremacy.[49]

The imprisonment of a senior alderman of Dublin was a grave course of action for the government to follow. To leave him to languish in prison for up to seven years was unprecedented, and this underscores the significance

---

40 This is the date recorded by the informants whose evidence is appended to Mullan's works. Mullan himself (*Idea. Tog.*) gives the date of Taylor's death as 29 January 1621 and the time as 6 p.m. **41** See note 3. **42** A copy is in PROI, T.1747. **43** Ibid., f. 4. **44** Mullan, *Idea Tog.* **45** Cf. *togatae constantiae* and *religionis Catholicae defensione interitus.* **46** Mullan, *Idea Tog.*, 198–201, 267, 278. **47** Mullan, *Epitome Tripartita.* **48** See note 3. **49** Lynch, *Alithinologia* (See note 39).

of Francis Taylor's recusancy. As a veteran merchant and councillor, he would have had the resources and connections to mollify his captors. He eschewed this course and chose to confess his faith in prison and ultimately to die there.

There is adequate testimony to the circumstances of Francis Taylor's confinement. The fact that his captors kept him in prison for as long as seven years in harsh conditions suggests that they intended him to die there. Mullan refers to the squalor, isolation, and coldness of the jail.[50] Even when his death seemed imminent enough to warrant the drawing up of a will on 4 January 1621, the authorities did not release him but allowed him to die in prison twenty-six days later. Thus Francis Taylor's death occurred in circumstances directly attributable to his staunch Catholicism: his commitment to the faith was the cause of his imprisonment, and the authorities did not intend that he should leave prison alive.

FAMA MARTYRII

John Mullan was so impressed with the story of Francis Taylor's life and death that he cast him in the role of a great Catholic champion in *Idea Togatae Constantiae*. Mullan stressed Taylor's patrician status in Dublin and showed that his standards in both public and private matters were exemplary. His contention with the Protestant officials is described in great detail, but is obviously a literary construct. The references to his imprisonment and death, however, are succinct and accurate. Mullan also included Francis Taylor in his martyrology, *Epitome Tripartita Martyrum*.

When Mullan was seeking more information on Taylor's experiences he applied to Archbishop Fleming and Fathers Rochford, Cahill, Nugent and Cusack in Dublin. They were able to supply the essential facts about his life from sources in the city, where his memory must have been fresh. John Lynch enshrined the details of Francis Taylor's martyrdom in his *Alithinologia*, published in 1664. His source was Mullan's *Idea Togatae Constantiae*.

The evidence for the sufferings and death of Francis Taylor was examined during the Ordinary Process held at Dublin in 1904 and was then submitted to the Holy See. In due course, the General Promoter of the

---

50 Mullan, *Epitome Tripartita*.

Faith gave his verdict on Francis Taylor's case in his *Disquisitio*, 161–3. Having discussed the evidence, he concluded thus:

> *Quare actoribus arbitrator esse concedendum, ut sacrorum rituum Congregationis periclitentur iudicium.*

The favourable verdict of the Sacred Congregation of Rites, in February 1915, for the introduction of the 257 cases of alleged martyrdom was confirmed by Pope Benedict XV. During the Apostolic Process, which was held at Dublin 1917–30, the case of Francis Taylor was again examined. The findings were then presented to the Holy See.

CHAPTER 10

Peter Higgins, OP

Augustine Valkenburg

EARLY LIFE

In contemporary documents, Peter Higgins' family name is spelt in a variety of ways: Higgin, Higgins, Hyggins and O'Higgins. Very little is known about him before February 1642. Neither the date nor the place of his birth can be established with certainty. But what is known suggests that he was born in Dublin or in its neighbourhood. It is significant that, when the army captured Naas, he surrendered to the earl of Ormonde and requested a safe-conduct to Dublin. Before his execution there he is reported[1] to have said in an address from the scaffold: 'In this city and in the country around it, where the king's writ is still said to run, I have always lived'. These words indicate that, by birth or by choice, he was a man of the Pale. Because of religious persecution there are no Catholic baptismal registers for the period.

Many Dominican records were lost or destroyed during the religious persecution in the seventeenth century. Accordingly, it is not known where or when Peter Higgins was received into the order. The first definite reference to him occurs in 1627, when his name as *P. Fr Petrus Heggin* appears on a list of Irish Dominicans resident in Spain. This forms part of a report on the Irish Dominican province presented to the Sacred Congregation *de Propaganda Fide* in the autumn of that year.[2] The use of the abbreviation P. for *Pater* shows that he was then a priest. It cannot be determined where or when he was ordained. More than twenty Dominican priories in Spain and Portugal received young Irishmen at this period, but the surviving records contain no reference to him. It is reasonable to assume that he was born *c.*1600.

The Ireland to which he returned in the 1630s enjoyed a measure of religious toleration because of the policies followed by Thomas Wentworth, the

---

1 John Punch, *D. Richardi Bellingi Vindiciae eversae per R.P. Fr. Ioannem Poncium . . . ea occasione exponitur, quibus potissimum viis Hibernia a parlamentariis subacta est* . . . (Paris, 1653), 39–41.
2 APF, SOCG, 294, ff. 102r-105r; printed in Moran, *Spicil. Ossor.*, i, 160.

lord deputy. Writing in November 1636 the latter declared: 'It were too much to distemper them [the Irish], by bringing plantations upon them and disturbing them in the exercise of their religion, so long as it is without scandal.'[3] The Dominicans quietly took up residence again in Naas, on part of the old site that had been confiscated at the Reformation. The reference[4] to William Pilsworth, Protestant bishop of Kildare, who had lived in Naas, indicates that Higgins was resident there before 1635, the year of the bishop's death. At the time of his arrest, Higgins was prior of the Naas community.

Some extreme Protestants did take scandal at the toleration of priests and friars, particularly in the Naas area, where Wentworth was building a great house at Jigginstown; and when he fell from power and was put on trial and executed this was one of the charges brought against him.[5]

ARREST AND IMPRISONMENT

This policy of toleration changed abruptly when the dispossessed Irish of Ulster rose in arms on 23 October 1641. Disturbances soon spread to other parts of the country. Protestants were driven from the lands they had occupied. A number were killed, and many more suffered great hardships. Most of those who managed to escape fled to Dublin.

The traditionally loyal Catholic gentry of the Pale offered their services to the government to help in putting down the rebellion. This offer was contemptuously refused, and it was made clear to them that all Catholics were regarded as rebels. At this time, the government was headed by two lords justices in the absence of a lord deputy. They were Sir William Parsons and Sir John Borlase. Both were Protestants of strong Puritan leanings and hostile to Catholics. The army commander was the young James Butler, marquis of Ormonde. He had been reared a Protestant, and remained one all his life, but he was not trusted by the lords justices because he was of Old English stock. They preferred to rely on the New English, especially Sir Charles Coote, whom they appointed governor of Dublin. They also issued a commission authorising him to execute summarily any Catholic priests and common Irish who fell into his hands. This he did on a large scale and

3 Wentworth to Sir John Coke, 28 November 1636, in *The earl of Stafforde's letters and dispatches*, ed. William Knowler (2 vols, Dublin, 1740), ii, 39. 4 Deposition of Canon William Pilsworth, early 1642. Dublin, TCD, MS F 2 6, ff. 1r-2r. 5 Sir Richard Cox, *Hibernia Anglicana* (2 vols, London, 1689–90), ii, 60.

with great cruelty in a series of punitive raids from Dublin, for he was even more hostile to the Catholic religion than the lords justices.

It was during these months of confusion and panic that Peter Higgins sought the protection of Ormonde and was brought to Dublin and imprisoned there. The sources for his imprisonment and execution (it is quite possible that he did not have a formal trial, even by the processes of martial law) fall into three main groups. They are:

1. Documents from Protestant refugees in 1642.[6] As is to be expected, such people at this time were very hostile to Catholics, but the deposition of Canon Pilsworth, if it refers to Peter Higgins (and this, as will be seen, is highly likely), is very much in his favour.
2. Documents emanating from the Dominican Order.
3. A number of extracts from controversial writings concerning the role of the marquis of Ormonde in Ireland in the 1640s. Despite their controversial nature, they do provide much credible detail concerning the martyrdom of Peter Higgins.

When the offer of the gentry of the Pale was rejected, and when Coote's raids indicated that no Catholic was safe, this traditionally loyal group was gradually forced into resistance. Disorders had already broken out among the lower classes, and terrified Protestants were fleeing to Dublin even from the Naas district only about twenty miles away. As the disorder grew, Peter Higgins was quite fearless in protecting Protestants. Later at Dublin many of them, in an effort to save his life, publicly acknowledged their indebtedness to him.[7] A Protestant clergyman, William Pilsworth, son of the bishop of Kildare who had lived at Naas and died in 1635, claimed that he had been rescued when actually on the gallows for his father's sake by 'a priest whom I never saw before'.[8] It seems very reasonable to assume that the unnamed priest was Peter Higgins.

On 31 January 1642 armed forces under the command of Ormonde set out from Dublin to attack the rebels at Naas. The attack proved successful.

---

6 'Examination of Thomas Greames concerning Peter Hyggins', 13 February 1641 [1642 N.S.]. Dublin, TCD, MS F 2 6, f. 15r; Deposition of Canon William Pilsworth, early 1642. Dublin, TCD, MS F 2 6, ff. 1r-2r; Robert Bysse to his brother William, Dublin, 16 February 1642. Dublin, TCD, MS F 3 11, f. 8.   7 Acts of the General Chapter of the Order of Friars Preachers held at Rome in May 1644, Rome, AGOP, III, 26, 119, printed in B. Reichert (ed.), *Acta Capitulorum Generalium Ordinis Praedicatorum*, vii (Rome, 1902), 206. Richard Bellings, *Annotationes in R.P.F. Joannis Poncii opus ... Parisiis editum anno MDCLIII, perutiles ...* (Paris, 1654), 159–61.   8 See note 4.

In the confusion, Peter Higgins came forward and sought Ormonde's protection. He asked to be brought to Dublin, saying that he was guilty of no crime, but that if any charge were brought against him he was willing to submit himself to trial. He could say this with some confidence because he had remained loyal to the crown since the outbreak of the rebellion and had saved Protestant lives.[9] Ormonde assured him that if any charge were brought he would get a fair trial by jury, and handed him over to the custody of the cavalry commander, Sir Thomas Armstrong.[10]

At this stage Sir Charles Coote appeared. According to the Lords Justices, his forces had been part of the expedition from Dublin,[11] but according to another source,[12] which seems more plausible, Coote, who had been conducting punitive expeditions all round the countryside, turned up in Naas by chance. This same account says he demanded the custody of the popish priest in virtue of his commission from the lords justices. Ormonde refused. Coote then instigated Ormonde's infantry to attack his cavalry. The infantry were mostly Protestant refugees, while the cavalry contained some Catholics.[13] The better-trained cavalry beat off the attack, and Peter Higgins went to Dublin in Ormonde's custody.

It soon became clear that there were limitations on Ormonde's power to protect him. Almost inevitably he was imprisoned: no known Catholic priest would have been allowed his liberty in Dublin at that time. Ormonde does seem to have done his best, assuring the lords justices of Higgins' loyalty, and proffering oral and written testimony from more than twenty Protestants, asserting that the priest had protected them when their lives were in danger and asking for his release.[14]

Though there were some hopes that he might be released, Peter Higgins remained in prison. Here he was visited by a fellow-Dominican in disguise and was able to receive the sacrament of penance.[15] The Dominican sources of the 1650s say that he was offered life and preferment if he would renounce the Catholic faith. Such an offer was made regularly and almost as a matter of routine to imprisoned Catholics in most circumstances, but one may have some doubts if it were made to Peter Higgins. In the circumstances of this time Parsons, Borlase, and Coote did not want his conversion. They wanted his life.

9 The charge made by a Protestant that he had supported the rebels may be safely dismissed. **10** John Punch, *D. Richardi Bellingi* (see note 1); Richard Bellings, *Annotationes* (see note 7); Edmund Borlase, *The history of the execrable Irish rebellion* (London, 1680), 264–5. **11** *Ormonde MSS*, new series, ii, 70. **12** Richard Bellings, *Annotationes* (see note 7). **13** *Letter of Mr Chappell of Dublin to a draper in London*, 20 January 1642 (copy in RIA, Haliday tracts, xx). **14** Acts of the General Chapter 1644 (see note 7); Richard Bellings, *Annotationes* (see note 7). **15** Acts of the General Chapter 1644.

TRIAL

The problem was to find a plausible charge to bring against him. Many Protestants had testified to his innocence of any guilt of rebellion and to his practical charity in saving their lives. There had been a royal proclamation of 8 March 1641 ordering all Catholic priests to leave the country or face a charge of treason.[16] This proclamation had been issued for England only, but it was not the first time a Dublin administration had stretched the law by extending English legislation to Ireland. A letter of Richard Boyle, earl of Cork, dated 20 July 1641, speaks of a priest who had already been executed under this edict and of others in prison who might be expected to meet the same fate.[17]

Early in the morning of 23 March 1642, one of Ormonde's kinsmen brought him the information that he had seen the body of Peter Higgins hanging on a scaffold. Ormonde taxed the lords justices with his death. They blamed Coote, saying that he had hanged Higgins without their knowledge, but when Ormonde demanded that he be brought to task for his crime, they refused.[18] It does appear certain that Coote played the leading role in bringing about the execution, but it is likely that the lords justices were privy to it in that they yielded to Coote's demand that he be hanged. The execution of Peter Higgins and other priests immediately became a real element in the reluctance of the Irish Catholics to trust Ormonde or to make a peace treaty with him in the King's name after Charles I had appointed him lord lieutenant in 1643.[19] But the version of events given by his defender Bellings seems the more likely, namely that in the case of Peter Higgins he had done all he could to protect him, but without success.

Bellings states explicitly that there was no civil trial. It is possible that there was not even the summary justice of a trial by court martial, and that Peter Higgins was simply taken out of prison and hanged early in the morning of 23 March 1642.

16 Steele, *Proclamations*, i, 224.   17 *Lismore Papers*, ed. A. B. Grosart (10 vols, London, 1886–8), 2nd series, iv, 205–7.   18 Richard Bellings, *Annotationes* (see note 7).   19 See, e.g., the memorandum of Bishop Nicholas French of Ferns in 1646, when a peace with Ormonde was being discussed (*Comment. Rinucc.*, ii, 291).

MARTYRDOM

The execution may have been carried out without Ormonde's knowledge, but there were eyewitnesses. This is stated explicitly by John Punch, who said that there were a number of them in Paris in the early 1650s, and that he had derived his information from them. There may have been Catholics among them, but probably most of them were Protestants, for many royalist Protestants had gone into exile with Charles II after his father had been executed in 1649. Punch says that Higgins declared on the scaffold that he died innocent of any crime, that he had always been loyal to his king, and that he had saved Protestant lives. He considered Ormonde with Coote and others guilty of bringing about his death, and he forgave them.

O'Daly[20] published his book in Lisbon in 1655.[21] Punch's work, published in Paris in 1653, would have been among his sources. He too gives a speech from the scaffold, but with a different emphasis. According to O'Daly, Higgins declared that he was being put to death solely on account of the Catholic faith, and as proof he produced a document sent to him only that morning by the viceroy[22] for signature, promising him freedom and rewards if he would apostatize. When he had ended his speech he threw this document to a friend among the bystanders.

O'Daly cites no source for his quite vivid account. It is possible that he had his information from eyewitnesses, but he does not say so. It is possible that Punch received the same information from eyewitnesses. However, he was writing in a strictly political context, and it was not his purpose to show that Higgins had died a martyr, but to charge Ormonde with complicity in his death. But here too the argument is from silence. However, the entry in the acts of the 1644 general chapter of the Dominicans does contain information which seems to bridge the two accounts, and its source can be traced. The entry states that on the scaffold Peter Higgins publicly proclaimed his loyalty to the Catholic faith and to his Dominican profession. (Punch adds that he publicly proclaimed his loyalty to the king.) The source of this information in the Dominican chapter acts is quite certainly the two Irish delegates to that chapter, John Nolan and Terence Albert

---

20 Dominic O'Daly, *Initium, incrementa et exitus familiae Geraldinorum, Desmoniae comitum ... ac persecutionis haereticorum descriptio ...* (Lisbon, 1655), 335–6. **21** The entry in the acts of the Dominican General Chapter of 1656 (Acts of the General Chapter of the Order of Friars Preachers held at Rome in May 1656, Rome, AGOP, III, 26, 157, printed in Riechert (ed.), op. cit. (see note 7), vii, 476), was clearly inspired by the publication of O'Daly's work the year before and is dependent on it. **22** In fact there was no serving viceroy at this time, only lords justices.

O'Brien, later to be bishop of Emly and himself a martyr. Their source of information, equally certainly, is the Dominican who in disguise visited Peter Higgins in prison. He was very probably Dominic Nugent, prior of the Dublin community. He was probably present at the execution (he had already shown his courage by visiting the prisoner), and even if he were not, he was well placed to get information from someone who was there.

Some of the Protestants there were moved by Higgins' words. They included some whose lives he had saved. Others, however, continued to insult his body even after he had been hanged. The body was exposed naked for mockery. It was not allowed burial in the city, but apparently permission was obtained to inter it outside the walls.[23]

MOTIVE FOR MARTYRDOM

In the light of what has been said above, it is clear that Peter Higgins died professing his loyalty not merely to his king but to his Catholic faith and to his religious profession. He had not sought martyrdom: indeed, what he had sought in the first instance was the protection of the royal government of Dublin. He soon found the protection promised him by Ormonde to be very uncertain. He was first imprisoned and then executed. The principal motive of those who put him to death was almost certainly to weaken the political position of Ormonde. In so far as they may have troubled to give any cloak of legality to their action, it would appear to have been by invoking the English proclamation of 8 March 1641, which banished all priests under pain of treason. It would not have been so easy to execute a Catholic layman in the circumstances. A Protestant, of course, would not have been executed. When the trap finally closed on Peter Higgins, he declared that he offered up his life not merely as a loyal subject unjustly executed for treason, but as a Catholic and a religious put to death by people who hated his faith and religious profession, that is, *in odium fidei*.

FAMA MARTYRII

Within his Dominican Order Peter Higgins was immediately accepted as a martyr. In addition to the sources used above, his name is included in a list

---

23 Acts of the General Chapter 1644 (see note 7).

of Dominican martyrs forwarded to the Internuncio in Flanders on 10 August 1658 in connection with an appeal for funds for the Irish Dominican College at Louvain.[24] The Irish martyrologists were fewer in number after the calamities of the mid-seventeenth century, but an account of Higgins' martyrdom was given by Bruodin in 1669.[25]

His fame spread among the Dominicans in Europe, with such works as that of Marchese (1668–79), translated into Spanish by Manrique (1690), and by the French translation of O'Daly's work by Joubert (1697). Two Irish Dominicans kept his memory alive through the eighteenth century: O'Heyne (1706)[26] and Burke (1762).[27] When Irish interest in the martyrs revived in the nineteenth century he was firmly established in the lists.

The evidence in his cause was examined during the Ordinary Process held in Dublin in 1904 and was then submitted to the Holy See. In due course the General Promoter of the Faith gave his verdict (*Disquisitio,* 172–8). He expressed reservations. He was not prepared to accept O'Daly's account as historical fact, and, relying heavily on Bellings, he concluded that Peter Higgins was put to death for political reasons: his execution was outrageously unjust, but he was not a martyr for the Catholic faith. His verdict was:

> *Ergo, quo huic Petri O'Higgins causae talis conditio fiat, ut ad sacrae Congregationis iudicium deferri possit, necesse est, haec dubia ita actorum studio atque industria dissolvantur, ut veritas rerum plane liquescat.*

In his reply (*Responsio ad Disquisitionem,* 143–61) the Advocate examined these arguments and adduced fresh evidence, notably the royal proclamation of 8 March 1641 and the letter of the earl of Cork.[28] He concluded: *Stant itaque firmae atque invictae probationes martyrii Dei servi.* The problem about this additional documentation is that there is no evidence that Peter Higgins was charged under the terms of the proclamation, and that the earl of Cork did not name the priest who was put to death under it. It may indeed be that he was so charged, though it would appear certain that he was not granted a civil trial, and it may be doubted if there was even a court

---

24 Felix O'Connor, OP, to Giralmo de Vecchii, Internuncio in Flanders, 10 August 1658, in APF, SOCG, 3709, ff. 312v-313r; printed in *Archiv. Hib.* 15 (1959), 32. **25** Anthony Bruodin, *Propugnaculum Catholicae Veritatis* (Prague, 1669), 731–2. **26** John O'Heyne, *Epilogus Chronologicus Exponens succincte conventus et fundationes sacri Ordinis Praedicatorum in regno Hyberniae, et nomina pariter illustrium filiorum eiusdem provinciae* (Louvain, 1706); ed. and trans. Ambrose Coleman (Dundalk, 1902). **27** Burke, *Hib. Dom.* **28** See notes 16, 17 above.

martial. At this time Dublin was full of Protestants who had fled from the Catholic insurgents in October 1641. They were being encouraged by the lords justices to record their suffering in written depositions designed to show that all Catholics, led by their priests, were guilty of insurrection and murder. At the same time, military forces were being organized to attack areas held by the Catholics. Among the commanders, Charles Coote was particularly ferocious in massacring Catholics and priests, whereas Ormonde was prepared to accept that there could be loyal Catholics, even loyal priests. Given these circumstances, the accounts given by Bellings and Borlase may be accepted as substantially true. Peter Higgins was put to death on the orders of Charles Coote with or, less probably, without the knowledge of the lords justices, possibly after a court martial, possibly even without one. He was put to death because he was a Catholic and a priest by those who wished to establish that all Catholics, and especially all priests, were traitors and murderers. Bellings and Borlase make it plain that Peter Higgins was neither. They depict him as a good and loyal man who had tried to restrain excesses, and for this there is supporting evidence. He was put to death because he was a Catholic and a priest, as he proclaimed from the scaffold.

In February 1915 Peter Higgins was included among the martyrs for the introduction of whose cause authorization was granted. Accordingly, the cause was examined at the Apostolic Process held in Dublin between 1917 and 1930. The findings were then presented to the Holy See.

CHAPTER II

Terence Albert O'Brien, OP

Augustine Valkenburg

EARLY LIFE

Terence O'Brien was born in 1601[1] at Tuogh, known today as Tower Hill, one mile south of Cappamore, in the county of Limerick and the diocese of Emly. Both his father and mother were of the noble family of O'Brien Arra, and they possessed an estate of about 2,000 acres.[2]

He began his education locally at Tuogh and continued it probably in the city of Limerick, a short distance away. Here he became a Dominican novice, probably in 1621, taking the name Albert in religion.[3] A detailed report to Propaganda in 1627[4] indicates that at this date the Dominicans were established in Ireland at twelve of their pre-Reformation foundations. Eight of these were in towns, where the friars lived in houses externally indistinguishable from others, but interiorly laid out with an oratory, dormitory, refectory, and everything needed for community life.

He completed his studies at Toledo in Spain.[5] His name appears among the students in a list of Irish Dominicans in Spain in 1627,[6] and a fellow-student testified twenty years later that he had been ordained in that year.[7]

---

1 The date is deduced from the evidence given to the Roman datary at the time of his epis-copal appointment (AV, Processus Datariae, 26, ff. 11r-13r); calendared in Cathaldus Giblin (ed.), 'The *Processus Datariae* and the appointment of Irish bishops in the seventeenth century', in *Father Luke Wadding*, 575–7. 2 Terence O'Brien's father died in 1623, and, in accordance with English law, an inquisition *post mortem* was held to determine his posses-sions and his heir. A transcript of this inquisition has survived (MacEnerney transcript of Limerick inquisitions, in PROI, 1A/53/34/45). Further details concerning the family lands will be found in *Civil Survey*, ii, 140, 143, 157, 160–2, 170; iv, 8–9, 11. 3 John Lynch, *De Praesulibus Hiberniae*, 1672 (Bibl. Mazar., MS 1869, 678–80); printed in Lynch, *De Praesulibus Hib.*, ii, 67–8. Again, the date is deduced from the evidence in the Datary Process. 4 APF, SOCG, 294, ff. 102r-105v; printed in Moran, *Spicil. Ossor.*, i, 156–61. 5 Acts of the General Chapter of the Order of Friars Preachers held at Rome in May 1656 (Rome, A.G.O.P., III, 26, 149–50); printed in B. Reichert (ed.), *Acta Capitulorum Generalium Ordinis Praedicatorum*, vii (Rome, 1902), 469–7; Lynch, *De Praesulibus Hib.* 6 Moran, *Spicil Ossor.*, i, 160. 7 *Processus Datariae*, loc. cit.

There is no record of his ordination in the diocesan archives at Toledo. He may have returned to Ireland to be ordained, probably by Richard Arthur, bishop of Limerick.

He was twice prior of what the sources describe as 'his native priory' of Limerick, and once of Lorrha, County Tipperary.[8] In 1643 he was elected provincial of the Irish province.[9] In that capacity he went to Rome for the general chapter of the order in 1644. He presented to the chapter a list of those Dominicans who had been martyred in Ireland, and was created Master of Sacred Theology by the Dominican master general.[10]

He returned to Ireland by way of Lisbon, with authority from the master general to visit as Provincial the two Irish houses there, one of friars and one of nuns.[11] The Dominican sources[12] and Lynch, who was relying on a Dominican source, state that he was appointed coadjutor bishop of his native diocese of Emly by Pope Urban VIII, and that he received information to this effect while he was in Lisbon.

The Consistorial record of his appointment as titular bishop of Clama and coadjutor to the ailing bishop of Emly is dated 11 March 1647.[13] It is certain that, as early as February 1645, his name was being put forward by interested parties in Ireland, the clergy and laity of Emly, some Irish bishops, and the supreme council of the Irish Confederate Catholics. When he was consecrated at Waterford by the papal nuncio, Archbishop Rinuccini, on 2 April 1648,[14] he became thereby bishop of Emly, because the old bishop had died in September 1646.

The disturbed state of Ireland may have been a factor in the delay of his consecration. The two witnesses examined in the Datary Process of investigation prior to his appointment were sufficiently well informed to allow their information on the diocese of Emly in the mid-1640s to be accepted as substantially correct. The diocese was small, eighteen or twenty parishes, with some religious houses where a few religious lived and also helped the diocesan clergy in the pastoral ministry. The cathedral town was small indeed, about forty houses with about two hundred people. The cathedral

8 Acts of the General Chapter 1656 (see note 5); Lynch, *De Praesulibus Hib.* 9 AGOP, IV, 78a, ff. 8r, 18r; printed in Hugh Fenning (ed.), 'Irish material in the registers of the Dominican masters-general, 1390–1649', in *Archivum Fratrum Praedicatorum* 39 (1969), 312–13. 10 Acts of the General Chapter 1656 (see note 5); Lynch, *De Praesulibus Hib.*; see also AGOP, IV, 78b, fol. 15v; printed in Fenning, loc. cit., 313.   11 Lynch, *De Praesulibus Hib.* 12 Dominic O'Daly, *Initium, incrementa et exitus familiae Geraldinorum, Desmoniae comitum … ac persecutionis haereticorum descriptio …* (Lisbon, 1655), 344–8; Acts of the General Chapter 1656 (see note 5).   13 Minutes of the Secret Consistory held on 11 March 1647 (AV, Acta Camerarii, 19, ff. 88v–89r); BV, MSS Barb. Lat., 2928, 35–6 [contemporary copy].   14 Lynch, *De Praesulibus Hib.*; see also *Comment. Rinucc.*, iii, 56.

as well as the town had been damaged in the previous year, but there was a priest there, and the services of religion were provided.

By the time Terence Albert O'Brien became bishop of Emly, the Irish Catholics had been trying to secure full freedom for the practice of their religion for more than six years by force of arms. This effort had disclosed serious differences between them. The Old English Catholics sought a negotiated agreement with the marquis of Ormond, the king's representative, which would allow them not only religious toleration but would guarantee their political and economic position. The papal nuncio, Archbishop Rinuccini, who had arrived in 1645, rejected such a compromise as totally unsatisfactory. In this he had the support of the Old Irish Catholics, who had already lost most of their property. Bishop O'Brien came of an Old Irish family which had not yet lost its property. He unshakeably supported the nuncio in making a settlement which would guarantee the full rights of the Catholic Church. It must have been a source of special pain to him that his own Dominican Order divided on the same racial lines as the generality of Irish Catholics.[15]

The disputes and divisions forced Rinuccini to leave the country early in 1649. In the following August, Oliver Cromwell and his army landed at Dublin. Cromwell found the divided Irish easy victims, and, by the time affairs in England forced him to return there in May 1650, he had conquered a great deal of the country.[16]

Cromwell was not prepared to grant any toleration at all to the Catholic Church. The rank and file of his army were kept in a state of hostility to popery in any guise by regular preaching. It was this army which had carried out the indiscriminate massacres at Drogheda and Wexford in 1649. For some time afterwards, Catholic priests had been indiscriminately killed when captured, and though a milder policy of rounding them up and shipping them abroad had begun to take shape, it was still made clear that there would be no toleration of popery whatsoever.

When he left Ireland, Cromwell had entrusted the command of his army to his son-in-law, Henry Ireton. Ireton was if anything more hostile to popery than was Cromwell. As a military commander, however, he was plodding where Cromwell was dashing, and it was not until the end of 1650 that his forces had advanced to the line of the Shannon.

Limerick, with its bridge across the river, was an important key to further

---

15 AGOP, IV, 87, ff. 53v, 110r; 91, fol. 48v; printed in Fenning, loc. cit., 325–7. **16** For the most recent study of the Cromwellian regime in Ireland, see P. J. Corish in *NHI*, iii, 336–86.

advance. When Ireton's army appeared outside its walls in June 1651, the bishop of Emly was within them. He had earlier retired to Connacht, but clearly had not yet given up hope that all might not yet be lost, as appears from a letter he wrote from Galway on 29 March to the Secretary of Propaganda.[17] This letter shows clearly his distress and depression at the calamities that had come on the Irish Catholics. But he could still place some hope in the difficulties Cromwell faced in England and the possibility that some help might come from the duke of Lorraine, a mercenary leader left idle after the ending of the Thirty Years War. Cromwell surmounted his difficulties, and there never really was any prospect of help from Lorraine, but the possibility kept a kind of glimmer of false hope alive.

The citizens of Limerick tried to negotiate terms of surrender. Ireton agreed to meet them, but refused to suspend siege operations while the negotiations were in progress. They broke down when Ireton made it clear that he would not allow toleration of the Catholic religion and would not grant any terms at all to the Catholic clergy. In the course of these negotiations, Ireton could learn who among the defenders were counselling the stiffest resistance. One of these was the bishop of Emly. O'Daly[18] says that he was offered a huge bribe and liberty to go abroad in safety if he changed his attitude, but he refused. There is independent testimony that a similar offer was made to the military commander of the city, Hugh Duff O'Neill, and that he too refused.[19] O'Daly too is the source of the story that Bishop O'Brien offered to surrender himself to Ireton, if he would agree to spare the rest of the clergy, despite their expressed view that such a handing over of an innocent person was immoral. O'Daly had his information on these points from Fabian Ryan, OP, who was in Limerick during the siege.

The siege dragged on for over five months. By the end of October, conditions inside the city were desperate. Provisions were running out, and there was an outbreak of the bubonic plague, which was widespread in the country at the time. A number of the defenders felt that now there was no option but to surrender, and terms were agreed on 27 October. No pardon was extended to the Catholic clergy, and about twenty people, including Hugh Duff O'Neill and the bishops of Limerick and Emly, were excluded from pardon by name.

Ireton's troops entered the city on 29 October. The bishop of Limerick

---

17 APF, SOCG, 298, ff. 864rv, 875r; printed in Moran, *Spicil. Ossor.*, i, 367–9.   **18** See note 12. Acts of the General Chapter 1656 (see note 5) makes the same statement. It may be taken as certain that in this it depends on O'Daly, so that both depend on Fabian Ryan, OP, who was in Limerick during the siege.   **19** Gilbert, *Contemp. Hist.*, iii, 267.

escaped by disguising himself as a soldier and marching out with them. O'Neill and others exempted from pardon surrendered themselves to Ireton at the city gate.[20] The bishop of Emly was not among them.

ARREST AND IMPRISONMENT

He was immediately arrested, together with Major General Purcell, in the plague-house where he was tending the sick, and chained hand and foot.[21]

TRIAL

His trial by court-martial followed immediately, and he was sentenced to death by hanging. He asked for the opportunity to confess, and his confession was heard in prison by a fellow-Dominican, Denis Hanrahan.[22] O'Daly is again the source for the story that at his trial the bishop foretold the coming death of Ireton. While O'Daly did have his information from an eye-witness, Fabian Ryan, OP, it is possible that this is an embellishment. Ireton did die of a fever on 26 November. Hanrahan, as recorded by Lynch, corroborates O'Daly's account of how, in his final delirium, Ireton was haunted by the fact that he had sent Bishop O'Brien to the gallows.

MARTYRDOM

The bishop was executed on the day following his trial, 30 October 1651. He went joyfully to his death. At the gallows he addressed the Catholics who crowded around, urging them to hold to their faith, to live good lives, and not to be cast down by the calamities which had come upon them. He then asked them to pray for him that he might be firm in enduring his fate.

He was then hanged. His body was left hanging for three hours. Stripped of everything except its undergarment, it was treated with every possible indignity, being spun around and beaten with muskets until it no longer had the appearance of a human being. The head was then cut off and spiked on

---

20 Ireton to William Lenthall, Speaker of the English parliament, 3 November 1651, ibid. 21 *Memoirs of Edmund Ludlow*, ed. C. H. Firth (2 vols, Oxford, 1894), i, 373. 22 Lynch, *De Praesulibus Hib.*; see also Edmund Borlase, *The history of the execrable Irish rebellion* (London, 1680), 299.

the river gate, where it remained fresh and incorrupt, because, people said, he had preserved his virginity throughout his life.[23] There is no record of where what remained of his body was buried.

MOTIVE FOR MARTYRDOM

The bishop and the three priests mentioned in Kearney's work[24] were put to death 'for being priests'. After Cromwell's ban on the Mass, he had functioned as a priest. Ireton blamed him for everything and stated that he hanged the bishop and Major General Purcell as 'original incendiaries of the rebellion', in a long letter to William Lenthall, the Speaker of parliament in London, on 3 November 1651.[25] But the bishop's corpse was treated with a barbarity that did not mark the other executions. Further, not all priests who fell into Ireton's hands were executed, nor were all those who were exempted from pardon by name. The most striking case is that of Hugh Duff O'Neill. He too had refused a proffered bribe and had been named as one to whom no pardon would be granted. Yet when he was brought before the court-martial, it was decided to send him a prisoner to London. Spain intervened diplomatically on his behalf, and he was released after a few months.[26] He had had a distinguished career in the Spanish army in the Low Countries, and his execution might have had international repercussions, especially after the first hesitation. No one taken at Limerick suffered such barbarities as Terence Albert O'Brien. The only possible explanation of why his dead body was treated as it was is that, as well as being instrumental in prolonging the siege, he was, as a friar and a bishop, a special symbol of the popery so hated by Ireton and his soldiers.

There can be no doubt that this was the thought central in the mind of the bishop when he went to the scaffold. As already noted, when the Irish Catholics rose in arms and proclaimed their cause to be for religion, king and country, serious divisions arose among them as to how the conflicting claims of these three objectives could be resolved. Terence Albert O'Brien was completely single-minded. For him the interests of the Catholic religion always came first: the defence of Limerick was the same as the defence of the Catholic religion. When the city could no longer be held, he did not

---

23 O'Daly, *Initium* (see note 12); Acts of the General Chapter 1656 (see note 5); Lynch, *De Praesulibus Hib.* **24** Treatise entitled *Memoriall of the war begun 1641*, written by Mr Kearney between February and May 1656. Bodl., Carte MSS, 64, fol. 458v. **25** Gilbert, *Contemp. Hist.*, iii, 265–8. **26** Corish in *NHI*, iii, 351.

try to escape or seek mercy. His address on the scaffold makes it clear beyond all doubt that as he faced death the only things in his mind were that the citizens of conquered Limerick should preserve their Catholic faith and that his own courage should not fail.

FAMA MARTYRII

Bishop O'Brien's contemporaries had no doubt that he had died a martyr. This is the testimony of the clergy and laity of the diocese of Emly in 1652.[27] Walter Lynch, bishop of Clonfert, said in that same year that he had died a martyr.[28] An Irish layman in 1656,[29] an Irish Franciscan in 1659,[30] two Irish Capuchins in the early 1660s,[31] and Nicholas French, Bishop of Ferns, in 1667[32] all describe him as a martyr. These men had all lived through the Cromwellian conquest, and knew the facts and the issues. Two Irish Dominicans, Fabian Ryan and Denis Hanrahan, who had been with him in Limerick, compiled detailed accounts of his martyrdom, which have been preserved in the works of O'Daly and Lynch. Felix O'Connor, OP, included his name in the list of Dominican martyrs he sent to the internuncio in Brussels in 1658.[33] After the general chapter of 1656, he was firmly established in the Dominican martyrologies, and he received special attention from the Irish Dominican writers in the eighteenth century: O'Heyne[34] (1706) and Burke[35] (1762). When general Irish interest in the martyrs revived in the nineteenth century, his name was always among them. Terence Albert O'Brien, as he is always known, continues to be venerated, particularly in his own diocese of Emly. On 8 October 1927, a small silver cross was given to the Irish Dominicans and is reverently preserved in their Limerick priory. The donor was the last surviving

---

27 Clergy and Nobles of the Diocese of Emly to Pope Innocent X, 23 April 1652. Rome, APF, Fondo di Vienna, 14, fol. 95r [contemporary copy]. 28 Walter Lynch, bishop of Clonfert, to the secretary of the Sacred Congregation *de Propaganda Fide*, Boffin, 31 August 1652 (Rome, APF, SOCG, 298, fol. 825r); printed in Moran, *Spicil. Ossor.*, i, 385. 29 Kearney, *Memoriall* (see note 24). 30 Conry, *Threnodia*, 62, 70; printed in *Archiv. Hib.* 13 (1947), 96, 100. 31 An account of Irish Catholic affairs compiled by Richard O'Ferrall and Robert O'Connell, 1660–2. *Comment. Rinucc.*, iv, 647. 32 [Nicholas French], *Vera descriptio moderni status Catholicorum in regno Hiberniae, et preces eorum ad Sanctissimum Dominum Clementem Papam Nonum* (Cologne, [1667]), 24–5; reprinted in Burke, *Hib. Dom.* 33 APF, SOCG, 370, ff. 312v-313r; printed in *Archiv. Hib.* 15 (1950), 32. 34 John O'Heyne, *Epilogus Chronologicus Exponens succincte conventus et fundationes sacri Ordinis Praedicatorum in regno Hyberniae, et nomina pariter illustrium filiorum eiusdem provinciae* (Louvain, 1706); ed. and trans. Ambrose Coleman (Dundalk, 1902). 35 See note 32.

member of a family that claimed descent from the O'Briens of Tuogh, and the tradition in the family was that this was the pectoral cross of Bishop Terence Albert O'Brien.[36]

The evidence in his cause was examined during the Ordinary Process held in Dublin in 1904 and was then submitted to the Holy See. In due course the General Promoter of the Faith gave his verdict. In his examination of the evidence (*Disquisitio*, 236–42) he argued that while beyond doubt Terence Albert O'Brien was immediately and widely venerated as a martyr, one could at the very least question if he had been put to death *in odium fidei*. He concluded:

> *Quare, aut Terentius, optimus ceteroque et sanctus vir, martyr non fuit aut, ut levissime dicam, de martyrio eius nequit nobis certo constare, neque mihi licet actorum petitioni concedere, ut causa eius ad sacram Congregationem deferatur.*

In a lengthy reply the Advocate (*Responsio ad Disquisitionem*, 177–200) stressed the fact that he had been immediately accepted as a martyr by very many people well placed to appreciate the situation in which, he argued, zeal for the defence of Limerick was zeal for the defence of the Catholic religion in the mind of a man so single-minded as Terence Albert O'Brien. Permission was granted to continue with his cause, which was further examined during the Apostolic Process held in Dublin between 1917 and 1930. The findings were then presented to the Holy See.

---

36 Michael Moloney, 'Terence Albert O'Brien, his pectoral cross, his kith and kin', in *Saint Munchin's Folk: Parish Annual* 1949 (Limerick, 1949), 17–31.

CHAPTER 12

John Kearney, OFM

Benignus Millett

EARLY LIFE

Within a year of John Kearney's death, his confrère and great friend, Joseph Sall, had written a life of this martyr.[1] Moreover, a *Vita Fratris Ioannis Kearny* was circulated among the Irish exiles in Europe during the Cromwellian persecution of the Catholic Church in Ireland.[2] Copies of a *vita* were being secretly passed around among priests in Ireland, and in 1656, or early in 1657, a copy came into the hands of the Superior of the Jesuit mission.[3] At Prague, Anthony Bruodin had a manuscript copy of a life written by Joseph Sall, OFM, and Canon Geoffrey Sall of Cashel, seemingly a *textus conflatus*. Bruodin based his account of Kearney's life and death on that *vita*.[4] Whenever he cites a written or printed source, Bruodin has been found to be accurate and reliable.

The information given here on John Kearney's early years, his capture, imprisonment, and death is taken from Bruodin's account unless otherwise noted. Some of the details which he gives can be controlled from other sources. There are two errors in his account, but they may not have originated with him.[5]

John Kearney was born in Cashel, County Tipperary, in 1619. His father's name was John, and his mother was Elizabeth Creagh, who was among the Catholic clergy, religious, and laity killed by Inchiquin's soldiers in Cashel

---

1 Joseph Sall, OFM, to an Irish confrère in Louvain, Avila (Spain), 16 January 1654: FLK, MS D 23, no. 1; printed in Millett, *Ir. Franciscans*, 263. 2 These *vitae* are discussed in section VI below. 3 Thomas Quin, *Relatio et conditio Catholicorum Hiberniae ab anno 1652 ad annum 1656*, 1656–7. Stonyhurst College Library, MS A IV, 11, no. 7, f. 1v (copy). 4 Anthony Bruodin, *Anatomicum Examen Inchiridii Apologetici seu famosi cuiusdam libelli a Thoma Carve (verius Carrano) sacerdote furtive publicati* (Prague, 1671), 233–59. 5 On page 253, ibid., when referring to Kearney's capture, it says that he was then Guardian of Cork friary. Either the scribe who made the MS copy of the *vita* used by Bruodin mistakenly transcribed *Corkagiensis* for *Carrigiennsis*, or Bruodin misread his manuscript. Kearney was still in Louvain on 15 June 1644, when he defended some theological theses. Accordingly, the statement on page 244, that towards the end of 1642 he got permission to return to Ireland and that he departed without delay, seems to be wrong. Perhaps Joseph Sall gave the wrong date in the *vita*.

Cathedral in 1647.[6] The Kearney (or O'Kearney) family were prominent in the town of Cashel as merchants and ecclesiastics for many centuries. Kearneys are regularly found as aldermen and burgesses in Cashel until the Cromwellian usurpation.[7] They were one of a group of families, including the Salls, Hacketts, Everards, and Creaghs, who were both prosperous and prominent in the life of the town and among whom there was considerable intermarriage.[8] All these families were staunchly Catholic, displaying the piety of the Counter-Reformation and giving many candidates to the diocesan priesthood and the religious life during the lifetime of the future martyr. The genuine loyalty of these Cashel families to the Catholic Church was due in no small measure to the pastoral zeal of the seminary priests, friars, and Jesuits, in south Tipperary. These factors played a large part in the formation of the young John Kearney and in his choice of profession.

In his parents' house he was trained in virtue, and from his seventh year he attended Mass daily. The residence of the Kearneys was during persecution the usual hiding-place for the religious of the town and district, especially the Franciscans. The Friars Minor, whose local friary had been suppressed in 1540, had re-established themselves as a community in Cashel, in a private residence, in 1618.[9] They taught Christian doctrine to young John Kearney in his own home. The Jesuits, who had been working zealously in the town for more than twenty years under Barnaby Kearney[10] and had opened a school there, also exercised a considerable influence on him. From them he learned the humanities. When he decided to become a religious, for a time he seriously thought of entering the Society of Jesus.

On parental advice, John Kearney consulted Joseph Everard, the minister provincial of the Friars Minor,[11] who knew him well.[12] Joseph Sall, a close

---

6 Her sufferings and death were examined during the Ordinary Process held at Dublin in 1904. 7 They had extensive lands, e.g. at Ballyduagh (near Cashel), Knockinglass, Clonbrogan and Cloneen. The head of the family was called 'Kearney Crux' or 'Kearney Bachall' because he was the hereditary custodian of the relic known as 'the staff of St Patrick', and he usually lived at Ballyduagh. When John Kearney was born (1619) the 'Kearney Crux' was Donagh Kearney, who was either a brother or a first cousin of the martyr's father. 8 For example, the James O'Kearney who was a student in the Irish College at Salamanca in 1620 was the son of Philip O'Kearney and Helen Sall, cf. *Archiv. Hib.* 3 (1914), 93–4. 9 *Anal. Hib.* 6 (1934), 147. 10 See Edmund Hogan, *Ibernia Ignatiana*, i (Dublin, 1880), 132, 171–2, 177, 187–90, 200, 216–19; *Wadding papers*, 587; *Comment. Rinucc.*, i, 87; iv, 67; Carlos Sommervogel, *Bibliothèque de la Compagnie de Jésus* (11 vols, Brussels/Paris, 1890–1932), iv, 957. Barnaby Kearney, SJ, was a brother of David Kearney, archbishop of Cashel 1603–24. 11 Joseph Everard, who was a native of Cashel, was minister provincial 1635–8 (see *Liber Lovan.*, 8–9). 12 In August 1629 Everard was the guardian of Cashel friary (ibid., 5). He probably hid in the Kearneys' house in 1630, when a warrant was issued for his arrest (see *Wadding Papers*, 408).

friend of Kearney, did likewise. Everard sent the two young men to the Franciscan friary in Kilkenny, where they were given the religious habit and commenced their canonical novitiate under Dominic Dempsey. No record of their religious profession has survived. A little less than six months after completing their noviciate, the two young friars were sent to Belgium to study for the priesthood. After a stormy crossing from Waterford they reached Bristol, and in due course made their way to Flanders, where they took up residence in St Anthony's College, Louvain, which had been founded in 1607 by the Irish Franciscans. They arrived there probably in 1638.[13] In the *studium* conducted by the Irish friars at St Anthony's[14] they were taught philosophy and then theology. John Kearney spent six years in Louvain. He received clerical tonsure and minor orders on 23 September 1639, and was ordained subdeacon on the following day. Three years later, on 20 September 1642, he was ordained priest by Jacobus Boonen, archbishop of Mechelen, in the parish church of St Catherine in Brussels.[15] On 15 June 1644, he publicly defended a series of theses *de iustitia et iure ad mentem doctoris subtilis* before his professor, Raymund Caron.[16] Shortly afterwards he left Louvain for Ireland.[17]

The ship on which he sailed was captured by English Parliamentarians. He was taken from Bristol to London, where he was imprisoned. In an effort to persuade him to renounce Catholicism, his jailers had him tortured. These tactics having proved unsuccessful, he was locked in a deep dungeon. Early in his captivity he had admitted during interrogation that he was a Catholic priest and a Franciscan friar. Three months after being put in the dungeon he was taken before a court and condemned to death. But on the night before he was due to be executed, he was helped by an English Catholic to escape from prison and flee to France. From there he travelled to Ireland, sailing from Calais to Wexford.

He then spent two years, until 1647 or shortly before,[18] teaching philos-

---

13 According to the *vita* recorded by Bruodin, Kearney spent six years in Louvain. He was still there in 1644 (see note 16 below).   **14** See Cathaldus Giblin, 'Hugh MacCaghwell, O.F.M., and Scotism at St Anthony's College, Louvain', in *De Doctrina Ioannis Duns Scoti*, iv (Rome, 1968), 375–97.   **15** 'Registrum Ordinationum 1629–1644' of the diocese of Mechelen. Mechelen, Aartsbisschoppelijk Archief, Acta Mechliniensia: Registrum 62, ff 116r, 117r, 155v.   **16** E.H.J. Reusens (ed.), *Documents relatifs à l'histoire de l'Université de Louvain ... 1425–1797*, v (Louvain, 1892), 428.   **17** The *vita* cited by Bruodin states that, towards the end of 1642, Kearney asked for and received, from his superiors, permission to return to Ireland, and that he did not delay long in Louvain after getting this written permission: '*Non diu ... cunctatus est*'. This cannot be correct. Either Joseph Sall's memory failed him, or 1642 is a misprint for 1644.   **18** The *tabula* of the provincial chapter of 1647 is extant. According to it, there was a *studium philosophicum* attached to Cashel friary, but as John Kearney was not

ophy in the friary in Cashel. During that time he also dedicated himself to the apostolate of preaching, in which he had considerable success, and his superiors received numerous requests from Cashel and neighbouring towns for his services. After this short stay in his native town, he was sent by his minister provincial, in response to repeated requests from the citizens, to the friary in Waterford city as master of novices and preacher. His preaching gave great satisfaction to both clergy and laity. In mid-August 1649, Oliver Cromwell landed with his troops at Dublin, and the Catholics in Leinster and Munster soon found themselves in danger. The *vita* as recorded by Bruodin states that John Kearney continued his priestly ministry in Waterford until the Cromwellian troops arrived in 1649, and then he went into hiding. Cromwell and his soldiers reached Waterford on 24 November 1649[19] and summoned the city to surrender. Knowing what had occurred at Wexford on 11 October, when a large number of laity and seven Franciscans had been put to death,[20] Kearney and his fellow-priests did not expect mercy.

The Catholic bishops of Ireland met at Clonmacnoise from 4 to 13 December 1649 to assess the situation. They issued three declarations.[21] Among other things, they stated that it was very clear that Oliver Cromwell planned to extirpate the Catholic religion in all the king's dominions. In his reply in 1650 to their declarations, Cromwell left them in no doubt regarding his attitude to bishops and priests, to Catholicism in general, and especially to the Mass.[22]

In the spring and summer of 1650 the conquest continued, but Cromwell himself returned to England on 26 May after the surrender of Clonmel (10 May). The city of Waterford surrendered on 6 August.[23] There is no evidence that John Kearney returned there. In August 1650, the Friars Minor held their provincial chapter in Connacht, at Kilconnell Friary. This chapter changed Kearney from Waterford city, but not from the united dioceses of Waterford and Lismore. It appointed him Guardian of the friary in Carrick-on-Suir,[24] about thirteen miles from Waterford. From this time onwards, until his capture, his life was a hunted one.

one of the lecturers appointed by that chapter to Cashel he must have taught there previous to the chapter (see *Liber Lovan.*, 18). **19** Gilbert, *Contemp. Hist.*, ii, 325. **20** See sources cited in Millett, *Ir. Franciscans*, 539. **21** *Comment. Rinucc.*, iv, 318–40. **22** See W.C. Abbott (ed.), *The writings and speeches of Oliver Cromwell* (4 vols, Cambridge, Mass., 1937–47), ii, 196–205. **23** Gilbert, *Contemp. Hist.*, iii, 219. **24** *Tabula* of the provincial chapter of the Friars Minor in Ireland, 1650. FLK, MS Christ 1, 64. Printed in *Liber Lovan.*, 36.

ARREST AND IMPRISONMENT

After the surrender of Fethard, of Clonmel, and of Waterford, in 1650, all the Catholic clergy and religious in south Tipperary and in County Waterford had to go into hiding. Kearney was stationed in the Suir valley, midway between Waterford and Clonmel. A contemporary report states that, by the end of October 1650, the Catholics had lost all their churches in the cities of Waterford and Kilkenny and in many towns, including Clonmel.[25] In common with many diocesan and regular priests in Munster, John Kearney decided to remain in Ireland to minister to the Catholics, despite the pleas of various lay and clerical friends that he should seek safety overseas. This is confirmed by the testimony of the Jesuit superior, Thomas Quin, who also pays tribute to Kearney's missionary work and his preaching.[26] In those early years of Puritan rule in Ireland, before the Cromwellian Act of Settlement had uprooted many of the Catholics in the provinces of Munster, Leinster, and Ulster, the priest was safest among his relatives and friends. John Kearney kept on the move, travelling between towns and villages. Day and night he worked in secret, saying Mass, administering the sacraments, and preaching.

On 4 October 1650, as a beginning of a new civil administration, Cromwell appointed four 'Commissioners of Parliament', one of whom, Edmund Ludlow, was even more uncompromising and radical than Cromwell himself. They divided the country up into precincts, each under a military governor. One precinct had its centre at Clonmel. This explains why so many captured priests and religious from south Tipperary, including Kearney, were imprisoned at Clonmel between 1652 and 1655 and there interrogated, and in some cases (e.g. John Kearney and William Tirry) put to death.

As soon as the conquest was effectively over in 1652, pressure mounted to implement the Act of Settlement of 1652 and to carry out quickly the great social upheaval which had been planned. This legislation, which came to be aimed almost exclusively at the Catholics, was so framed that no person of any property could hope to escape.[27] The second serious impact of the Cromwellian settlement was in matters of religion. There was to be no toleration of papists. It was hoped that those priests who had not fled the country would, from the beginning of 1653, willingly go abroad, at least

25 *Comment. Rinucc.*, iv, 468. **26** See note 3. **27** For details, and for sources cited, see P.J. Corish in *NHI*, iii, 353–86.

out of fear of the new, very severe legislation. On 6 January 1653, the commissioners issued a proclamation banishing from the country within twenty days of its publication all Jesuits, seminary priests, and all other priests, and stating that those who did not withdraw from Ireland within the prescribed period or who returned from exile were to be subject to the penalties of the English statute of 1585 (27 Eliz., c. 2) against Catholic clergy. This proclamation was published at Clonmel on 21 January 1653.[28] The commissioners quickly found out that the priests of Ireland did not go abroad as readily as the soldiers. Accordingly, to discover and punish those who would not, the government offered a reward for their capture, fixed at £5 in 1653.[29]

John Kearney did not present himself for deportation, but endeavoured to continue his priestly work in secret. But the circumstances had changed. After the publication of the proclamation of banishment, Kearney and his fellow-priests who had previously taken refuge in the houses of relatives and friends were reluctant to continue to do so, because the Elizabethan statute which the proclamation applied made it a felony for anyone to harbour or assist a priest. Despite several appeals for a suspension of the proclamation, the commissioners insisted that the harsh legislation against priests be strictly enforced and increased the pressure by issuing a special declaration on 19 February.[30] At about the beginning of March, Kearney was captured at Cashel. The exact date is not known. He fell into the hands of a certain Captain (or Colonel) Wilmer who was in command of a company of soldiers.[31] He was bound and locked up. A short time later he was taken to Clonmel, the administrative centre of the precinct. There Colonel Jerome Sankey, the precinct's military governor, ordered him to be thrown into jail, to join other Catholic prisoners, clerical and lay. The imprisoned priests are not named, but there were Franciscans among them, and they helped John Kearney to prepare himself for death.[32]

·

28 J.P. Prendergast, *The Cromwellian settlement of Ireland* (2nd ed., London, 1870), 319–20. **29** For some details on the application of this penal legislation, taken from the administrative records (printed) and other contemporary sources, see R.D. Edwards, 'Irish Catholics and the Puritan revolution', in *Father Luke Wadding*, 93–118; Benignus Millett, 'Survival and Reorganisation, 1650–95', in Corish, *Ir. Catholicism*, iii, ch. 7, 1–12. **30** *Archiv Hib.* 7 (1918–21), 41. **31** No officer of this name has been traced. A William Willer was among the signatories of the articles of agreement within the city of Limerick in April 1652, cf. *Archiv. Hib.* 6 (1917), 66. **32** It is possible that one of them was Raymund English, OFM, who was one of six priests in Clonmel jail in 1653–4; see Patrick Power, *Waterford and Lismore: a compendious history of the united dioceses* (Cork, 1937), 368.

TRIAL

Kearney was tried and sentenced the day after he was imprisoned at Clonmel. It is described in the *vita* recorded by Bruodin as the feast-day of St Joachim, i.e. 20 March in the liturgical calendar then in use among the Franciscans. But this *vita* was written overseas, and it is therefore safe to assume that it followed the Gregorian calendar and that Kearney's trial was held in Clonmel on 10 March. On that day all the imprisoned priests, including Kearney, were taken from jail and brought before a court presided over by Sankey.

John Kearney was expressly accused of having celebrated Mass and administered the sacraments in various places in Munster and of having strengthened the Catholics in their faith and prevented their conversion from popery.[33] In other words, he was charged with having functioned as a priest in defiance of the law. Kearney admitted that he was a Catholic priest and said that it was his priestly duty to offer Mass and administer the sacraments required by a Catholic people. Sankey straightaway condemned Kearney to death and ordered the other clerical prisoners to be banished from the country.

But frequently capital punishment was not imposed on captured priests, who were deported instead of being executed. In Clonmel, on 10 March, Kearney alone was sentenced to death. The other priests were sentenced to banishment. The proclamation of banishment had been promulgated at Clonmel on 21 January. The twenty days' grace allowed had expired on 10 February. Therefore the other accused priests, if captured after 10 February, would have been deemed at law automatically guilty of high treason by the mere fact that they had remained in the country, and so were subject to the death penalty.

MARTYRDOM

Immediately after sentence was passed on him, Kearney was led back to prison. Back in jail he prepared himself for death by putting aside the lay clothes which he wore as a disguise over his religious habit. Though it is not explicitly stated in the *vita* cited by Bruodin that the execution was carried

---

33 Treatise entitled *Memoriall of the war begun 1641*, written by Mr Kearney between February and May 1656. Bodl., Carte MSS, 64, f. 458v; cf. Quin, *Relatio et conditio* (see note 3); Bruodin, *Anatomicum Examen*.

out the day after sentence was passed, it is clear from internal evidence that this was so. It is stated explicitly that Kearney died at 11 a.m. on a Friday in the year 1653 at the age of thirty-four. In 1653, 21 March new style (11 March old style) was a Friday.

Clad in his Franciscan habit, with rosary attached, and with a cross in his hand, John Kearney was taken from the jail[34] out into the town to the scaffold.[35] A crowd quickly gathered, comprising Catholics and Puritans, the latter scoffing in amazement at the strangely dressed prisoner. When he reached the place of execution, Kearney knelt down and with tears in his eyes prayed briefly. He then ascended the steps and got permission from the commander of the company of soldiers to address the crowd. The *vita* cited by Bruodin gives his exact words, which may mean that Canon Geoffrey Sall, its co-author, heard them or got them from someone who did. Kearney told his listeners that he was captured, imprisoned, charged, and sentenced to death because he had celebrated Masses, administered the sacraments, and confirmed the people in their loyalty to the Catholic faith, and for no other reason. He said that he had admitted to all this during his trial, and that he now publicly professed his faith in the Catholic Church as the one true Church and willingly died for this, relying confidently on the merits of Christ. The sentence was then carried out. Two of the sources explicitly say that he was hanged.[36]

Sankey gave permission to Kearney's friends for the removal of his body, which they brought to Cashel and buried in the chapter hall of the suppressed friary.

V. MOTIVE FOR MARTYRDOM

John Kearney was condemned to death because he had functioned as a priest in defiance of the proclamation of 6 January 1653. At his trial witnesses were produced who charged him with high treason, stating that in various places he had celebrated Mass, given the sacraments and cate-

---

34 The jail is not specified. According to the survey taken at Clonmel on 9 August 1655, there were three jails in the town: the county jail, beside the town hall, near the centre of the town; the shire jail 'under the West Court house' and a stone house in the middle of the town, on the south side, the lower part of which (presumably the basement) was used as a common jail (*Civil Survey*, i, 387–8).   35 The scaffold possibly was erected in Martyr Lane (now Market Street). It is possible, but not likely, that it was outside the north gate, on Gibbet Hill (now Gallows Hill); see W. P. Burke, *History of Clonmel* (Waterford, 1907), 56–7, 170–1. 36 Quin, *Relatio et conditio* (note 3); Bruodin, *Anatomicum Examen*.

chised the people. He readily admitted this and strenuously defended his right to officiate as a priest.

His refusal to leave the kingdom, or to have declared, at the appropriate time, his willingness to depart, meant that at law he was deemed guilty of treason, for which the punishment was death. So also were the priests who were imprisoned with him at Clonmel. But they were sentenced to banishment, not to death. Kearney, it is clear, was specifically charged with having exercised his priesthood.[37] He admitted that he was guilty, but showed no regrets. On the contrary, he refused to apologize or to be intimidated by threats;[38] instead he put up a spirited defence and insisted that the laws which forbade him to function as a priest were unjust.[39] These emphatic pronouncements probably angered Sankey, who decided to apply the full penalty allowed by law. The *Memoriall of the War begun 1641* says that John Kearney and the other three victims whom it names were put to death 'for being priests'.

FAMA MARTYRII

Among the Catholic bystanders, including Kearney's friends, who witnessed his death, the *fama martyrii* was instant, and they greatly helped to spread this reputation. From them came the story of the alleged miracle during the funeral procession from Clonmel to Cashel, which was incorporated into the composite *vita* written by Joseph Sall and Canon Geoffrey Sall. It is clear that the young John Kearney had rapidly gained a reputation for himself as a zealous priest and an eloquent preacher in south Tipperary and in the lower valley of the Suir. Joseph Sall, who knew him since childhood and had received his religious and priestly formation with him, described him as a companion of the greatest integrity.[40] Impressive in his living, he obviously was equally impressive in his dying. His fellow-priests were convinced that he was a martyr. The diocesan and regular priests of south Tipperary, all of whom were his friends and some his relatives, played a major role in spreading his reputation of martyrdom at home and abroad. A large number of them were deported or fled the country in 1653 and 1654. After settling down temporarily in Flanders, France, or Spain, they kept in contact by letter with each other and with other priests from the same district who had fled the country earlier. This kept the *fama martyrii* alive.

---

37 See note 33 above. **38** Quin, *Relatio et conditio.* **39** Bruodin, *Anatomicum Examen.* **40** See note 1.

Within much less than a year after his execution, a life of John Kearney had been written by his friend and confrère Joseph Sall, who sent it from Spain to Louvain with his letter of 16 January 1654. Sall, who had left Ireland before John Kearney's capture, had no first-hand information on the martyrdom. His letter was probably addressed to John Colgan, OFM, the distinguished Irish hagiographer at St Anthony's College in Louvain. It may well have been Colgan who persuaded Canon Geoffrey Sall to write an account of the martyrdom, i.e. to add to the *vita* written by Joseph Sall. According to Bruodin, the *vita* used by him had both the friar and the canon as its authors. As mentioned above, it was, apparently, a *textus conflatus* made up of two accounts.

In his report on the Irish Church for the years 1652–6, Thomas Quin, SJ, made reference to the martyrdom of two Franciscan priests, John Kearney and John Daton (the latter of whom was executed in Kilkenny in 1654), and said that he was enclosing lives of the two martyrs with his report. He did not name the author of either life. Among the papers of John Colgan which were preserved at Louvain in St Anthony's College until the French Revolution, it was noted that there were '*Vitae Patrum Joannis Daton et Joannis Kearny*'.[41] Writing from Arras on 26 January 1657, Peter Creagh, SJ, mentioned that he had in his possession an account of Kearney's martyrdom written by a Father John Sall.[42] This may have been a completely independent account. On the other hand, Creagh may have intended Joseph Sall, whom he mistakenly called John. An exhaustive search in various archives and libraries in Europe since 1976 has failed to find any manuscript life of the martyr.

Some priests from south Tipperary smuggled relics of John Kearney to France. In his letter, Creagh told Conway that, one or two years earlier, their cousin Geoffrey Sall (probably to be identified with Canon Geoffrey Sall, the co-author of the *vita*) had sent on to him from Paris a little piece of Kearney's habit and a few of his hairs. In Arras, Creagh treasured these relics and told Conway that they 'wrought many evident miracles in this town'. The same Geoffrey Sall, or someone else, sent some relics of Kearney to the martyr's Irish confrères at Louvain. There they remained until 1797, when with some of the contents of the archives of St Anthony's College they were taken for safety to St Isidore's College in Rome, whence they were removed to the Franciscan Friary at Merchant's Quay, Dublin, in 1872. Since 1947, they have

---

41 *HMC, Fourth Report*, app. 1, 612.   **42** Peter Creagh, SJ, to Walter Conway, Canon of the diocese of Cashel, Arras, 26 January 1657. FLK, MS D 23, no. 2 (contemporary copy). Printed in Millett, *Ir. Franciscans*, 261–2.

been in the Franciscan Library at Killiney, County Dublin.[43] The folded seventeenth-century paper in which the relics of John Kearney are packed has an inscription which reads: '*Ex tunica, chorda, et capillis P. Joannis Carneii cuius vitam et martyrium . . .*', the remainder of the inscription being illegible owing to corrosion of the paper. The tiny packet contains a small piece of grey cloth (from Kearney's habit) and a small fragment of rough hemp. The relics of the martyr's hairs have disappeared. During the Ordinary Process in 1904, these relics were mentioned, but the inscription was misread and the relics attributed in error to another friar martyr.

Peter Creagh's letter provides strong evidence of a flourishing *fama martyrii* among some Irish exiles and among the laity at Arras, less than four years after Kearney's death. Creagh was anxious to foster devotion to the martyr at Arras, and asked Canon Conway to get some Irish Franciscan at Louvain who knew Kearney to draw a picture of him. We do not know if any such painting was made.

Kearney's death occurred too late to be mentioned by any of the Irish martyrologists. The only major work to record his martyrdom was Bruodin's *Anatomicum Examen*. This appeared in 1671. But eight years earlier the Irish minister provincial had included Kearney's name in the list of Franciscan martyrs which he sent to Rome for presentation at a general chapter.[44] In the eighteenth and nineteenth centuries, the reputation of martyrdom faded away, until reawakened by the martyrologies of O'Reilly and Murphy, and by Moran's study of the sufferings of the Catholics of Ireland under the Puritans.

During the Ordinary Process *de fama martyrii* held at Dublin in 1904 the case of John Kearney was examined in detail and the findings were submitted to the Holy See. In due course the General Promoter of the Faith, in his *Disquisitio*, 282–3, reviewed the evidence and concluded thus:

Haec igitur historia sacram Congregationem latere non debet.

As a result of this favourable verdict, Kearney's case was among the 260 examined during the Apostolic Process held at Dublin between 1917 and 1930. The findings were then presented to the Holy See.

43 FLK, MS D 23, no. 4. 44 List of Irish Franciscan martyrs compiled by Anthony Doherty, OFM, Minister Provincial of Ireland, July 1663. FLK, MS D 1, 880 (authenticated copy); A.S.I., MS W 5, 5 (authenticated copy). List printed in Millett, *Ir. Franciscans*, 538–40, in *Ann. Min.*, ad an. 1662, no. XIV, and, with some slight inaccuracies, in Moran, *Spicil. Ossor.*, i, 437.

CHAPTER 13

William Tirry, OSA

Francis X. Martin

EARLY LIFE

William Tirry was born in the city of Cork in 1608. His family were patrician merchants who had been prominent in Cork civic life for centuries. In such small cities, the merchant families formed close-knit communities – William's mother, Joan, appears to have been closely related to his father, Robert. These families also regularly married into the landed gentry – Robert Tirry's sister, Joan, married Dominick Sarsfield, Viscount Kilmallock.[1] Such families were at the very centre of the efforts to establish the Counter-Reformation in Ireland. Robert's brother, William's uncle, also William Tirry, was provided to the united dioceses of Cork and Cloyne on 24 January 1622, and consecrated on 4 April 1623; he died in 1646.[2]

The future martyr was brought up in a household where Catholicism of the Counter-Reformation was almost certainly a personal conviction. This led him to become an Augustinian friar. There are no extant records of his religious profession or of his priestly ordination. Because no Catholic institutions of learning were allowed in Ireland at the time, he, like many others, had to go to Catholic Europe to complete his education.

He went first to Valladolid,[3] and thence to Paris, where he was in 1635 and 1636. His Prior at the Collège des Grands Augustins was a noted leader of the Augustinian reform, Archange Guin.[4] A note on page 7 of James O'Mahony's *Sanguinea Eremus*[5] in the Bibliothèque Royale, Brussels, refers

---

1 For details, see *Archiv. Hib.* 20 (1957), 79, note 4.   2 James O'Mahony, *Sanguinea Eremus Martyrum Hibernia Ord. Eremit. S. P. Augustini* (Brussels, 1655), 7–9. Printed in *Archiv. Hib.* 15 (1950), 84–7. See the testimony of Walter Conway, canon of the diocese of Cashel, Brussels, 25 June 1655: Paris, Archives Nationales, Registre +3640, ff 89v–93r.; printed in *Archiv. Hib.* 20 (1957), 90–7. See also the narrative of William Tirry's imprisonment and death, written *c.*1655 by Robert O'Connell – *Comment. Rinucc.*, v, 192–7; *HBC*, 395.   3 Testimony of Walter Conway, see note 2 above.   4 Official list of the Augustinian community at the Collège des Grands Augustins, Paris, in 1636. AGA, MS Ff 25, 202. See James O'Mahony, OSA, to Archange Guin, OSA, Prior of the Collège des Grands Augustins, Paris, Brussels, 26 June 1655. Paris, Archives Nationales, Registre S +3640, ff 87v–88r. Printed in *Archiv. Hib.* 20 (1957), 78–80.   5 See note 2 above.

to William Tirry as *qui studentis laurea fuit insignitus Parisiis die 4 Augusti 1635.*
Vide lib. I contractuum, f. 536. This apparently means that he was admitted to
the higher course, preparing for the lectorate in theology at Paris.
Unfortunately, this '*lib. I contractuum*' cannot be traced, and Tirry's name does
not appear in the surviving list of doctors of theology who were alumni of
the Paris college, compiled about 1654, but it is clear that he was being
steadily schooled in the discipline of the reformed religious orders and in
theological learning.

When he had completed his theological studies in Paris, he spent some
time in Brussels before returning to Ireland.[6] His stay in Brussels must have
been a short one, for he had returned to Ireland 'a few years' before the
outbreak of hostilities there in 1641.[7] In Ireland, in the late 1630s, the religious orders were able to live in community, and Tirry was attached to the
Augustinian house in his native Cork.[8] However, it was not easy for a
person of his social standing to remain always within the community. He
spent about four months as secretary to his uncle, the bishop,[9] but though
he relinquished this post to return to his community, he was shortly afterwards prevailed upon to become chaplain to his uncle by marriage, Viscount
Kilmallock, and to act as tutor to his two sons.[10]

When war broke out in 1641, William Tirry's native city of Cork became
the headquarters of the Protestants of Munster, and remained under their
control for the whole decade of the 1640s. William may have continued as
chaplain and tutor to Viscount Kilmallock for some time, but at the provincial chapter of 1646 he was appointed *socius* to the incoming provincial,
Denis O'Driscoll,[11] and in consequence was to be his close associate for the
three-year term of his office. Almost certainly they were stationed at
Fethard, County Tipperary, where O'Driscoll became Prior in 1649.

William Tirry was appointed prior of Skreen, County Meath, at the
Augustinian provincial chapter held on 15 June 1649.[12] However, it is most
unlikely that he ever took up residence there, for Oliver Cromwell landed
at Dublin just two months later, on 15 August, and soon the area around
Skreen was under the control of forces of the English Commonwealth. By
the end of the year, they held a coastal strip stretching from Derry in the

---

6 James O'Mahony to Filippo Visconti, Brussels, 7 November 1654. AGA, MS Dd 89,
268–78. Printed in *Archiv. Hib.* 20 (1957), 111–14; O'Mahony, *Sanguinea Eremus*; Testimony
of Walter Conway (see note 2); *Archiv. Hib.* 20 (1957), 70.   7 *Comment.Rinucc.*   8 Ibid.
9 O'Mahony, *Sanguinea Eremus*; Testimony of Walter Conway (see note 2).   10 O'Mahony,
Sanguinea Eremus; *Comment. Rinucc.*   11 O'Mahony to Archange Guin, 26 June 1655 (see
note 4).   12 Acts of the Irish Franciscan Provincial Chapter held at Fethard, County
Tipperary, 15 June 1649. AGA, MS Ff 22, f. 1417r.

north to a point west of Cork in the south, and, by the middle of 1650, William Tirry was probably living in territory occupied by the Commonwealth forces.

All the sources are agreed that, for three years before his arrest at Easter 1654, he was living in seclusion at Fethard, County Tipperary, under the protection of another relative by marriage among the landed gentry, the widowed Mrs Amy Everard.[13] Here he acted as tutor to her only surviving son, made himself available to all who came seeking the sacraments, and spent most of his time in prayer and mortification.

ARREST AND IMPRISONMENT

He was arrested on Holy Saturday, 25 March 1654.[14] He had been betrayed by three informers, who wished to collect the £5 paid to those who supplied information leading to the capture of a priest.[15] When the soldiers broke into his retreat they found him vested for Mass. In his desk they found writings in defence of the Catholic faith and against Protestant beliefs.[16] He was brought to Clonmel, where he was committed to jail with other priests. Here he remained for nearly a month, giving edification to all by his life of prayer and mortification. The circumstances of his arrest made it unlikely that he would escape the death penalty.[17]

TRIAL

At this time, all Catholic clerics in Ireland were adjudged automatically guilty of high treason and therefore subject to the death penalty by the mere fact of their presence in the country; this was a provision of an English statute of 1585

13 For details see *Archiv. Hib.* 20 (1957), 89, note 1.   **14** James O'Mahony, OSA, Irish prior provincial to Filippo Visconti, OSA, prior general of the Hermits of St Augustine, Brussels, 4 September 1654. AGA, MS Dd 89, 207–10. Printed in *Archiv. Hib.* 20 (1957), 108–9; Testimony of Walter Conway (see note 2); O'Mahony to Archange Guin, 26 June 1655 (see note 4). The statement that he was arrested on Ash Wednesday (*Comment. Rinucc.*) must be simply an error.   **15** James O'Mahony to Filippo Visconti, Brussels, 26 December 1654. AGA, MS Ff 22, f. 1443r., printed in *Archiv. Hib.*, 20 (1957), 118; Testimony of Walter Conway (see note 2). See J.P. Prendergast, *The Cromwellian settlement of Ireland* (2nd ed, revised, London, 1870), 320–2.   **16** Testimony of Matthew Fogarty, OFMCap, 6 April 1655. Paris, Archives Nationales, Registre S +3640, ff 88r-89v., printed in *Archiv. Hib.* 20 (1957), 80–9; *Comment. Rinucc.*   **17** O'Mahony to Filippo Visconti, 4 September 1654 (see note 14); Testimony of Walter Conway (see note 2).

(27 Eliz., c. 2), extended to Ireland by proclamation on 6 January 1653. However, the capital penalty was by no means always enforced, the government being normally content with banishing captured priests.

The first distinction made among the group of priests in jail in Clonmel was between seculars and regulars. On 23 April, the four secular priests were sentenced to banishment. William Tirry and another friar, Matthew Fogarty, OFMCap, were brought to trial on 26 April before a jury of twelve men and Commonwealth judges, including Mr Paris and Colonel Solomon Richards. The charge against both was the same: that they were guilty of high treason by virtue of being in the country contrary to the proclamation of 6 January 1653. Tirry's reply was that he had no wish to defy the Commonwealth government in temporal affairs, for in such matters he recognised it as the highest authority in the country, but in matters of religion and conscience he had to obey his religious superiors and the pope, and in consequence he had no option but to remain in Ireland. A debate on what appears to have been the problem of conflicting loyalties seems to have gone decidedly in Tirry's favour.[18]

The two friars had been given the benefit of trial by jury, but it would appear that the members of the jury were very much under the influence of the local civil and military authorities. The jury seems to have had little hesitation in finding the two friars guilty as charged (in fact they did not make any defence). They were sentenced to death by hanging,[19] and they accepted the sentence joyfully. Until Tirry's execution on 2 May, they were permitted lenient custody, in the form of house arrest, and a great number of people were given access to them.[20]

MARTYRDOM

On the morning of Monday, 1 May, William Tirry and a layman, Peter Power, were told that they were to die, and were given twenty-four hours to prepare themselves. Fogarty was told that he would be hanged later – in fact he was held in prison for several further months and then banished abroad.[21] At nine o'clock the next morning, 2 May,[22] the jailer, Richard

18 O'Mahony to Filippo Visconti, 4 September 1654 (see note 14); O'Mahony to Filippo Visconti, 7 November 1654 (see note 6); O'Mahony, *Sanguinea Eremus*; Testimony of Matthew Fogarty (see note 16); Testimony of Walter Conway (see note 2). 19 Testimony of Matthew Fogarty; Testimony of Walter Conway. 20 Ibid. 21 O'Mahony to Archange Guin, 26 June 1655 (see note 4). 22 The date as given in *Comment. Rinucc. (2° Maii 1654*

Rouse, informed Tirry that he must be manacled in order to bring him to
the gallows. Tirry went in chains, wearing the religious tonsure, dressed in
his black Augustinian habit, and reciting the rosary.[23]

Great crowds – one source says about a thousand people[24] – had gathered to seek his final blessing. He was allowed to address them from the
scaffold, despite the efforts of a Protestant minister to have him silenced. The
minister tried to divert him from his theme by engaging him in religious
controversy, but was quickly silenced by Tirry. The friar's theme was simple:
there is only one true Church, whose head is the pope: pope and Church
are to be obeyed. He publicly forgave the three men who had betrayed him,
and, as already noted, stated explicitly that he had been offered life and
favour, if he would renounce his religion.[25]

He was then hanged.[26] The crowd rushed forward with cloths to soak up
the blood which gushed from his nostrils, and many of them were prepared
to pay high prices to the Protestants for what they believed were relics of a
martyr. The Protestants themselves were impressed and moved by his death.
He was buried with some ceremony in the ruins of the Augustinian friary
at Fethard, County Tipperary, in the grounds, according to all the evidence,
rather than in the church.[27] It has not been possible to locate his grave.

MOTIVE FOR MARTYRDOM

William Tirry was put to death because he was a priest, and had remained
in Ireland and functioned as a priest after the edict of banishment. Under
its terms, although he fully accepted the authority of the government in
temporal matters, he was guilty of treason and subject to the death penalty.
The *Memoriall of the War begun 1641*[28] says that Tirry and the other three
victims whom it names were put to death 'for being priests'.

Yet not all the priests brought to trial under this draconian edict were
executed: Matthew Fogarty is only one of many who were merely
banished.[29] Why Tirry was hanged and Fogarty banished must remain a

---

stylo Ibernico, proindeque veteri, sed 22° Aprilis stylo Romano) can only be regarded as a slip by a
normally careful author.   **23** Testimony of Walter Conway; *Comment. Rinucc.*   **24** Testi-
mony of Matthew Fogarty (see note 16).   **25** Testimony of Walter Conway; *Comment.
Rinucc.*   **26** The statement that he was hanged, drawn and quartered (*Comment. Rinucc.*) is
wrong. This punishment was not inflicted under the Commonwealth.   **27** Testimony of
Walter Conway; O'Mahony to Archange Guin, 26 June 1655 (see note 4); *Comment.
Rinucc.*   **28** Treatise entitled *Memoriall of the war begun 1641*, written by Mr Kearney between
February and May 1656: Bodl., Carte MSS, 64, f. 458v.   **29** *Comment. Rinucc.*, v, 197–9.

matter for speculation. It may be that the distinction was made because Tirry had a more important political background, being the nephew of Viscount Kilmallock, but this would appear the less likely explanation. It is quite possible that there was an element of chance, in that Tirry was the first to be tried and sentenced, and logically therefore the first to be summoned to execution. It may be suggested that the longer Fogarty remained in jail the better became the prospect that his sentence would be commuted to banishment. The logical procedure would seem to be that the two condemned together should be executed together. In fact a layman, Peter Power, was executed on the same occasion as Tirry, and their executions were linked for no apparent reason, whereas Fogarty was left waiting for death but ultimately was saved by being banished abroad.

The question remains therefore: why was Tirry sent to the scaffold? It may well be because he was captured vested for Mass, *flagrante delicto*; and the Mass was held in detestation by the Commonwealth authorities. The fact that a manuscript work composed by him discrediting Protestantism was found among his effects is mentioned both by Fogarty and Robert O'Connell, OFMCap, as an even more serious consideration.[30] The accounts of his trial do seem to suggest that while neither friar tried to defend or exculpate himself – and indeed there was no legal defence – Tirry gives the impression of being the more unyielding. On the scaffold, he said explicitly that he had been offered life and favour if he would become a Protestant.[31] There is no improbability in this statement: such an offer must have been made routinely, even regularly made. It is likely that it was also made to Matthew Fogarty and rejected by him; but there is a suggestion that Tirry rejected it brusquely. He might very well have escaped with banishment had he been less emphatic in proclaiming his allegiance to the Catholic Church and his positive rejection of Protestantism.

FAMA MARTYRII

As already noted, Tirry's death made an immediate impression. The Protestants were impressed; Catholics treasured his relics; and miracles were recorded as having been obtained through his intercession.[32] The interest expressed by the Augustinian prior general, Filippo Visconti, induced the

---

30 These are the two reasons advanced by Fogarty (see note 16) and O'Connell (see note 2). **31** Testimony of Walter Conway; *Comment. Rinucc.* **32** O'Mahony, *Sanguinea Eremus*; Testimony of Walter Conway (see note 2).

Irish provincial, James O'Mahony, to publish the *Sanguinea Eremus* in 1655. However, this rhetorical pamphlet seems to have made little impression except on the Augustinians. Only three copies are known to have survived, and Irish writers of the second half of the seventeenth century either ignore it[33] or mention it with little enthusiasm.[34]

Nevertheless, when interest in the martyrs revived in the nineteenth-century writers included Tirry in their lists.[35]

The case of William Tirry was examined at the Ordinary Process held in Dublin in 1904, and the findings were submitted to the Holy See. Through a strange oversight by the postulator, Tirry's name was omitted from the list of martyrs submitted to the Sacred Congregation. In due course the General Promoter of the Faith, having examined the evidence, concluded as follows (*Disquisitio*, 290–1):

> His documentis perspectis, idoneam existimarem hanc causam, de qua coram sacrorum rituum Congregatione esset disputandum, si quid tamen, de Gulielmi Tirrey affirmando martyrio, actores petiissent. Sed nescio qua postulatoris oblivione commissum est, ut, qui Augustinianos reliquos omnes sodales, qui in Sanguinea eremo, pro fide catholica defendenda, interfecti narrantur, in suum catalogum retulerit, hunc unum, de quo in eo documento plurima narrantur, imo, ad cuius historiam posteris tradendam, id documentum exaratum potissimum videtur, hunc unum, dico, praetermiserit (Proc. fol. 30). Legitime ergo petant actores oportet et de Gulielmi martyrio quaestio instituatur testesque rite ante excutiantur, quam disceptari liceat, an haec causa sit sacrae Congregationi credenda. Idque cum agent, necesse etiam erit, integrum locum historiae legationis nuncii Rinuccini ab eis proferri, in quo de Gulielmi martyrio agitur. Nam eminentissimus testis vicesimus ex hac historia ea retulit (Summ. pagg. 1417, 1418 par. 144), quae martyrium sequuta sunt. At non minus ea cognoscere refert, quae ante martyrium atque in ipso martyrio, ab historiae scriptore accidisse narrantur.

The Advocate, in his reply (*Responsio ad Disquisitionem*, 30–8), stated emphatically that Tirry's name *had* been presented. As a result, his name

---

33 O'Connell, *Comment. Rinucc.*, v, 192–7; Lynch, *De Praesulibus Hiberniae*, 1672. Bibl. Mazar., MS 1869, 678–80; printed in Lynch, *De Praesulibus Hib.*, ii, 158. **34** Anthony Bruodin, *Propugnaculum Catholicae Veritatis* (Prague, 1669), 727. **35** E.g. Denis Murphy, *Our martyrs* (Dublin, 1896), 358–60.

appeared in the list of martyrs, the introduction of whose cause was authorized by the Holy See in 1915. His cause was examined during the Apostolic Process held at Dublin between 1917 and 1930. The findings were then presented to the Holy See.

Important new documentation in support of his cause has been located and published over the past forty years.[36]

---

36 F.X. Martin (ed.), 'The Tirry documents in the Archives de France, Paris', in *Archiv. Hib.* 20 (1957), 69–97; M.B. Hackett (ed.), 'The Tirry documents in the Augustinian General Archives', ibid., 98–122.

The historiography of the martyrs

Benignus Millett, OFM

There are no judicial or court records for most of the Irish martyrs because most of them were condemned at summary trials under martial law. Therefore, while the testimony of eyewitnesses of their death – if any such be extant – is of primary value, the evidence for their martyrdom provided by their contemporaries and by the martyrologists is of special significance. Accordingly, certain aspects of the historiography of the Irish martyrs demand investigation. It is important to determine how individual martyrologists obtained their information. Were they eyewitnesses of the events they reported? Did they depend on first-hand knowledge? How reliable were their sources? Did the martyrologists approach their task with enlightened critical skill, or were they enthusiastic amateurs whose writings show little or no degree of restraint? If and when they depended on the researches of others, did they acknowledge such direct borrowings?

The relevant historiography must be seen in its contemporary setting. In the sixteenth and seventeenth centuries, the need – acutely felt to defend the Church against Protestant attack – contributed gradually to the emergence of Church history through a reappraisal of the sources and a subjection of them, in greater or lesser degree, to comment and criticism. In 1584, the Roman martyrology was officially published by Gregory XIII. The labours in this field during the 1580s by Baronius and his associates may have prompted John Howlin to compile his work on the Irish martyrs. Even before the critical method had taken a firm hold some volumes of history – such as Gonzaga's monumental tome on the Franciscan Order (1587) – had begun to appear. Between 1588 and 1605, twelve volumes of the *Annales Ecclesiastici* by Caesar Baronius were published, and this for reasons which were frankly apologetic, as he readily admitted.

In due course, this work inspired the scholars of the great religious orders to produce somewhat similar studies, characterized more and more, as the seventeenth century progressed, by the new methodological spirit. For example, the Franciscans, Dominicans and Jesuits published encyclopaedic works on their own history, several of which contain accounts of the sufferings and death of their Irish confrères. The scholarship of Luke Wadding, OFM, and Jean Bolland, SJ, both of whom wrote on Irish martyrs, has to a remarkable degree stood the test of an ever-developing critical spirit. Many chroniclers, historians and bibliographers, especially his own religious brethren, have borrowed directly from Luke Wadding. These later Franciscan writers copied information on the friar martyrs – e.g. on Bishop Patrick O'Healy and Conn O'Rourke – from entries printed by Wadding in one or other of his works. Bolland's name is associated principally with hagiography. The earliest attempts at methodical hagiographical criticism date from the beginning of the seventeenth century, from the scholarly work of Héribert Rosweyde, SJ, in Flanders which was successfully continued by Jean Bolland and led to the great co-operative enterprise of the Bollandists. The Irish Franciscan historians at Louvain and Rome fell under the spell of the Bollandists.[1] The new critical method inspired two Irish Franciscans with Louvain associations, Donagh Mooney[2] and Francis O'Mahony,[3] who in the second and third decades of the seventeenth

---

1 There was a regular correspondence between the Bollandists and these Irish friars (see Patrick Fleming's posthumous publication *Collectanea Sacra* (Louvain, 1667), 212, where he says, in reference to Jonas's life of St Columbanus: *cuius mihi copiam fecit R. P. Heribertus Rosweyde*). There was a fruitful exchange of views and information between the Franciscans at St Anthony's, Louvain, and the Bollandists, and there is plenty of evidence of mutual borrowing in the works of each. For details, see Canice Mooney, 'Father John Colgan, OFM, his work and times and literary milieu', in Terence O'Donnell (ed.), *Father John Colgan, OFM, 1592–1658* (Dublin, 1959), 19, note 29; see also Fergal Grannell, 'Letters of Daniel Papebroch, SJ, to Francis Harold, OFM (1665–1690)', in *Archivum Franciscanum Historicum*, lix (1966), 385–455. **2** Donagh Mooney began his novitiate in the friary of Donegal in the autumn of 1600 and was one of the last friars to escape when the friary was attacked in early August 1601 by an English and Irish army led by the ambitious Niall Garbh O'Donnell. He was sent to Multyfarnham to complete his novitiate, and he was there when that friary was sacked on 1–2 October. As a prisoner in Sir Francis Shane's castle at Ballymore, he made his religious profession to the imprisoned minister provincial in the presence of the dean of Armagh and the Franciscan bishop of Kilmore. He escaped from the castle and in due course was ordained priest. On 23 November 1607 he was appointed the first guardian of the new College of St Anthony at Louvain. Mooney was the minister provincial of the Franciscans in Ireland 1615–18. See *Anal. Hib.* 6 (1934), 40, 49, 93–6, 109–10, 124. **3** Francis O'Mahoney, also known as Francis Matthews from the Latinized form of his name, 'Franciscus Matheus', a native of Cork and baptized Edmund O'Mahony, was received into the order of Friars Minor at St Anthony's College, Louvain, on 1 July 1614 and made religious profession there the following year. While pursuing studies at St Anthony's he was promoted to orders, being ordained priest at Brussels on 28 February 1619. He was still at Louvain at the end of that year, when he was appointed preacher and confessor. In the early 1620s he became guardian of Cork friary, and on the death of the minister provincial, Nicholas Shea, in March 1625 he was chosen as vicar provincial. He retained this office until the Chapter held at Multyfarnham on 20 August 1626, at which he was elected minister provincial. The Provincial Chapter of 1629 elected him guardian of St Anthony's College in Louvain, where he remained, according to his own statement, for four and a half years. He was again chosen as guardian of Cork friary in 1641, and when the Catholics under

century wrote histories of the Franciscan province of Ireland in which they incorporated every scrap of information they could find on their martyred confrères. But even before the advent of Jean Bolland, hagiography was in favour, and David Rothe, the future Irish martyrologist, who was educated at Douai in the final decade of the sixteenth century, came under its influence.[4] He certainly would have been acquainted with the *Sanctorum Priscorum Patrum Vitae* (8 vols, Venice/Rome, 1551–60) by Luigi Lippomano and *De Probatis Sanctorum Historiis* (6 vols, Cologne, 1570–5) by the Carthusian Lawrence Surius, for both collections enjoyed a considerable reputation. And he may have personally known Rosweyde. The erudite and versatile Henry Fitzsimon, SJ, also came under these cultural influences; in 1593 he was sent to study theology in Louvain, where he made the intimate acquaintance of Rosweyde, as he stated in his *Brittannomachia*. This precursor of the Bollandists seemingly instilled into him the need for careful research,[5] and Fitzsimon, despite many other commitments, accepted the challenge, for he was capable of prodigies of industry and endurance.

Among the Irish martyrologists a mere handful emerge as outstanding. All, however, contributed significantly to the *fama martyrii*. Many recorded some details, perhaps not always very important, about individual martyrs, which were not known to other martyrologists. On the other hand, there are great similarities between the accounts of several martyrdoms, which strongly suggest that there were borrowings, even if no dependence was acknowledged.

The earliest written account of any of these martyrs may have been the relevant entry[6] for 1579 in the Annals of Loch Cé, which describes briefly the martyrdom of Bishop Patrick O'Healy, OFM, and Conn O'Rourke, OFM. On the face of it, it seems to be a completely independent account, standing aloof from all others, being the only reference to the martyrdom in a native Irish source. While the writer of this entry[7] cannot be described

Donough McCarthy, Viscount Muskerry, were trying to win control of the city during the Confederate war he was arrested in 1643 by order of Murrough O'Brien, Lord Inchiquin. After examination under torture he was hanged. See *Liber Lovan.*, 4, 6, 8; Canice Mooney, *The Friars of Broad Lane: the story of a Franciscan friary in Cork, 1229–1977*, ed. B. Egan (Cork, 1977), 44–6. **4** Later he published, besides his *Analecta Sacra*, a Latin life of St Brigid of Kildare in 1620, and in 1621 the *Hibernia Resurgens*, a defence of Ireland and its saints against the Scot, Thomas Dempster. **5** In his book on the Mass he refers to twenty years' research on the question of the first arrival of Christianity in Ireland (see Henry Fitzsimon, *The justification and exposition of the divine sacrifice of the Masse* [Douai, 1611], 119). **6** It may have been written in 1579, but perhaps not until a little later, i.e. between 1580 and 1588. There are also some problems regarding the identification of the scribe. **7** Brian Mac Diarmada or, more likely, a scribe employed by him.

as a martyrologist, his source may ultimately have been the same as the one from which the first martyrologist, the Englishman Thomas Bourchier, drew his information.

This probably was someone who was present at the execution of the two Franciscans and brought the story to Conn O'Rourke's brother, from whom the annalist learned of it. And, seemingly, it was someone from O'Rourke's native district who sent or brought word of the execution to Paris, where Bourchier heard of it. The information was specific, with a wealth of detail. Bourchier probably heard it at the friary from the other of the two friars – i.e. the companion of Friar Conn – who had arrived from Sligo, probably in 1575 or 1576.[8] The only Irish friar known for certain to have been in Paris in 1580 was the young Seán (or John) Ó Cathasaigh, OFM, then aged thirty,[9] who was provided to Killala as bishop on 11 July 1580[10] and, to judge from his family name, was probably from County Roscommon or County Mayo. There is another possibility, namely, that word of the executions was sent or brought to Paris by one of the Franciscans of Askeaton or Adare. These religious houses were not far from Kilmallock, and despite the adverse circumstances, communities of friars were still functioning in both places. There is no indication from Bourchier concerning the identity of his source; but because his description of the capture, interrogation and execution of the two friars is not short, vague and generic, but detailed, clear-cut and positive, this suggests that the informant who came to Paris was conversant with the facts of the case, either because he had been present at the events recorded or because he had questioned closely someone who had been there.

Francesco Gonzaga's account of the same martyrdom, published in 1587,[11] depends to a considerable extent on Bourchier's, as the internal evidence shows. He probably also heard of it from the youthful bishop-elect, Seán Ó Cathasaigh, who was in Rome when provided to Killala in July 1580.[12] However, Gonzaga, who also records the martyrdom of two

---

8 PRO, S.P., 63/58/2 i, intelligence report from France, undated but endorsed at Cork, 19 Feb. 1576 [1577 N.S.]. It was enclosed with letter of Sir William Drury to Walsingham, Dungarvan, 14 Apr. 1577. The report comments: 'The two friers that caine from Sligoye (whereof Oruorke his bastarde son is one) are in Parris at the chardge of Jeames [Fitzmaurice].' See also *Cal. S.P. Ire., 1574–85*, 112.   **9** See *Archiv. Hib.* 5 (1916), 162.   **10** Ibid. 174.   **11** Franciscus Gonzaga, *De Origine Seraphicae Religionis Franciscanae* (Rome, 1587), 846–7.   **12** At the consistory at which he was provided to Killala, it was announced that he had already made the prescribed profession of faith (*Archiv. Hib.* 5 [1916], 174). Gonzaga, who must have first met Ó Cathasaigh in Paris, was elected minister general at a chapter held in Paris at Pentecost 1579. He was in Rome in November 1579 and seemingly remained there, with occasional visits to Italian provinces, until 1583, when he went to Spain

Irish friars not mentioned by Bourchier, had other avenues of information open to him as minister general. One of his sources must have been the minister provincial of the province of Ireland, whom he would have met at the general congregation of the order at Toledo in 1583 and whose seal of office he describes.[13]

Also in 1587 another martyrologist, the Englishman Richard Verstegan,[14] published accounts of the martyrdom of O'Healy and O'Rourke and of the torture and execution of Archbishop Dermot O'Hurley in his *Theatrum Crudelitatum Haereticorum nostri temporis* (Antwerp, 1587), 80. His sources for these Irish cases are not known. It has to be remembered that Verstegan was still in England when the first occurred (August 1579), and that, when Archbishop O'Hurley was hanged (June 1584), he was in Rome, whence he returned towards the end of 1584 to Paris, where he remained until early in 1587, when he moved to Antwerp. Accordingly, he may have heard oral reports from Irish or English exiles. Both accounts by Verstegan are very brief and accurate. Because he does not give O'Rourke's name or the date of that martyrdom, it seems that he had not read or used Bourchier's description before his text was printed.[15] Another English martyrologist, John Bridgewater, reported the same martyrdoms in 1588.[16] He borrowed directly from Verstegan, whom he quoted word for word.

The Jesuit John Howlin was the first of the modern Irish martyrologists.[17] In his *Perbreve Compendium,* this meticulous chronicler lists forty-five victims of the religious persecution in Ireland, of whom eleven are on our

---

to prepare for a general congregation (see Paolo M. Sevesi, *L'Ordine dei Frati Minori* [2 pts, 3 vols, Milan, 1924–60], pt 2, i, 20–1).   **13** Gonzaga, op. cit. 846.   **14** This English Catholic (*c.* 1550–1640), who went into exile in 1582, was an author, publisher and engraver. He became the chief publisher and distributor of recusant books printed at Antwerp. With the publication of his *Theatrum Crudelitatum,* which had at least eight editions between 1587 and 1607, he also became one of the leading martyrologists in the closing years of Elizabeth's reign.   **15** See A. G. Petti, 'Richard Verstegan and Catholic Martyrologies of the Later Elizabethan Period', in *Recusant History* 5 (1959–60), 64–90. For a bibliography of his writings see *Recusant History* 7 (1963–4), 82–103.   **16** John Bridgewater, *Concertatio Ecclesiae Catholicae in Anglia* (2nd ed, Trier, 1588). The accounts of the Irish executions are printed on the recto and verso of the first folio (not numbered) immediately following the conclusion of Part II of the *Concertatio* on f. 212. This work first appeared in 1583. Then Bridgewater, using the tautonym Ioannes Aquaepontanus, published this enlarged edition.   **17** Born in Wexford in 1543 or 1544, Howlin was a priest when he entered the Society of Jesus at Rome in 1583. So far as is known, he was in Ireland at the time of the execution of O'Healy and O'Rourke. He describes it with a certain amount of vivid detail which would seem to indicate that he got his account from some person who had witnessed it. From 1589 to his death ten years later he was in Lisbon, where he was in close contact with Irish sailors and other exiles from Ireland who used the port of Lisbon, and may have received some information on the martyrs from one or other of them. See T.J. Morrissey, *James Archer of Kilkenny, an Elizabethan Jesuit* (Dublin, 1979), 5.

list. It is possible that he was present at the martyrdom of O'Healy and O'Rourke, for he was in Ireland at that time, but it is unlikely, because, careful recorder that he was, he would have admitted this. His informant was probably James Archer, SJ, who had been in Kilmallock. His account of Archbishop Dermot O'Hurley probably came from a report of Charles Lea, SJ, who had been imprisoned with the archbishop and used his medical skill to assuage the pain and injuries caused by the torture. But Howlin has no information on O'Hurley prior to his capture. And he states, wrongly, that the archbishop was hanged 'circa annum 1585 mense maio'. Apart from this, his account is accurate, if skimpy. He correctly records that the citizens of Dublin were not aware that the archbishop was being hanged, because the authorities arranged for the execution to be carried out secretly and very early in the morning. In the case of the priest Maurice MacKenraghty, Howlin noted that he got his facts from three trustworthy eye-witnesses. One of them was preparing the altar for the priest when the raid occurred. The other two, a priest and a nobleman, were natives of Clonmel and well known to Howlin. Being from Wexford, Howlin, who was then in Ireland, may have been in Wexford town when the laymen Matthew Lambert, Robert Meyler, Patrick Cavanagh, Edward Cheevers and companions were put to death in 1581. If he were not present at the events he records, then he obviously checked carefully with someone who had been. The martyrologist knew Margaret Bermingham personally and, as he states, was an eye-witness of her several attempts to have her son reconciled with the Church. He was in close contact with her and certain members of her family. Accordingly, his entry dealing with her sufferings for the Catholic faith is based on what he heard from those who witnessed them at close quarters.

David Rothe was the leading Irish martyrologist.[18] Some of the sources

18 David Rothe (1573–1650) was the outstanding Irish martyrologist of his time. Educated at Douai, where he became prefect of the Irish College, he then went to Spain, and in the summer of 1601 from there to Rome. Peter Lombard, the exiled archbishop of Armagh, sent him to Ireland as vice-primate in 1609 or 1610 with the Pope's approval. From 1618 until his death he was bishop of Ossory. At Paris in 1616 Rothe first published his *Analecta Sacra*. The projected work was to contain three parts, but this Paris edition had Part I only. Another edition, containing Parts I and II, appeared at Cologne in 1617. Then in 1619 his *De Processu Martyriali* was published at Cologne as the promised Part III. These Cologne printings were published under the pseudonym 'T.N. philadelphus'. While on his visit to Spain in 1601 Rothe spent some time in Salamanca. He may have seen and used Howlin's *Perbreve Compendium*, if it was then in the Irish College. The accounts of the martyrdom by Bourchier and Verstegan, or the reprint of the latter by Bridgewater, may have supplied him with information on the deaths of O'Healy and O'Rourke. *Cal. Carew MSS, 1603–24*, 286; *Archiv. Hib.* 2 (1913), 9; 3 (1914), 298; 4 (1915), 227–8; Lynch, *De Praesulibus Hib.*, i, 379; William

used in his *De Processu Martyriali* are known to us from the text itself. For example, he cites Bishop Conor O'Devany's *Index Martyrialis* twice. In the preliminary, unpaginated section of his work, when he treats of the martyred Brian Carolan he refers to the *Index* and states that he possesses a copy. He mentions it again in reference to the Franciscan Nial O'Boyle. Presumably he used O'Devany's brief text for a number of his own short entries. Bishop O'Devany, who had lived through the whole of Elizabeth's reign and for the first nine years of James I's, was acquainted with many of the martyrs of the Elizabethan era. To preserve their memory he had compiled this list, which contained the basic facts, i.e. the name of each martyr, and the date, place and circumstances of death. There were at least two copies of this catalogue or list. The second known copy is mentioned by Christopher Holywood, superior of the Irish Jesuit mission, in his report for 1612.[19] Holywood states that, shortly before his capture, O'Devany forwarded to the Jesuits his list of all the bishops and priests (beginning with Primate Creagh) who had suffered martyrdom, and asked them to vindicate their memory.

There is also incontrovertible evidence that, in at least one case, Rothe used Howlin's *Perbreve Compendium*. When treating of the martyrdom of Maurice MacKenraghty, he refers, on p. 156 of his *De Processu*, to Howlin's manuscript without mentioning the author's name, and then, on p. 157, he accurately quotes thirteen lines of text from it. Rothe, who was educated at Douai, spent some time in Salamanca.[20] While there, he could have seen Howlin's text and made extracts from it. Another explanation, and the more likely one, is that he asked someone in Spain to copy the relevant passage on MacKenraghty and forward it to him in Ireland. For some entries in his work, Rothe appears to have given a summary of what he found in other printed martyrologies. However, it must be stressed that Rothe, writing in

Carrigam, *The history and antiquities of the diocese of Ossory* (4 vols, Dublin, 1905), i, 86–112. **19** ARSI, MSS Anglia, 41, f. 53v. Born at Artane, County Dublin, Holywood entered the Society of Jesus at Verdun in June 1584 and studied at Pont-à-Mousson, where he was ordained priest in 1592 or 1593. He taught theology successively at Dole and Padua. In 1598 he was appointed superior of the Jesuit mission to Ireland, newly undertaken at the request of Clement VIII, but he was captured by the English when on his way to Ireland in 1599 and cast into prison. After his release he was able to enter Ireland in 1604 and for the next twenty-two years was busily engaged in organizing the mission. He died in office in Dublin. Holywood was a priest of great personal integrity, learning and patent missionary zeal. He was also a writer of no mean distinction. Many reports and letters penned by him have survived, some of which have been printed. See Carlos Sommervogel, *Bibliothèque de la Compagnie de Jésus* (11 vols, Brussels/Paris, 1890–1932), iv, 446–7. Many of his letters are printed in Edmund Hogan, *Ibernia Ignatiana*, i (Dublin, 1880). **20** See Lynch, *De Praesulibus Hib.*, i, 379; see also *Archiv. Hib.* 2 (1913), 9.

Ireland in the second decade of the seventeenth century, was in a position
to check and verify details of some cases of reputed martyrdom with
eyewitnesses, relatives and people in a position to know the facts. The
obvious men for him to have approached for information on the execution
of the priest Maurice MacKenraghty in Clonmel on 20 April 1585 were the
Jesuit priests Nicholas Leynach, Andrew Mulroney, and Thomas Shine.
These were all natives of Clonmel, and were adolescents or young men at
the time of MacKenraghty's death. Leynach and Shine were working in the
town and its neighbourhood when Rothe was writing his account. The
letter of Robert Rochford, SJ, on the martyrdom, which Rothe printed on
pp. 160–2, must have been given to him by one of these three Clonmel
Jesuits.

In his account of the martyred archbishop of Cashel, Dermot O'Hurley,
Rothe, on pp. 65–7, explicitly cites one of the sources he consulted, i.e.
Stanyhurst's *Brevis Praemunitio*, 29–30, from which he printed a lengthy
extract.[21]

He gives a wealth of detail on the archbishop's activities from the time
he arrived back in Ireland and on what happened to him in prison. Much
of this latter account, when checked against the official letters in the State
papers, is found to be accurate. What he writes about O'Hurley's movements before his capture cannot be controlled so easily, but it is clear that
he consulted a number of sources, oral and written. When writing (p. 60)
about the archbishop's contacts with Thomas Butler, Earl of Ormond, he
uses the phrase *nec desunt qui asserunt*. On this point, Rothe was favourably
placed to seek information, for he was a relative of Ormond's relatives, the
Butlers of Kilcash.[22] He was also able to ask relatives and friends of the
martyr about the imprisonment, for, unlike Howlin and other earlier
martyrologists, he mentions (on pp. 69–70) that O'Hurley, after being
tortured, was visited in prison by his only sister Honora, who tried to
persuade him to submit. Rothe's account, on pp. 102–44 of *De Processu*, of

---

21 Richard Stanihurst, *Brevis Praemunitio pro Futura Concertatione cum Jacobo Usserio* (2nd ed,
Douai, 1615). Richard Stanyhurst, born in Dublin in 1547, was a polymath who is best
known for his historical and chorographical accounts of later sixteenth-century Ireland.
While at Oxford he befriended Edmund Campion and probably under his influence became
a staunch proponent of the Counter-Reformation. Stanyhurst settled in the Spanish
Netherlands in the early 1580s and received a pension from the Spanish Crown. After a
number of years spent as a diplomat he eventually entered the Society of Jesus, and on being
ordained about 1606 was appointed one of the chaplains to the Archdukes Albert and Isabella
at their court in Brussels. He died there in 1618. 22 Bishop Rothe's paternal grandmother
was Ellen Butler, a first cousin of Piers Butler, eighth earl of Ormond (see Carrigan, *The
history and antiquities of the diocese of Ossory* [Dublin, 1905], iii, 76).

the martyrdom of Bishop Conor O'Devany and Patrick O'Loughran is lengthy, with no source cited. Rothe, of course, knew his fellow-bishop. Moreover, he would have had no problem about verifying details of his report, which could be checked with eyewitnesses. In his preface, he stated that he had exercised all diligence to discover the truth and to be sure about what he reported on the Irish martyrs.[23]

This martyrology was available to Philip O'Sullivan Beare[24] and John Mullan.[25] The former, who treats of many martyrs, including six on the present list, names no source. It is certain that Mullan used Rothe's martyrology, for he cites it three times in his *Epitome*,[26] which is the most comprehensive of the Irish martyrologies. Among the numerous Irish martyrs and confessors who suffered for the Catholic faith, it lists: five archbishops (including Dermot O'Hurley); thirteen bishops (including Patrick O'Healy and Conor O'Devany); twenty-two secular priests (including

---

23 In the unpaginated preface he wrote: *Horum ego praescius, et meae pariter imbecillitatis conscius, quamquam me neutiquam arguat mea mens praetermissi laboris et diligentiae, qua debui potuique uti in conquirenda veritate et certitudine eorum quae commemoro de nostris illis pugilibus.* **24** Philip O'Sullivan Beare, *Historiae Catholicae Iberniae Compendium* (Lisbon, 1621). He prints accounts of the martyrdom of Bishop O'Healy and Conn O'Rourke (ff 90r-91v), Archbishop O'Hurley (ff 102v-104v), Dominic Collins (f. 185r) and Bishop O'Devany and Patrick O'Loughran (ff 230v-236r). Philip O'Sullivan Beare (*c.* 1590–1650?), born on the island of Dursey, near the coast of west Cork, was one of the youngest of the seventeen children of Dermot O'Sullivan and his wife Johanna MacSweeney. After the defeat of the Irish armies at Kinsale he was sent with others to Spain and arrived at Corunna in February 1602. Philip was taught grammar, physics and philosophy at the College of St James of Compostella. When he had completed his studies he received a commission in the Spanish navy from Philip III. By temperament a studious man, Philip O'Sullivan Beare was one of those scholarly Irish exiles, and the only non-cleric among them, who wrote historical works in defence of their native land to counteract the propaganda of certain contemporary English and Anglo-Irish writers. His purpose, therefore, was polemical. In his work he was influenced and helped by the Irish in Spain, and especially by Father Patrick Synott, his former teacher, and by two Jesuits, Michael Cantwell and Richard Conway. His best-known work is the *Historiae Catholicae Iberniae Compendium*, the greater part of which is taken up with an account of the Elizabethan wars in Ireland. He was interested in Irish hagiography and in the 1630s was in correspondence with the Bollandists. For an account of his life and family, and for his work as an historian, see *Selections from the Zoilomastix of Philip O'Sullivan Beare*, ed. T.J. O'Donnell (Dublin, 1960), VI–XIX; and see *Studies*, 19 (1930), 211–26. See also Paul Grosjean, 'Hibernia a schedis Bollandianis' in *Anal. Boll.*, 50 (1932), 39–46. **25** John Mullan, a native of Cork, was a member of the Congregation of the Oratory and professor of 'theology, history and public eloquence' in Paris, possibly at the Sorbonne. Lynch, *De Praesulibus Hib.*, ii, 160. His book, published in 1629, consists of (i) *Idea Togatae Constantiae*; and (ii), with separate title-page, *Epitome Tripartita Martyrum*, so called because it treated of the martyrs of England, Ireland and Scotland. The Irish martyrs are treated of in 'Epitome secunda de martyribus Iberniae'. Some copies have in addition two letters giving details of the death of Francis Taylor. **26** John Mullan (Molanus), *Epitome Tripartita Martyrum* (Paris, 1629), 82, 90–1, 96. This work, with separate title-page, is printed at the end of his *Idea Togatae Constantiae*.

Maurice MacKenraghty and Patrick O' Loughran), together with six others listed as confessors; sixteen regular priests and brothers (including Conn O'Rourke, coupled with O'Healy, and Dominic Collins); twenty-nine laymen (including Robert Meyler, Edward Cheevers, Patrick Cavanagh and Matthew Lambert, and Francis Taylor), together with thirteen confessors and twenty unnamed lay martyrs; and two women (including Margaret Ball, née Bermingham). Accordingly thirteen on the present list appear in his martyrology.

Rothe's volume was issued too late to be used by Fitzsimon for his catalogue.[27] Verstegan's *Theatrum* was known to the Jesuit scholar, who also had access to information on some martyrs through the Irish Franciscans at Louvain and through his confrère Christopher Holywood, superior of the Irish mission, who corresponded with him.[28] John Coppinger may have seen Rothe's martyrology before sending his own[29] to the printers. If so, he makes no direct reference to it.

It might be argued that some of his entries – e.g. those on the priest Richard French and the laymen James Dowdal of Drogheda, Patrick Hayes and Peter Meyler – appear to be based on Rothe, but the evidence is purely internal and not conclusive. Coppinger, according to the seventeenth-century scholar John Lynch,[30] was a native of Cork, a priest, and a bachelor of sacred theology. He should probably be identified with the 'Johannes Copingerus' who was at the Irish College in Salamanca in September 1598.[31] It seems that while there he read Howlin's manuscript. The text of his martyrology shows that some entries in it – e.g. that on the priest Laurence Moore – depend on Howlin, and that others – e.g. those on Archbishop Nicholas Skerret and Bishops William Walsh, Hugh Lacy,

---

27 Henry Fitzsimon, *Catalogus Praecipuorum Sanctorum Hiberniae* (Liège, 1619). The author did not hesitate to include in his list of Irish saints Archbishop O'Hurley, Bishop O'Healy and other martyrs. **28** See BR, MS 2158–67, ff 10–15. **29** John Coppinger, *The Theatre of Catholique and Protestant Religion* (Saint-Omer, 1620). The title-page of this work says: 'Written by I.C. Student in Divinitie'. Even in recent years, there has been some confusion about the identity of the author. Bruodin took him to be one John Good, an English priest who worked in Limerick in Elizabeth's reign (cf. Anthony Bruodin, *Propugnaculum Catholicae Veritatis* [Prague, 1669] 424). **30** Lynch, *De Praesulibus Hib.*, ii, 159–60. John Lynch (c.1599 – c.1677), who used the pseudonym 'Eudoxius Alithinologus', was a distinguished classical scholar and historian who became archdeacon of Tuam c.1630. After the capture of Galway in 1652, he fled to France, where he remained until his death. Both this work, which, as he states in a brief note to the reader, was completed in July 1660, and the *Supplementum Alithinologiae* (1667) were published to refute certain statements in a report submitted to the Sacred Congregation *de Propaganda Fide* by Richard O'Ferrall, OFM Cap. His published works would seem to indicate that he succeeded in bringing many of his papers with him when he escaped from Ireland. **31** *Archiv. Hib.* 2 (1913), 9, 36.

Thomas Leverous and Maurice O'Brien – were probably compiled from notes made from Howlin's text. Moreover, Coppinger, who according to Lynch resided for a time in County Kildare and preached throughout Leinster, must have picked up information on certain martyrs from acquaintances in Ireland and from Irishmen living in exile. He mentions by name nine of those on the present list, together with the chaplain of Bishop O'Devany, but his treatment of the seventy-nine martyrs he presents is not totally reliable.[32]

The martyrology which Francis O'Mahony inserted into his history of the Irish Franciscans (1629) relied on sources apparently not available to the other martyrologists for many of the friar martyrs. But he did have a copy of Gonzaga's history of the order at his disposal, and also one of Antonio Daza's *Chrónica General de N.P.S. Francisco*, for he explicitly refers to them at the beginning of his *Brevis Synopsis*.[33] So his information on Bishop Patrick O'Healy and Conn O'Rourke and two others not on our list may have come from there. Historians have found Francis O'Mahony accurate and trustworthy. The martyrology which his namesake James O'Mahony, the exiled provincial of the Irish Augustinians, published anonymously at Brussels in 1655, treats of those Irish Augustinian friars who suffered for their loyalty to the Catholic faith during the Puritan regime in Ireland.[34] In all, he treats of twenty-six friars and also of the Augustinian bishop of Waterford. His longest entry is on William Tirry of the present list. His principal source of information on Tirry was one of the martyr's fellow-prisoners and his confessor, Canon Walter Conway of Cashel diocese, whom he mentions twice in the text (pp. 8, 9), and some other priests who were eye witnesses. They visited O'Mahony in Brussels and brought him relics of the martyr.[35] For reasons which have not yet been satisfactorily explained, O'Mahony's *Sanguinea Eremus* was scarcely noticed by Irish historians of the seventeenth and later centuries, with the exception of Bruodin, or indeed by non-Irish Augustinians until 1860.[36] But James O'Mahony repeated his information on Tirry in his correspondence with the French historian Augustin Lubin, OSA, who included the Irish martyr in his *Orbis Augustinianus* (Paris, 1659). Father William Meagher's list

---

32 Besides some minor inaccuracies, there are one or two major errors: e.g. he makes Matthew Lambert a priest. 33 See *Anal. Hib.* 6 (1934), 143. 34 James O'Mahony, *Sanguinea Eremus Martyrum Hiberniae Ord. Eremit. S.P. Augustini* (Brussels, 1655). Only three copies of this very rare booklet have been traced. The text was edited, with a critical introduction, by F. X. Martin in *Archiv. Hib.* 15 (1950), 74–91. 35 See *Archiv. Hib.* 20 (1957), 109. 36 See comments by F. X. Martin in *Archiv. Hib.* 15 (1950), 77.

of names and brief accounts of Irish Augustinian victims of the Cromwellian persecution was written too early to include Tirry.[37]

The martyrdom of the Dominican Peter Higgins in 1642 was duly reported to the General Chapter of his order held at Rome in 1644, and the printed acts of that Chapter contain an account of it. The printed acts of the next two Chapters, in 1650 and 1656, also refer to his martyrdom. The execution of his confrère Bishop Terence Albert O'Brien on 30 October 1651 was reported in the acts of the 1656 General Chapter. These printed accounts were the sources used by the non-Irish Dominican historians and martyrologists. For example, in his *Sacro Diario Domenicano* (6 vols, Naples, 1668–79), Domenico N. Marchese based his account of Higgins on that printed in the acts of the 1644 Chapter. This popular work, many times reprinted, appeared in a Spanish translation by Alonso Manrique in 1691. Marchese's description of the death of Bishop O'Brien was taken from the acts of the 1656 Chapter, as was Vincenzo Fontana's in his *Monumenta Dominicana* (Rome, 1675) and M. de Vienna's in his *L'Anée Dominicaine* (Paris, 1679). Fontana also relied on the 1656 acts for his accounts of Peter Higgins's death, but Manoel de Lima utilized the 1644 acts.[38] All these martyrological entries, and others by Fontana[39] and Cavalieri,[40] either depend directly on the acts of the General Chapters or derive indirectly from the same sources by interdependent borrowings.

In 1650, when Father Luke Wadding published at Rome his Franciscan bibliography, the *Scriptores Ordinis Minorum*, he added a useful appendix containing a Franciscan martyrology entitled *Syllabus Fratrum Minorum qui pro fide Catholica a Christianae religionis hostibus interempti sunt*. Arranged in alphabetical order according to religious names, it contains twenty Irish Franciscan martyrs, including three on the present list – Bishop Patrick O'Healy, Conn O'Rourke and Bishop Conor O'Devany – and also Patrick O'Loughran (in association with O'Devany). All the entries are brief. They contain no new evidence, being dependent on existing accounts, both printed and in manuscript. But the usually accurate and attentive Wadding made two errors. The first was due to forgetfulness. In the *Syllabus* he noted that David Rothe dedicated Part II of his *Analecta Sacra* to Bishop

---

37 It is contained in a letter of William Meagher (or O'Meagher), OSA, to Filippo Visconti, prior general of the Hermits of St Augustine, 28 Oct. 1650 (see *Archiv. Hib.* 20 (1957), 104, note 1). 38 Manoel De Lima, *Agiologio Dominico: Vidas dos Santos, Beatos, Martyres e outras persoas veneraveis da Ordem dos Prégadoros ...* (4 vols, Lisbon, 1709–12), i, 220–1. 39 Vincenzo Fontana, *Sacrum Theatrum Dominicanum* (2 vols, Rome, 1666), i, 205. 40 Giovanni Cavalieri, *Galleria de'sommi Pontefici, Patriarchi, Arcivescovi e Vescovi dell'Ordine de'Predicatori* (2 vols, Benevento, 1696), i, 602–3.

O'Devany, and he also recorded in the *Scriptores* that Rothe gave a description of O'Devany's martyrdom in Part III, i.e. his *De Processu Martyriali*. But
having given in the *Syllabus* the date of martyrdom as 1 February, Wadding
left a blank space for the year, presumably intending to satisfy himself
regarding the calendar being followed before inserting the year. Rothe,
whose volume he had, twice mentions the exact date,[41] as does Francis
O'Mahony in his *Brevis Synopsis*,[42] a manuscript copy of which was also in
Wadding's possession.[43] Accordingly, it seems that, through an oversight,
Wadding forgot to write in the year before sending his text to the printers.
The second error concerns the year of Patrick O'Healy's martyrdom. His
entry on Bishop O'Healy in the *Syllabus* confidently gives 22 August 1578
as the date of martyrdom. But in the second volume of his *Annales
Minorum*, published in 1628, he gave, with reference to Gonzaga, the correct
year (1579),[44] which he then changed to 1578 in the third volume.[45] Two
other sources which he had – i.e. the brief accounts by Rothe and Francis
O'Mahony – give 1579. But Wadding also had a manuscript copy of
Donagh Mooney's history of the Irish province of the Friars Minor,[46]
which has three references to the martyrdom with three different dates.

Being a scholar imbued with the new critical spirit, Wadding had tried
to reconcile the conflicting dates. Apparently, he then recalled Howlin's
manuscript from his Salamanca days and either consulted his notes or had
someone check the text for him. But an examination of Howlin's manuscript shows that it gave the year 1578, which was later cancelled and '1579'
written overhead. Wadding's scientific method was adequate, but some vital
historical data, particularly about the movements of Sir William Drury and
the arrival in Ireland of the Fitzmaurice expedition, were not available to
him.

In 1659, Maurice Conry, an Irish Friar Minor who had spent thirty
months in prison for the faith in England from August 1655,[47] published at
Innsbruck a slender volume entitled *Threnodia Hiberno-Catholica, sive planctus
universalis totius cleri et populi regni Hiberniae*. A somewhat restless character,
with proven scholarly ability and literary tastes,[48] he disguised the author's
identity under the pseudonym Maurice Morison. His book of 72 pages
describes the sufferings of the Irish Catholics under the Puritans. On pp.

41 David Rothe, *De Processu Martyriali quorundam fidei pugilum in Hibernia* (Cologne, 1619),
103, 143. 42 A.S.I., MS W 28. 2, pp. 70, 74; printed in *Anal. Hib.* 6 (1934), 177, 178. 43 See
Wadding, *Scriptores*, 123. 44 *Ann. Min.*, ad an. 1291, no. LI. 45 Ibid. ad an. 1302, no. XII.
46 Wadding, *Scriptores*, 104. 47 See Millett, *Ir. Franciscans*, 276–8, 328–30. 48 Ibid. 329,
488, 490.

51–8, he printed brief catalogues of Irish saints who preached the gospel of Christ in other lands. He treats of the martyrs on pp. 61–72, mentioning that there were 153 in the reign of Elizabeth. Of the recent victims, he names one archbishop and four bishops, including Bishop O'Brien of the present list, and two Franciscans, and adds that there were forty-six other Friars Minor and many victims from among the Dominicans, Augustinians and secular clergy, from the other religious and the various categories of laity. Then, with some brief historical facts, he lists twenty-three from the ranks of the laity and Brian Fitzpatrick, a priest of Ossory diocese. It is not a very informative book, for its author was short of facts (though this did not deter him from his set purpose of awakening sympathy in Europe for his suffering fellow-countrymen).

The so-called Harold manuscript, preserved in the archives of St Isidore's College, Rome,[49] deals with Irish Franciscan bishops, writers, and martyrs, and was written between 1654 and 1658, apparently at Rome, with many additions inserted between 1657 and 1664.[50] The martyrology comprises slightly less than a third of the extant text, and it is restricted to the period from 1640 to the late 1650s. Though it is an Irish Franciscan martyrology, it treats briefly of three other martyrs. In all, the author mentions by name, with salient details, one archbishop, one secular priest, one Dominican, and thirty-three Franciscans. But many Franciscan martyrs of these decades are omitted, including John Kearney. This martyrologist, like Maurice Conry, was restricted to the information available to him from letters and reports, oral and written, which had reached him in exile. The official list of Irish Franciscan martyrs for the years 1641–61, which was prepared for the general chapter of 1664 by the Irish minister provincial, Anthony Doherty, in July 1663,[51] contains the names of twenty-nine Friars Minor, including John Kearney, and one secular priest who was a Franciscan tertiary. But it is merely a list of names without any biographical details or facts about each martyrdom.

The two Irish Capuchin historians, Richard O'Ferrall and Robert O'Connell, are not reckoned among the martyrologists. Nevertheless, their monumental history of the Irish Confederate Wars and the nunciature of Archbishop Rinuccini, which was composed between 1661 and 1666, and remained unpublished until the last century,[52] contains descriptions of the

---

49 A.S.I., MS W 28. 1.   **50** See Millett, *Ir. Franciscans*, 244.   **51** Ibid. 535–41, for information on the manuscript copies and for the edited text of the list and accompanying documents.   **52** Under the title *Commentarius Rinuccinianus, de Sedis Apostolicae Legatione ad Foederatos Hiberniae Catholicos per annos 1645–9*, ed. Stanislaus Kavanagh (6 vols, Dublin,

sufferings and death of many priests and bishops in the 1640s and early 1650s.[53] It has lengthy accounts of the martyrdom of three clerics on the present list: Peter Higgins, OP, Bishop Terence Albert O'Brien, OP, and William Tirry, OSA.[54] And in each of these three cases the authors are careful to cite their sources. The provenance of their information on Tirry is of particular interest. It came from their confrère Matthew Fogarty, who had been imprisoned with Tirry. Fogarty had also been condemned to be hanged, but his sentence was commuted to exile, and after being transferred to prison at Waterford he was eventually deported to France. He reached La Rochelle on 14 August 1654, some three and a half months after Tirry's execution, and from there made his way to the Irish Capuchin friary at Charleville,[55] where he gave the details on Tirry's imprisonment and death to Robert O'Connell. In none of these cases did the Capuchin authors borrow their material from any of the existing martyrologies. Apparently the *Sanguinea Eremus* was not known to them.

Anthony Bruodin, a Friar Minor from Thomond and the last of the Irish martyrologists, though not always an entirely successful one, was a member of the Bohemian province of the Franciscans[56] when he published at Prague in 1669 his *Propugnaculum Catholicae Veritatis*. This bulky octavo volume of more than eleven hundred pages was written to refute a fellow-Irishman and priest, Thomas Carew (or Carve), whose *Itinerarium* and other writings published between 1639 and 1666 had given great offence to Irishmen abroad and, in the opinion of Bruodin, had discredited Ireland among his European contemporaries. Its chief purpose, therefore, was polemical.

But the *Propugnaculum* has a rather large section which is devoted to the Irish victims of religious persecution, with a wealth of information, not always accurate, on martyrs. A modern scholar and fellow religious has poured scorn on Bruodin as a martyrologist, describing him as a first-class

1932–49).   **53** For example: Henry White; Denis O'Connor; Francis O'Mahony, OFM; Archbishop Malachy O'Quealy of Tuam; Bishop Boetius MacEgan of Ross; Bishop Heber MacMahon of Clogher; John Daton, OFM (see *Comment. Rinucc.*, i, 302, 304, 305, 488; ii, 36–9, 291; iv, 392–3, 397–9; v, 158–61).   **54** Ibid. i, 302–3; ii, 291; iv, 647–52; v, 193–7. **55** Ibid. v, 197–9.   **56** Anthony Bruodin (or MacBrody) was an Irish Franciscan from Ballyhogan in County Clare, who studied at St Isidore's College in Rome, which he left in 1649. He lectured in philosophy in the Irish Franciscan College in Prague up to 1651. Having taken up residence in the friary of Our Lady of the Snows, Prague, he taught philosophy and then theology there and in the archiepiscopal seminary for more than twelve years and was incorporated into the Bohemian province of the Friars Minor, of which he remained a member until 1675, when he rejoined the Irish province and its college in Prague. (See Millett, *Ir. Franciscans*, 151–2).

propagandist who, when given merely a martyr's name, could with vivid imagination construct all further details of martyrdom with the greatest facility.[57] But a careful examination of Bruodin's text shows that this scathing criticism is not valid for the reign of Elizabeth I or for those martyrs in later years for whom Bruodin had written sources. It must be admitted that, for those martyrs concerning whom he had nothing more reliable than oral reports or stories, as apparently was the case for some from the 1640s and 1650s, his reporting has been found to be quite inaccurate, at least in a small number of cases, and therefore untrustworthy.

On pp. 424–5, Bruodin gives some of the written sources. The list is quite impressive.[58] He also mentions a work in manuscript on the Irish martyrs said to have been written by Matthew Magrath (or Creagh),[59] vicar general of Killaloe, which was preserved in the Irish Franciscan College in Prague since 1660, when it was brought there by Daniel Conry, a relative of the vicar general. Nothing is known of this martyrology. Later in his text, in his accounts of individual martyrs, he refers to other printed sources: for example, on p. 697 to Maurice Conry's *Threnodia*, and on p. 721 to James O'Mahony's *Sanguinea Eremus*. It is not certain that Bruodin consulted all these works, but the internal evidence clearly establishes that he read some of them.

Among the very large number of martyrs whose sufferings and death are recorded in the *Propugnaculum* all but four[60] of the martyrs on the present list are recorded. Bruodin's account of Bishop Patrick O'Healy and Conn O'Rourke (pp. 433–7) depends in part on Wadding's *Syllabus*, from which he repeated the incorrect date 22 August 1578, and to a much greater extent

---

57 Brendan Jennings, 'The Irish Franciscans in Prague', in *Studies* 28 (1939), 220. Father Jennings offered no annotated evidence in support of his adverse criticism. But his severe opinion of Bruodin as a martyrologist has been repeated by others, without any critical appraisal (see, e.g. Thomas Wall, 'Bards and Bruodins', in *Father Luke Wadding*, 447–8). **58** David Rothe's *Analecta Sacra*; John Coppinger's *Theatre of Catholique and Protestant Religion*; Faustino Tasso's history in Italian of the Franciscan families, covering the years 1567–80; Thomas Bourchier's work on the Franciscan martyrs; Francesco Gonzaga's history of the Franciscan Order; Barezzo Barezzi's additional Part IV to his Italian version of Mark of Lisbon's *Chronica Ordinis Minorum*; Nicholas Sanders's posthumous work *De Origine ac Progressu Schismatis Anglicani liber*; Luke Wadding's *Syllabus*; Arthur Monstier's Franciscan martyrology; Philip Alegambe's work on Jesuit martyrs – his *Mortes Illustres* – with, as Bruodin specifically states, the continuation by John Nadasi. **59** He calls the author 'Matthaeus Chrahius, Diaecesis Laonensis in Hibernia' and states that in the manuscript itself it is said that it was written by him (cf. Bruodin, op. cit. 425). **60** Margaret Bermingham, Francis Taylor, John Kearney and William Tirry. The omission of Tirry is strange because the *Sanguinea Eremus*, which was used by Bruodin (op. cit. 721) for his entry on Donagh O'Kennedy, OSA, carries a longer account of Tirry's martyrdom than any for the other Augustinian martyrs.

on Gonzaga's *De Origine Seraphicae Religionis Franciscanae*, from which he took, among many other details, the date 1577 for that of O'Healy's visit to Rome. He also refers to Monstier's martyrology. His report on Matthew Lambert and on Cheevers, Meyler and Cavanagh (pp. 442–3) clearly depends on Coppinger's *Theatre*. On pp. 446–8, he has a succinct account of Archbishop O'Hurley's martyrdom which derives, in part, from Coppinger, who wrongly states that the archbishop was executed in May 1584. Likewise there appears to be a dependence on Coppinger for his description of Maurice MacKenraghty (pp. 448–9); in his *Theatre* Coppinger does not specify Clonmel as the town where this priest was imprisoned and killed, and Bruodin incorrectly presumed that the events narrated took place in MacKenraghty's native Kilmallock. He also gives 25 February (*recte* 20 April) 1585 as the date of the martyrdom. In his account of Dominic Collins (pp. 470–1), which appears to be a synopsis of some Jesuit version, Bruodin erroneously described him as a priest. His entry on Bishop Conor O'Devany and Patrick O'Loughran (pp. 497–9) is short but accurate. Bruodin expressly states that he learned of these events from trustworthy people in Ireland, and in particular from a distinguished layman from his native Thomond, Boetius Clancy, who was in Dublin when the martyrdom occurred. Although the year cited is incorrect, the entry on Peter Higgins, OP (pp. 731–2), is reasonably accurate. The source of this information is not immediately obvious. Bruodin may have taken it from some Dominican author. His account of the hanging of Bishop Terence Albert O'Brien in 1651 (p. 706) is brief and is perhaps based on Conry's *Threnodia*.

In 1671, Anthony Bruodin continued his literary controversy with Thomas Carew with the publication of his *Anatomicum Examen*[61] at Prague under the pseudonym Cornelius O'Mollony. Dissecting paragraph by paragraph the reply to the *Propugnaculum*, Carew's *Inchiridion*, he refuted with ease his opponent's attempt to prove that some Irish bishops, priests and friars had been put to death for military reasons and therefore were not martyrs. Of particular interest is his reply on pp. 58–63 to Carew's printed assertion that he had never heard of the martyrdom of Archbishop Dermot O'Hurley. Bruodin referred him to the relevant passage in the *Theatre of Catholique and Protestant Religion* and then printed verbatim Coppinger's account in English. To Carew's charge that the account he had published of

---

61 The full title is *Anatomicum Examen Inchiridii Apologettici seu famosi cuiusdam libelli, a Thoma Carve (verus Carrano) sacerdote Hiberno furtive publicati.*

the martyrdom of Father Francis O'Mahony was a fable, Bruodin retorted first by citing the General Chapter of the Franciscan Order held at Toledo in 1644, and then by stating that Conry had briefly mentioned the martyrdom in his *Threnodia* and by repeating verbatim the account given by Wadding in the *Scriptores Ordinis Minorum*.[62] At the end of the *Anatomicum Examen*, on pp. 233–66, he printed an additional Irish Franciscan martyrology, which, as the title explains, records the names of those martyrs from the province of Ireland who were not mentioned in his catalogue in the *Propugnaculum*. In all, he records details on twenty-two friar martyrs. All the entries are rather brief, except the first one, which deals with John Kearney, who is on the present list. His lengthy account of Kearney (pp. 233–59) is based on a *vita* of the martyr written by Joseph Sall, OFM, and Canon Geoffrey Sall, a manuscript copy of which Bruodin had beside him as he wrote.[63] His accuracy in citing texts from Wadding and Coppinger suggests that he was equally careful here. In fact, unlike his account, of the other twenty-one friar martyrs, that of John Kearney is prefaced with a title, *Vita Martyris Joannis Kernei*, which seems to indicate that he copied word for word from the manuscript. He mentions no source for the others in this martyrology, and none can be readily determined.

Some of the Irish martyrologies mentioned above – e.g. Rothe's *De Processu Martyriali*, James O'Mahony's *Sanguinea Eremus*, Conry's *Threnodia* – were printed in order to make the Catholics of Europe aware of the sufferings of the Irish for their faith. Not all the sources available to the martyrologist have survived the upheavals of the last four centuries. Indeed, any sincere attempt at presenting the case for the Irish martyrs of the sixteenth and seventeenth centuries must accept that there are some vital pieces, concerned with the ecclesiastical and civil situation in the country, missing from the puzzle because of the destruction of contemporary records.[64]

---

62 Wadding, *Scriptores*, 122–3. Bruodin cited the rather long entry accurately, but changed the date at the end from 1644 to 1642.   **63** [Bruodin], *Anatomicum Examen*, 258.   **64** The dates of all documents are given exactly as in the originals. When presenting or citing documents and letters which were written in Ireland or England after October 1582 we have always adhered to the style of dating in use in both countries up to 1752, i.e. the 'old style' or Julian calendar. It should be noted also that during the period with which we are dealing the year was sometimes computed as beginning on Lady Day, 25 March, and not on 1 January. Accordingly the date '23 March 1641' emanating from a source in Ireland may sometimes be the equivalent 23 March 1642 according to modern reckoning. Documents and letters originating in Italy, Spain, France and the Low Countries bear dates according to the Gregorian calendar. The date of martyrdom is in all cases according to the Julian calendar.

List of contributors

Patrick J. Corish, Professor Emeritus of Modern History, National University of Ireland, Maynooth

Benignus Millett, OFM, Franciscan House of Studies, Dún Mhuire, Seafield Road, Killiney, Co. Dublin

†John J. Meagher, formerly parish priest of Dalkey, archdiocese of Dublin, former editor of *Reportorium Novum*

Ciarán Brady, Senior Lecturer, Department of Modern History, Trinity College, Dublin

†James Coombes, former parish priest of Timoleague, diocese of Ross

Proinsias Ó Fionnagáin, SJ, author, Jesuit Community, St Francis Xavier's, Upper Gardiner Street, Dublin 1

Kieran Devlin, parish priest, Gortin (Badoney Lower), 17 Chapel Lane, Omagh, Co. Tyrone

Colm Lennon, Associate Professor, Department of Modern History, National University of Ireland, Maynooth

†Augustine Valkenburg, OP, formerly of St Catherine's Dominican Priory, Newry, Co. Down

†Francis X. Martin, OSA, formerly Professor of Medieval History, University College, Dublin